LOVE LETTERS

Love Letters

An Anthology from the British Isles
975-1944

edited by
JAMES TURNER

CASSELL · LONDON

CASSELL & COMPANY LTD
35 Red Lion Square, London, WC1
Melbourne, Sydney, Toronto
Johannesburg, Auckland

First published 1970

I.S.B.N. 0 304 93485 2

Printed in Great Britain by
The Camelot Press Ltd, London and Southampton
F.570

ACKNOWLEDGEMENTS

The author wishes to acknowledge permission to quote copyright material from the sources stated:

The late Mr E. V. Lucas and Methuen & Co. Ltd: *The Gentle Art*, 1907

Mr Gavin Bone and The Clarendon Press, Oxford: *Anglo-Saxon Poetry*, 1943

Mr John Fenn, Mrs Archer-Hind and J. M. Dent & Sons Ltd: *The Paston Letters* 2 vols. Everyman's Library, 1951

Miss Margaret Sanders and Sir Isaac Pitman & Sons Ltd: *Intimate Letters of England's Kings*, 1959

The Trustees of the British Museum: Harleian 4031. folio 11v., and Harleian 36. folios 268–269

Miss Barbara Winchester & Jonathan Cape Ltd: *Tudor Family Portrait*, 1955

The late Sir Rennell Rodd and Macmillan & Co. Ltd: *Sir Walter Raleigh*, 1904

Mr Philip Wayne and Longmans, Green & Co. Ltd: *The Personal Art*, 1949

Mr Martin Freeman and Hutchinson Publishing Group Ltd: *Vanessa and Her Correspondence with Jonathan Swift*, Selwyn & Blount, 1921

The late R. Brimley Johnson and The Bodley Head Ltd: *The Letters of Robert Burns, The Letters of Percy Bysshe Shelley* and *The Letters of Laurence Sterne*; and the same author for *The Letters of Richard Steele*, Quill Library, 1937

Mr Robert Halsband and The Clarendon Press, Oxford: *The Complete Letters of Lady Mary Wortley Montagu*, 1965

John Murray (Publishers) Ltd: *George Crabbe and His Times 1754–1832* by René Huchon, 1907

Rev John C. Hill, M.A., and J. M. Dent & Sons Ltd: *The Love Songs and Heroines of Robert Burns*, Medill McBride Co. Inc. N.Y., 1962

Mr Hugh Tours and Victor Gollancz Ltd: *The Life and Letters of Emma Hamilton*, 1963

Mr Geoffrey Rawson and J. M. Dent & Sons Ltd: *Nelson's Letters*, 1960

Mr Guy Pocock and J. M. Dent & Sons Ltd: *The Letters of Charles Lamb*, 1945. Two volumes

Mr C. R. Leslie, R.A., and BPC Publishing Ltd: *Memoirs of the Life of John Constable, R.A.*, John Lehmann, 1949

Mr John Lock, Canon W. T. Dixon and Thomas Nelson & Sons Ltd: *A Man of Sorrow*, 1965

Mr R. G. Howarth and J. M. Dent & Sons Ltd: *The Letters of Lord Byron*, selected and edited by R. G. Howarth, 1949

The Executors of the late M. Buxton Forman and the Oxford University Press: *The Letters of John Keats*, 1952

Miss Trudy Bliss and Victor Gollancz Ltd: *Jane Welsh Carlyle: A New Selection of Her Letters*, 1950

Mr Dormer Creston and Eyre & Spottiswoode (Publishers) Ltd: *Andromeda in Wimpole Street*, 1950

Miss H. E. Litchfield and the Cambridge University Press: *Emma Darwin—a Century of Family Letters*, 1904

Sir Ralph Millais, Sir William James, the Trustees of the Estate of John Ruskin and George Allen & Unwin Ltd: *The Order of Release*, John Murray, 1948

Mr Derek Patmore and George Bell & Sons Ltd: *Selected Poems of Coventry Patmore*, Chatto & Windus, 1941

The late Miss Nancy Spain and Ward, Lock & Co. Ltd: *The Beeton Story*, 1956

The late Mr C. D. Medley and Rupert Hart-Davis Ltd: *George Moore—Letters to Lady Cunard*, 1957

J. M. Dent & Sons Ltd: *R. L. Stevenson—Virginibus Puerisque and Familiar Studies of Men and Books*, Everyman's Library, 1948

Messrs Letcher & Son and Legatees of the Estate of the late Dame Ethel Smyth: *Impressions that Remained*, Vol. 1. Longmans, Green & Co. Ltd, 1919

Miss D. E. Collins, Miss Maisie Ward, A. P. Watt & Son and Messrs Sheed & Ward Ltd: *Gilbert Keith Chesterton*, 1945

Countess Barcynska and Hurst and Blackett Ltd: *Caradoc Evans*, 1948

The Society of Authors and the Estate of the late Katherine Mansfield: *Letters of Katherine Mansfield to John Middleton Murry*, Constable & Co. Ltd, 1951

The late Sir Harold Nicolson and Wm. Collins Son & Co. Ltd: *Harold Nicolson. Diaries and Letters*, ed. Nigel Nicolson. 1930–1939, Vol. 1

Mr Filson Young, William Hodge & Co. Ltd and London Express News and Feature Services: *Trial of Frederick Bywaters and Edith Thompson* in Notable British Trials Series, 1923

Mr Constantine FitzGibbon and J. M. Dent & Sons Ltd: *Selected Letters of Dylan Thomas*, 1966

The late Alun Lewis, Mr Ian Hamilton and George Allen & Unwin Ltd: *Selected Poetry and Prose*, 1966

THANKS

I would like to express my thanks to Mr W. Best Harris, Librarian of the Central Lending Library, Plymouth, for his help and encouragement, and to Mr James Smith, of the same library, for his patience and tireless searching for and obtaining rare and necessary books; to Mr Patrick Drake, Librarian of the Newquay Public Library for the loan of books and suggestions; to Dr Desmond Flower for reading the manuscript while it was in progress and suggesting revisions; to Mr and Mrs Peter Ford for the loan of books, and last, but by no means least, to Mrs Phyllis Barker for her excellent typing of the manuscript.

CONTENTS

INTRODUCTION

Valerie was 10 years old, a year older than I and in a different classroom of the local school. I saw her daily, since not only did we haunt the same corridors in the large country house which was the school, but we lived four doors away from each other in houses which had been built about 1900 and were all exactly the same. They had long gardens behind them, a small formal garden in front and wooden palings shutting them off from the road. The palings were exactly suited to hiding love letters. Thinking of her now—or saying her name, I can remember nothing about her at all but the fact that she existed.

There was an added, fearful joy in writing my first love letter to her. What an extraordinary thing it was that the youthful passion engendered in my mind and body by the sight and speech, the tough, the gentle mockery (even at that age) of my beloved Valerie, could be so increased as soon as I took a pen in hand, as if the thread of passion was running from my mind's vision, from my memory, down my arm and out at my fingers on to the pink paper.

This was to be young and in love for the first time; the joy was secret not only to Valerie but to myself. Nothing would have happened if I had not been alone to write my letter, knowing that she only would see the results of my labour. The pleasure, too, consisted in the thought of her fingers reaching out into the space of the wooden fence and withdrawing the paper; in the warmth of her hand or her immature bosom engendering its own passion to that of mine. It was a peculiar effusion of calf love made doubly wonderful by the secrecy and by the space between our two homes. And then the affront; the discovery of a note she had not taken or had been prevented from taking. The confrontation by my parents with the 'hideous' writing—so that it seemed as if a boy of 9 had committed some obscene act. The opening into daylight of the almost sacred words—not only to be laughed at by brothers and sisters—but to be an occasion for disapproval. The daylight was dark indeed. I might, then, be forbidden to write such letters to Valerie or to receive hers. But I saw her every day. Yet the Valerie I saw was different from the Valerie to whom I wrote letters. And this, too, is an odd thing about love letters. Is it that in receiving such a letter the lover herself becomes a different person because she is handling and reading something only written for her eyes and which, in its full implications, is meaningless to anyone else? Is it that the magic of love words—even the simple words of such children as we were—creates a different person when they are read in private? That the mention of such simple biological details as the colour of her eyes, the shape of her lips, or her glowing skin, does actually cause the eyes to be bluer or the skin to glow brighter? Who but the lover can say? Who but the lover can know the alarming significance of such words as 'darling' or 'I love you'? One thing is certain; no one was ever made anything but better for reading them.

Only at the discovery and banning of further letters did the first realisation of a world outside of love (which had not existed while I was writing and receiving the letters) force its meaning upon me. It was a lesson in circumspection. And further, a lesson in the fickleness of women. For, although it had been Valerie who had not collected the letter and therefore led to its discovery, I was doubly blamed. First by my parents for writing it; and secondly by Valerie herself who, with deadly unreasonableness, accused me of not finding a more secure hiding place.

'If I had done that,' I replied—put fearfully into the wrong for the first time—'you would never have found it at all. You wouldn't have known where to look.'

She merely shook her fair head and walked away with the air of a girl who, if there had been a love letter hidden anywhere within a mile of her home, would have found it.

The secret cabinets of Kings and Queens must have held love letters of exquisite passion, for they had the time for such things. Even the three old ladies—Lady Dorchester, Lady Orkney and the Duchess of Portsmouth—who met one night at the Court of George I, must have received and treasured such letters. They had been respectively the mistresses of James II, William III and Charles II. Lady Dorchester said to the others 'God! Who would have thought we three whores should have met here!' If the love letters of these three old ladies were extant what treasures they would be!

Love letters, all down the years, reflect not only the absurdity of the writers (and to a philosopher there is nothing to equal the absurdity of a man in love) but the age in which they were written, from 'A Husband's Message' before history began, to George Moore writing to Maud Cunard, in July 1905:

'For years I shall remember how you came down to Seaford House in your electric brougham. That vehicle is forever enshrined in my memory. You can never—and for this I pity you—you can never form an idea of the wonder it is to me to see you—to think you and to dream you.'

But then in the same letter he wrote:

'Egotism is the god that inspires the letter-writer and good letters are all about the letter-writer.'[1]

How true this is of love letters! For love has a style of its own which is compounded of the memory of past delights and future enjoyments, of events in which the lover can project his love to his beloved and, sometimes, of secret codes.

George Birbeck Hill, second son of Arthur Hill, brother of Sir Rowland Hill, wrote love letters to his fiancée, Annie Scott, daughter of a Wigan solicitor. 'I suppose,' he wrote, 'there is nothing in lovers' letters, at least people say so; but there is a good deal of happiness in saying that nothing.'

I think he was right about the happiness but wrong about there being nothing in lover's letters. For love letters reflect every

[1] *George Moore—Letters to Lady Cunard, 1895–1933.* Rupert Hart-Davis, 1957.

degree of emotion from the freezing point of indifference, to the fever heat of madness; all the emotions of the mind, heart and soul. Surprise, interest, attachment and jealousy; affection, folly, suspicion and despair; faith, loyalty, self-sacrifice and devotion are fully revealed in such letters.

Rousseau says that to write a good love letter we must begin without knowing what we mean to say and finish without knowing what we have written. This is rather like Columbus who when he set out did not know where he was going; when he reached land did not know where he was, and when he got back home did not know where he had been. In short, both are half-truths. Most of the letters collected in this book are by people who knew quite clearly what they intended to say.

It is inevitable that, for the early days, when the majority were illiterate and women uneducated, few love letters exist. Not quite the earliest love letter in English is that in which Lady Pelham informs Sir John Pelham of the siege of Pevensey Castle. These early letters, as with the Pastons, were generally mixed up with sieges and battles, since sieges and battles, if you had any property at all—certainly if you owned a castle, made up most of the day's work. The letter is dated 1399:

'My dear Lord,

'I recommend me to your high lordship, with heart and body and all my poor might. And with all this I thank you as my dear Lord, dearest and best beloved of all earthly lords. I say for me, and thank you, my dear Lord, with all this that I said before for your comfortable letter that you sent me from Pontefract, that came to me on Mary Magdalen's day; for by my troth I was never so glad as when I heard by your letter that ye were strong enough with the Grace of God to keep you from the malice of your enemies. And, dear Lord, if it like to your high Lordship that as soon as ye might that I might hear of your gracious speed, which God Almighty continue and increase. And, my dear Lord, if it like you to know *my* fare, I am here laid by in a manner of a siege with the County of Sussex, Surrey and a great parcel of Kent, so that I may not go out nor no victuals get me, but with much hazard. Wherefore, my dear, if it like you by the advice of your wise counsel for to set remedy to the salvation of your castle and withstand the malice of the shires

4

aforesaid. And also that ye be fully informed of the great malice-workers in these shires which have so despitefully wrought to you, and to your castle, to your men, and to your tenants; for this country have they wasted for a great while.

'Farewell, my dear Lord! the Holy Trinity keep you from your enemies, and soon send me good tidings of you. Written at Pevensey, in the castle, on St. Jacob's day last past, by your own poor J. PELHAM. To my true Lord.'[1]

For the uneducated, one supposes, the carving of 'I love you' on an oak tree in Sherwood Forest or Savernake or the Weald, or just outside any English village, was enough to satisfy 'the language of the heart'. The style, as it were, lay in the carving and the speed in which the graffiti were overgrown. Such love letters are still to be seen on the beech trees in the village of Belchamp Walter, in Essex, where some German prisoner-of-war, stationed at the camp at Borley in 1944, has inscribed the three words, surrounded by a heart, in the greening bark. Perhaps they were the only English words he knew.

Today few write love letters since passion can be conveyed so easily in person and a ball-point pen does not lend itself, by virtue of its impermanency, to emotional crises. Nina Epton, in her book *Love and the English* (Cassell, 1960), described that rarity —a love-letter writer of the twentieth century who will write a letter for you for thirty shillings. This professional, Andrew Bainbridge, when asked why there was a custom for his services, replied: 'We live in an age of specialisation. Outside their own speciality, many people lack confidence'—and besides—'It takes too much time.' We can only be thankful that the love-letter writers of the past had all the time in the world to write and were educated and civilised.

And even if people today did write love letters (and after all mass-produced Valentines are very much coming back into vogue), the letters they write are no longer preserved. Neither a ball-point, nor a typewriter and certainly not that modern horror, the Thermo-Fax machine, are proper vehicles for conveying passion. The truth is that love letters are old-fashioned and the terms of endearment largely meaningless. If passion is put on paper at all, and put on paper by the actual hand of man or woman, it is in poetry which equally does not lend itself to machine-writing.

[1] Quoted from *The Gentlest Art*, E. V. Lucas. Methuen, 1907.

Once again it is left to the poet to enshrine an immortality of which the vast number of today's lovers have no conception and care nothing about. The pill has killed more secrets than those of the womb. Wit is drowned in the long hair of 'beat' groups and their followers; and the course of true love is no longer a cottage in the country but a 'pad' in the latest fashionable part of town. The truth is, today romance is dead. All that remains is sex.

But in between the early days and today! In between are the great centuries of letter writing (not only love letters either), the great permanencies of love letters, the seventeenth, eighteenth and nineteenth centuries. In between are the wonderful refinement of Elizabeth Barrett and Robert Browning; Emma Hart's coy letters and the agony of Nelson's consummate passion; Hazlitt's pain and the tender calf love of the boy of nine who wrote love letters to the composer Dame Ethel Smyth. Such letters rise to the height of passion in those of Keats to Fanny Brawne which tear the heart with an almost unbearable agony.

Yet with the passion and love what interests one about these love letters is not only the love—not only the slow flowering of a romance—but what the lover was doing at the time of writing. Nelson about to fight Trafalgar; Horace Walpole building Strawberry Hill while he is writing to the Misses Berry, Charles Lamb begging Frances Kelly, the actress, to come to dinner. Hazlitt again, throwing away the locket which contained the hair of the servant girl, Sarah Walker, who jilted him; George Moore in the Holy Land researching for his novel *The Brook Kerith*; or Conrad Russell who loved Lady Diana Cooper as much as George Moore loved Lady Cunard (and in rather the same way), writing about his farm at Mells; and his cheese-making; and his reading of St. Augustine. It is as if the love is inseparable from what the lover is doing and that the two go together, each inspiring the other with an extraordinary light.

Few love letters give reasons for loving, and even when they do, the reasons would not satisfy a logician or a philosopher—though they might well satisfy a poet. In one sense all the letters are different; in another they are but so many repetitions of that model of love letters, the famous letter of Sir John Falstaff to Mistress Anne Page, in the second act of *The Merry Wives of Windsor*:

6

'Ask me no reason why I love you; for though love uses reason for his physician, he admits him not for his counsellor. You are not young, no more am I; go to then, there's sympathy; you are merry, so am I—ha! ha! then there's more sympathy; you love sack and so do I; would you desire better sympathy? Let it suffice thee, Mistress Page—at the least if the love of a soldier can suffice—that I love thee. I will not say pity me; 'tis not a soldier-like phrase; but I say, love me. By me

> 'Thine own true knight,
> By day or night,
> Or any kind of light,
> With all his might,
> For three to fight.

JOHN FALSTAF'

The good manners of Henry's love letters to Anne Boleyn are not invalidated by the fact that later he cut off her head. For good manners are the essence of all love letters. A man may not be intellectually at his best when writing to his mistress, but at least he is on his best behaviour; and where he does catalogue his faults it is only that they shall be excused. 'The style of letters ought to be free, easy and natural,' said Walsh, 'as near approaching to familiar conversation as possible. The two best qualities in conversation are, good humour and good breeding; those letters are certainly the best that show the most of these qualities.'

No man ever asked a woman to love him because he was a murderer. True he might well murder for love of a woman, but it is not he himself the woman loves so much as the power or the lust provided by his act.

And yet in that strange case of Edith Thompson and Frederick Bywaters it comes very near to it. Whether Edith Thompson did help or arrange that fearful murder of her husband in a suburban street or not, she certainly studied ways to kill and wrote of them in her love letters to Bywaters. Naturally when such letters were read out in the light of open court they were damning. But you wonder when you read the full case whether she was only parading herself to her lover as a *femme fatale* and never meant him to go so far. Certainly she cannot have meant him to plunge a knife into her husband's neck in the street.

7

But murderers are sometimes as unreasonable as lovers. William Gardiner, of Peasenhall in Suffolk, sat with his feet in Rose Harsent's lap in the old Doctor's Chapel between morning and evening service. Yet he killed her, so it would seem, a few days later by the back stairs of the house where she was a maidservant. And much hung on what the Prosecution called 'The Letter of Assignation' which William wrote to Rose:

'Dear R,—I will try to see you to-night at twelve o'clock at your Place if you Put a light in your window at ten o'clock for about ten minutes. Then you can take it out again. Dont have a light in your Room at twelve as I will come round to the back.'

This must surely be accounted a love letter as fatal for Rose as Edith Thompson's to Frederick Bywaters were for her husband.

Perhaps good manners did not come into the love letters of these murderers, but they certainly do into those of Charles Darwin and G. K. Chesterton inquiring of houses in which to live (and love) and in Stevenson's *On Falling in Love*, which is really a love letter to Fanny Osbourne, *née* Vandergrift, an American whom he met at Grez-sur-Loing, and who became his wife.

Of course, with the exception of a few—such as those of Horace Walpole or of Steele—we were never meant to see these letters. It is our good fortune that we can for, as Dr. Johnson said to Boswell one afternoon as he opened a note which his servant brought him: 'An odd thought strikes me; we shall receive no letters in the grave.'

I have entitled the sections by the name of the key-figure on whom the letters centre.

8

ANGLO-SAXON

One of the earliest love letters is the Anglo-Saxon, 'The Husband's Message', preserved in the tenth-century miscellany called *The Exeter Book*. This is not the letter of one of the great Heroes, Beowulf for example, but the cry, the longing of all ancient classical wanderers and seafarers. One sees them, men larger than life, in their frail craft, waiting for dawnlight or sailing the northern seas in winter. Everything to them was a miracle and a danger, small islands were huge unknown fish, thunder the wrath of their gods, a safe harbour a goddess's blessing. What a curious, fearless light these ancient explorers held in their blue eyes. To be exiled, as was the writer of this letter, was, in fact, to have to 'explore beyond the seas'. Their horizons were limitless. Their world, a world that was at its beginning, unbounded.

THE HUSBAND'S MESSAGE

Here am I fresh from the barque,
From long wandering free.
Thou shalt know the dear love of thy lord,
For he says it in me
That thy faith may repose on the truth of his word.
See! he graved in this bough,
And bids it bring to thought
The hours when gold-bedecked you heard his vow,
Ere feud had wrought
His exile and your parting at the end—
Bright hours when, love scarce grown, you stood his friend.
Hear then his charge to thee:—
When the first cuckoo's throat
Sends shrilly its sad note
At the edges of the sea,
Set out and stir the wave,
Let no man stay your vow,
But climb on the shoulder brave
Of a ship with a southerly prow,
To seek beyond the sea-gull's home
The joyful man who waits there till you come!
He has conquered all his woes:
He will have no lack of steeds,
Of drink, joy, treasure; no foes;
But bright cups and glowing deeds,
And best of all, you, Princess, for his wife!
And often he mutters a rune.
Calling on Sigel and Wyn,
And swearing, if he has life,
(I have heard him) the very tune
Of those oaths he will hold to the letter
Once made by you two when the world went better.

PASTON LETTERS

Even today that part of the Norfolk coast where the village of
Paston lies, some twenty miles from Norwich, can be a desolate
place. In the 1400's, under the weak king Henry VI, when the
Paston family flourished, fought their feuds, fell in love and
engaged in endless lawsuits, the coast was much grimmer. To
stand on the beach behind Caistor Castle which the Pastons
lost, recaptured and lost again, is to be reminded not only of that
hard-headed business family but also of the Wanderers and Seafarers of Anglo-Saxon poetry, though four hundred years separate
them. To marry for love in those days was rare; a daughter was a
business asset and was treated as such. Which makes the love of
Margery, Margaret's daughter, for Richard Calle, John Paston's
bailiff and general agent, all the more poignant.

The Letters, first published by the antiquary Le Neve, are a
priceless collection of correspondence of the Paston family and
others, stretching from 1422 to 1509.

2   *Richard Calle to Margery Paston*

1469

MINE own lady and mistress, and before God very true wife,
I with heart full sorrowful recommend me unto you, as he that

cannot be merry, nor nought shall be till it be otherwise with us than it is yet, for this life that we lead now is neither pleasure to God nor to the world, considering the great bond of matrimony that is made betwixt us, and also the great love that hath been and as I trust yet is betwixt us, and as on my part never greater; wherefore I beseech Almighty God comfort us as soon as it pleaseth him, for we that ought of very right to be most together are most asunder, meseemeth it is a thousand year ago since that I spake with you, I had lever than all the good in the world I might be with you; alas, alas! good lady, full little remember they what they do that keep us thus asunder, four times in the year are they accursed that let matrimony; it causeth many men to deem in them they have large conscience in other matters as well as herein; but what lady suffer as ye have done; and make you as merry as ye can, for I wis, lady, at the long way, God will of his righteousness help his servants that mean truly, and would live according to his laws, &c.

I understand, lady, ye have had as much sorrow for me as any gentlewoman hath had in the world, as would God all that sorrow that ye have had had rested upon me, and that ye had been discharged of it, for I wis, Lady, it is to me a death to hear that ye be entreated otherwise than ye ought to be; this is a painful life that we lead, I cannot live thus without it be a great displeasure to God.

Also like you to weet that I had sent you a letter by my lad from London, and he told me he might not speak with you, there was made so great await upon him and upon you both: he told me John Thresher came to him in your name, and said that ye sent him to my lad for a letter or a token which I should have sent you, but he trust him not, he would not deliver him none; after that he brought him a ring, saying that ye sent it him, commanding him that he should deliver the letter or token to him, which I conceive since by my lad it was not by your sending, it was by my mistress and Sir James's advice; alas! what mean they? I suppose they deem we be not ensured together, and if they so do I marvel, for then they are not well advised, remembering the plainness that I brake to my mistress at the beginning, and I suppose by you, both, and ye did as ye ought to do of very right, and if ye have done the contrary, as I have been informed ye have done, ye did neither conciensly nor to the pleasure of God,

12

without ye did it for fear and for the time, to please such as were at that time about you; and if ye did it for this cause, it was a reasonable cause, considering the great and importable calling upon that ye had, and many an untrue tale was made to you of me, which, God know it, I was never guilty of.

My lad told me that my mistress your mother asked him if he had brought any letter to you, and many other things she bare him on hand, and among all other at the last she said to him that I would not make her privy to the beginning, but she supposed I would at the ending; and as to that God knoweth she knew it first of me and none other; I wot not what her mistress-ship meaneth, for by my troth there is no gentlewoman alive that my heart tendereth more than it doth her, nor is loather to displease, saving only your person, which of very right I ought to tender and love best, for I am bound thereto by the law of God, and so will do while that I live whatsoever fall of it; I suppose and ye tell them sadly the truth, they will not damn their souls for us; though I tell them the truth they will not believe me as well as they will do you, and therefore, good lady, at the reverence of God be plain to them and tell the truth, and if they will in no wise agree thereto, betwixt God, the devil, and them be it, and that peril that we should be in I beseech God it may lie upon them and not upon us; I am heavy and sorry to remember their disposition. God send them grace to guide all things well, as well I would they did; God be their guide, and send them peace and rest, &c.

I marvel much that they should take this matter so heedely as I understand they do, remembering it is in such case as it cannot be remedied, and my desert upon every behalf it is for to be thought there should be none obstacle against it; and also the worshipful that is in them is not in your marriage, it is in their own marriage, which I beseech God send them such as may be to their worship and pleasure to God, and to their hearts' ease, for else were it great pity. Mistress, I am afraid to write to you, for I understand ye have showed my letters that I have sent you before this time; but I pray you let no creature see this letter, as soon as ye have read it let it be burnt, for I would no man should see it in no wise; ye had no writing from me this two year, nor I will not send you no more, therefore I remit all this matter to your wisdom; Almighty Jesus preserve, keep, and [give] you your heart's desire, which I wot well should be to God's pleasure, &c.

13

This letter was written with as great pain as ever wrote I thing in my life, for in good faith I have been right sick, and yet am not verily at ease, God amend it, &c.

RICHARD CALLE

3 *Margery Brews to John Paston*

Topcroft, February 1476

A GIRL'S LOVE LETTER

Unto my right well-beloved valentine, John Paston, Esq., be this Bill delivered, &c.

RIGHT reverend and worshipful, and my right well-beloved Valentine, I recommend me unto you, full heartily desiring to hear of your welfare, which I beseech Almighty God long for to preserve unto his pleasure and your heart's desire.

And if it please you to hear of my welfare, I am not in good heele of body nor of heart, nor shall be till I hear from you;

For there wottys [knows] no creature what pain that I endure, And for to be dead [for my life], I dare it not dyscur' [discover].

And my lady my mother hath laboured the matter to my father full diligently, but she can no more get than ye know of, for the which God knoweth I am full sorry. But if that ye love me, as I trust verily that ye do, ye will not leave me therefore; for if that ye had not half the livelihood that ye have, for to do the greatest labour that any woman alive might, I would not forsake you.

And if ye command me to keep me true wherever I go,
I wis I will de all my might you to love, and never no mo.
And if my friends say that I do amiss,
They shall not me let so for to do,
Mine heart me bids evermore to love you
Truly over all earthly thing,
And if they be never so wrath,
I trust it shall be better in time coming.

14

No more to you at this time, but the Holy Trinity have you in keeping; and I beseech you that this bill be not seen of none earthly creature save only yourself, &c.

And this letter was endited at Topcroft, with full heavy heart, &c.

By your own

MARGERY BREWS

KING HENRY VIII

The love letters which Henry VIII wrote to Anne Boleyn, probably while he was in the process of being divorced from his first wife, Catherine of Aragon, were stolen by the Papal envoy and are still at the Vatican. The King was first attracted to Anne on her return from France where she had attended on his sister, Mary, second queen of Louis XII. Anne, the daughter of Sir Thomas Boleyn, is described as being 'dark, vivacious, accomplished, unscrupulous and wanton'. She was married to Henry in the spring of 1533. In the following September she gave birth to her only surviving child, Elizabeth, future Queen of England. No doubt Anne's downfall was her own fault, she was too much in love with love. Her adultery with several men being discovered, she was beheaded in the Tower in 1536. Henry was already in love with Jane Seymour. Anne wrote her last letter to Henry in May 1536.

Henry's letters are practical and written in the idiom of the period. Yet one feels he was genuinely in love with Anne. They echo, however, that time when Kings and the aristocracy had little to do but hunt and sing madrigals. The corridors and passages of Hampton Court rang to such songs as Henry's 'Greensleeves'. The Court was a hive of love intrigue and to put oneself in the position of being beheaded may have been exciting and one way to overcome boredom. Anything was better in those days, than being exiled to one's estates where the only companions were peasants and serving maids.

To My Mistress

As the time seems very long since I heard from you, or concerning your health, the great love I have for you constrains me to send this bearer, to be better informed both of your health and pleasure, particularly because, since my last parting with you, I have been told that you have entirely changed the mind in which I left you, and that you neither mean to come to court with your mother, nor any other way; which report, if true, I cannot enough marvel at, being persuaded in my own mind that I have never committed any offence against you.

And it seems hard, in return for the great love I bear you, to be kept at a distance from the person and presence of the woman in the world that I value the most; and if you loved with as much affection as I hope you do, I am sure that the distance of our two persons would be equally irksome to you—though this does not belong so much to the mistress as to the servant.

Consider well, my mistress, how greatly your absence afflicts me. I hope it is not your will that it should be so. But if I heard for certain that you yourself desire it, I could but mourn my ill fortune, and strive by degrees to abate of my folly. And so, for lack of time, I make an end of this rude letter, beseeching you to give the bearer credence in all he will tell you from me.

Written by the hand of your entire servant,

H.R.

[no date]

By revolving in my mind the contents of your last letters, I have put myself into great agony, not knowing how to interpret them—whether to my disadvantage (as I understand some of them) or not. I beseech you earnestly to let me know your real mind as to the love between us two. It is needful for me to obtain this answer, having been for a whole year wounded with the dart of love, and not yet assured whether I shall succeed in finding a place in your heart and affection.

This uncertainty has hindered me of late from declaring you my mistress, lest it should prove that you only entertain for me an ordinary regard. But if you please to do the duty of a true and loyal mistress, and give up yourself heart and body to me, who will be, as I have been, your most loyal servant (if your rigour does not forbid me), I promise you that not only the name shall be given you, but also that I will take you for my mistress, casting off all others that are in competition with you out of my thoughts and affections, and serving you only.

I beg you to give an entire answer to this my rude letter, that I may know on what and how far I may depend; but if it does not please you to answer me in writing, let me know some place where I may have it by word of mouth, and I will go thither with all my heart.

No more, for fear of tiring you.

Written by the hand of him who would willing remain

Yours,

H. REX

6 *King Henry VIII to Lady Anne Boleyn*

1528

My Mistress and My Friend,

My heart and I surrender ourselves into your hands, and we supplicate to be commended to your good graces, and that by absence your affections may not be diminished to us. For that would be to augment our pain, which would be a great pity, since absence gives enough and more than I ever thought could be felt. This brings to my mind a fact in astronomy, which is, that the further the poles are from the sun, notwithstanding, the more scorching is his heat. Thus it is with our love; absence has placed distance between us, nevertheless fervour increases—at least on my part. I hope the same from you, assuring you that in my case the anguish of absence is so great, that it would be intolerable

18

were it not for the firm hope I have of your indissoluble affection towards me.

In order to remind you of it, and because I cannot in person be in your presence, I sent you the thing which comes nearest that is possible; that is to say, my picture, and the whole device, which you already know of, set in bracelets, wishing myself in their place when it pleaseth you. This is from the hand of your servant and friend.

H.R.

7 King Henry VIII to Lady Anne Boleyn

1528

The reasonable request in your last letter, with the pleasure also that I take to know them true, causes me to send you these news. The legate whom we most desire arrived at Paris on Sunday or Monday last, so that I trust by the next Monday to hear of his arrival at Calais. And then I trust within a while after to enjoy that which I have so longed for, to God's pleasure, and both our comforts.

No more to you at this present, mine own darling, for lack of time. But I would that you were in my arms, or I in yours—for I think it long since I kissed you.

Written after the killing of a hart, at eleven of the clock; purposing with God's grace, to-morrow, mighty timely, to kill another, by the hand which, I trust, shortly shall be yours.

HENRY R.

8 Anne Boleyn's last letter to King Henry VIII

1536

Sr.

Yor graces displeasure, and my Imprisonment are things so Strange unto me, and what to write or what to excuse, I am

19

altogether ignoraunt, wheras you send unto me (willinge me to confesse a truth and so to obtaine y^{or} favour) by such a one, whom you knowe to be my anciente professed enemy, I no sooner received this message by hym, then I right conceived y^{or} meaninge; and if as you saie confessinge a truth in deed, may procure my safty, I shall with all willingnesse and duty perfourme y^{or} Command; but let not y^{or} grace ever emagine that y^{or} poore wife, will ever be brought to acknowledge fault where not so much as a thought therof proceaded, and to speake a truth, never prince had wiffe more Loyall in all dutye, and in all true affection, than you have ever found in An Bollen, with which name and place I could willinglie have contented my self, if so god and y^r graces pleasure had been pleased. Neither did I at any tyme so farre forget my selfe in my exaltation, or received queenship but that I always looked for such an alteration as nowe I find, for the ground of my preferment beinge on no surere foundation than y^r graces fancy, ye least alteration, I knew was fitt and sufficient to drawe that fancy to some other subject.

You have chosen me from a lowe estate to be y^r Queen and Companion, farre beyond my deserte or desire, if then you found me worthy of such honour, good y^r grace, let not any light fancy or badd counsell of my enemys, withdraw y^r princely favour from me, neither let that staine, that unworthy stayne of a disloyall hearte towards y^r grace ever cast so foul a blott on y^{or} most dutifull wiffe and ye infant princesse y^r daughter; try me good kinge, but let me have a lawfull tryall, and let not my sworne enemys sitt as my accusers and judges; yea lett me receive an open tryall, for my truth shall feare no open shames; then shall you see either my innocency cleared, y^r suspicion and conscience satisfied, the ignominy and slander of ye world stopped, or my guilt openly declared; so that what so ever God or you may determine of me, y^r grace may be freed from an open censure, and my offence being so lawfully proved, y^r grace is at liberte, both before God and man, not only to execute worthy punishment on me as an unfaithfull wiffe, but to followe y^r affection allreddy setled on that partie, for whose sake I come now as I am, whose name I could some good while sith have pointed unto y^r grace, beinge not ignoraunt of my suspicion therein.

But if you have alreddy determined of me, and that not only my death but an infamous slander must bring you the injoying y^r

desired happiness, then I desire of God that he will pardon your greate synne herein, and likewise my enemys, the instruments thereof; and if he will not call you to a straight accounte for y^r unprincely and cruell usage of me, at his generall Judgement Seatt, where both you and my selfe must shortly appeare, and in whose right judgement I doubt not (what so ever ye worlde may thinke of me), my innocence shall be openly knowne, and sufficiently cleared; my last and only request shall be, that my selfe may only beare ye burthen of y^r graces displeasure, and that it may not touch the innocent soules of those poore gentlemen whom as I understand are likewise in straight imprisonment for my sake; If ever I have found favour in y^r sight; if ever ye name of An Bullen have been pleasinge to y^r eares lett me obtain this last request. And I will so leave to trouble y^r grace any furthere, with my earnest praiers to ye Trinity to have y^r grace in hys good keepinge, and to direct you in all your actions. From my dolfull prison in the Tower this 6 of May,

Y^r most loyall and faithfull wiffe

A.B.

9 King Henry VIII to Lady Jane Seymour

1536

My dear Friend and Mistress,

The bearer of these few lines from thy entirely devoted servant will deliver into thy fair hands a token of my true affection for thee, hoping you will keep it for ever in your sincere love for me. Advertising you that there is a ballad made lately of great derision against us, which if it go abroad and is seen by you, I pray you to pay no manner of regard to it. I am not at present informed who is the setter forth of this malignant writing: but if he is found out, he shall be straitly punished for it.

For the things ye lacked, I have minded my lord to supply them to you as soon as he could buy them. Thus hoping shortly to receive you in these arms, I end for the present,

Your own loving servant and sovereign,

H.R.

c. 1514   c. 1590

JOHN JOHNSON

John Johnson was a Tudor cloth merchant. He met and fell in love with Sabine and they were married sometime after 1538. His business took him abroad a good deal, mostly to Calais, from where he wrote loving (and sometimes teasing) letters to his new wife, once or twice a week.

John became something of a dandy. In Miss Barbara Winchester's *Tudor Family Portrait* we read how, while he was courting Sabine, he suddenly took it into his head to become fashionable. Splendid lawn shirts and new shoes adorned his latest wardrobe. We can imagine him strutting about Calais in striped satin doublets, gold and silver lace and, best of all, Spanish cloaks. When John, in one of his letters from Calais, teased Sabine about his landlady, Mrs. Margaret Baynham, she saw red. She went across immediately to see what was going on. She need not have worried or braved the cold November crossing. John was in bed with a cold. The fine clothes, when he was better again, were for Sabine alone.

Jesus anno 1545, the 8 in November,
at Calais.

In most loving wise I have me commended unto you, trusting
of your health. Your letter of the 2nd of this present month I
received this day, and perceive that ye received my letter by
Dunkerley but the day before. If he rode about the country with
the gelding I bought of him fourteen days or he came at you, he
played a knavish part with me, and show him, and that I am not
content to be so used at his hands.

My coming into England shall be, if God send me life and
health, eight or ten days before Christmas, and therefore within
this fourteen days I will write to you against what time ye shall
send up my horse to London. The death is here not very sore;
howbeit, we be all in God's hands: as it pleaseth him, so be it.
I will keep myself for your sake as well as I can, and at my coming
home I am content ye have the keeping of me. Howbeit, I may not
be no more shrewdly spoken to, nor yet curstly looked on!

As for the sale of M. Griffin's wool I force not of, but that
my father hath disappointed me of his wools it grieveth me. I
perceive now his friendship is but feigned—howbeit, I trust I shall
live. If ye either speak or send to him, let no less be declared
than that I conceive it unkindly, as I have no other cause.

I perceive ye have sent Richard to London for £40. I pray
you, desire Harrison to get as long time of Mr. Bickill's as he can
for his wools, for I can now appoint him no more money before
Christmas. Desire Harrison to show you how much wool I shall
have of him above 2,000 stone, for I esteem to have above by the
money he hath had of me.

I pray you, send for no more money to London before
Christmas, for I have none to spare. As the Lord knoweth, to
whom I commit you in haste, going to my bed at ten of the clock
at night—and would ye were in my bed to tarry me! I bid you
Goodnight, good wife sometimes!

By your loving husband,

JOHN JOHNSON

Clapthorn Manor—1545

I am glad to hear that I did please you so well at your last being at home, praying to the Lord to give me grace that I may do always so; and whereas you do wish yourself at home (I would no less), and desiring you most heartily to come home so soon as you can, and keep yourself well, good husband. . . .

SIR CHRISTOPHER HATTON

Sir Christopher Hatton was a member of the court which tried the Babington conspirators and who, therefore, condemned Chidiock Tichborne to death.[1] He was an accomplished man who loved dancing, became Lord Chancellor and one of Queen Elizabeth's favourites. He was the son of William Hatton of Holdenby, Northants. The Queen showered gifts on him from estates to positions of power and trust. A rumour (as with many of her favourites) got about that he was her lover.

Besides trying the Babington conspirators he was one of the commissioners who condemned Mary Queen of Scots to death. Friend of the poet Edmund Spenser, his name is perpetuated in Hatton Garden. He married the lady to whom he wrote the following letter, Alice, daughter of Thomas Fanshaw of Ware Park, Hertfordshire.

12   *Sir Christopher Hatton to Alice Fanshaw*

[no date]

Sweete Mres Ales,

As I never liked yᵉ amorous gallants of our tyme yᵗ make a traffique of lovinge and a trade of dissemblinge, lovinge whom

_____
[1] See letter 13.

ere they see, and ownlie lovinge whilst they see; soe am I not composed of soe hard a mettle but y^t fine beautie can pearce, and compleate perfections ravish, my admiringe soule. Hithertoe have I beene good tutor to my owne youthfull fancies, makinge keepe whom [home] in a plain whomly breast; but, since of late y^r beauty procured them a litle liberty, they are flowne abroade and have burnte theire winges in affections flame, soe y^t I feare they will never flye whome againe. I have ofte observed it to bee ye effect of base and a dull discerninge eie to dote upon every obiect without distinction, and have markt it out as true property of ye fierie soule to honour chast beauty where ever it harbers, and to love ye verie windowes of y^t house where soe faire a guest as vertue soiourneth. In which sole regarde my iudgment and affection, of olde enimyes, provinge true friends, are resolved for ever to dwell together, my affection commendinge my iudgment for soe faire a choice, my iudgment applaudinge my affection for her eager persute of soe woorthy a game. Both which ioyntlie dedicate unto yow, upon this paper altar, love answearable to y^r owne vertuous desertes, and farr more then these fewe lines, the stammeringe servantes of a speackinge mynde, can utter.

Onely thus y^r vertue made mee to wounder; from admiration sprunge my love; from unspotted love this letter, the atturnie of cause which must often plead for mee in the court of beautie, since ye disadvantage of ye tymes, my many iealious observers prevent my presence. Maye it therfore plaese yow to answeare my love with likinge, and my letters hereafter with a line or twoo; y^t both of us, disaccustomed to this newe theame of love, maye write y^t freely with our tongues, devided with modestie and reverence, could hardly utter.

Meane tyme receave from him y^t loves yow woorthylie his harte (beecause hee hath nothinge deerer then his harte), vowed to bee an aerternall bed for y^r love to rest on. Receave the wish of y^r full content from him who must live discontented, tyll expiringe, and extracted favour set a period to his chast longinge desires.

Yrs, in all harty affection,

CHR. HATTON

Thus have I rudely rigde this paper saile,
Soone maye hee waufted bee with happie gaile;
Nor needs it piratts feare, for, though it die,
Loves endles trafique in this breast doth lie.

CHIDIOCK TICHBORNE

Chidiock Tichborne joined the conspirators of the Babington plot and, like them, was caught. Anthony Babington was associated with Mary Queen of Scots in Paris and, on his return to London, he became the leader of a plot to murder Elizabeth and organise a general rising of Catholics and to liberate Mary. Walsingham's spies, however, intercepted his letters to Mary. He and five others, amongst whom were Tichborne, were imprisoned in the Tower. All were condemned to death for high treason and executed.

This is the letter Chidiock wrote to his wife shortly before he died.

13 Chidiock Tichborne to his wife

[1586]

To ye most lovinge wife alive, I commend me unto her and desire God to blesse her with all happiness, pray for her dead husband and be of good comfort, for I hope in Jesus Christ this morninge, to see the face of my Maker and redeemer in the most joyfull throan of his glorious kingdome, Commende me to all my friends and desire them to pray for me, and in all charitie to pardon me, if I have offended them, Commend me to my six

28

Sisters poore desolate soules; advise them to serve god, for without him no goodness is to be expected here, were it possible, my litle Sister Babb, the darlinge of my race might be bred by her, god would rewarde her; but I do her wronge I confesse that hath my desolate negligence too litle for her selfe, to add a further charge unto her. Deere wife forgive me, that hath by these meanes impoverished her fortunes; patience and pardon good wife I crave, make of these our necesseties a virtue, and lay no further burthen on my necke than hath alreadie borne, there be certaine debts that I owe; because I knowe not the order of the Lawe. Piteouse it hath taken from me all, forfeited by my course of offense to Her Majesty.

I cannot advise ye to benefite me herein, but if there fallout wherewithal lett them be discharged for godes sake. I will not that you should trouble yo.selfe with the performance of these matters, my owne heart, but make it knowne to my uncles and desire them, for the honour of god and ease of their sowls, to take care of them, as they may and specially care of my Sisters bringing opp . . .

Now Sweet Cheeke, what is left now to bestowe on thee, a Small joynture, a Small recompense for thy deserving, these legacies followinge to be thine owne. God of his infinite goodnes give thee grace alwaies to remaine his true and faithfull Servant who, that through the merites of his bitter and blessed passion, thou maiest become . . . of his kingdom with the blessed women in heaven . . . May the Holy Ghost comfort thee with all necessaries for the wealth of thy soul in the World to come, where untill it shall please almighty god I meete thee, farewell lovinge Wife, ffarewell the dearest to me on all ye Earthe, ffarewell, by the hand from the hearte of the most faithfull lovinge husbande

CHIDEOCK TICHEBURN

1552   1618

SIR WALTER RALEIGH

Once more a letter from a man about to die. Sir Walter Raleigh, one of the most brilliant Elizabethans, yet spent thirteen years in prison under James I. Even if it is true that he had a large amount of comfort and freedom in the Bloody Tower, where his wife and daughter lived with him, it was absurd to shut away such a man whose life was brilliant with enterprises of all kinds and who could have added so much lustre to James's reign. He was born at a farmhouse, Hayes, near Budleigh Salterton; married one of Elizabeth's Maids of Honour, Elizabeth Throgmorton, and used his imprisonment to write essays and poems and his famous *History of the World* to 130 B.C.

James was finally persuaded to release Raleigh to undertake an expedition to the Orinoco for gold. The Treasury was hard up and needed the services of the one man who could have succeeded, for Raleigh was obsessed with stories of El Dorado, which never existed, but which attracted adventurers of all kinds.

The Adventure (for such it was) was a complete failure and James, disappointed at the lack of gold, arrested Raleigh once more. He was conveniently accused of the old crime of high treason for which he had originally been imprisoned and on 29th October 1618 he was beheaded in Westminster Palace Yard.

You shall receive, dear wife, my last words in these my last lines. My love I send you, that you may keep it when I am dead; and my counsel, that you may remember it when I am no more. I would not with my last will present you with sorrows, dear Bess. Let them go to the grave with me, and be buried with me in the dust. And, seeing it is not the will of God that ever I shall see you in this life, bear my destruction gently, and with a heart like yourself.

First, I send you all the thanks my heart can conceive, or my pen express, for your many troubles and cares taken for me, which —though they have not taken effect as you wished—yet my debt is to you never the less; but pay it I never shall in this world.

Secondly, I beseech you, for the love you bare me living, that you do not hide yourself many days, but by your travail seek to help your miserable fortunes, and the right of your poor child. Your mourning cannot avail me that am but dust.

You shall understand that my lands were conveyed to my child *bona fide*. The writings were drawn at midsummer was twelvemonth, as divers can witness. My honest cousin Brett can testify so much, and Dalberie, too, can remember somewhat therein. And I trust my blood will quench their malice that desire my slaughter; and that they will not also seek to kill you and yours with extreme poverty. To what friend to direct thee I know not, for all mine have left me in the true time of trial; and I plainly perceive that my death was determined from the first day. Most sorry I am (as God knoweth) that, being thus surprised with death, I can leave you no better estate. I meant you all mine office of wines, or that I could purchase by selling it; half my stuff and jewels, but some few for my boy. But God hath prevented all my determinations; the great God that worketh all in all. If you can live free from want, care for no more; for the rest is but vanity. Love God, and begin betimes to repose yourself on Him; therein you shall find true and lasting riches, and endless comfort. For the rest, when you have travelled and wearied your thoughts on all sorts of worldly cogitations, you shall sit down by Sorrow in the end. Teach your son also to serve and fear God while he is young, that the fear of God may grow up in him. Then will God be a husband unto you, and a father unto him; a husband and a father which can never be taken from you.

Bayly oweth me two hundred pounds, and Adrian six hundred pounds. In Jersey, also, I have much owing me. The arrearages of the wines will pay my debts. And, howsoever, for my soul's health, I beseech you pay all poor men. When I am gone no doubt you shall be sought unto by many, for the world thinks that I was very rich; but take heed of the pretences of men and of their affections; for they last but in honest and worthy men. And no greater misery can befall you in this life than to become a prey, and after to be despised. I speak it (God knows) not to dissuade you from marriage—for that will be best for you—both in respect of God and of the world. As for me, I am no more yours, nor you mine. Death hath cut us asunder; and God hath divided me from the world, and you from me.

Remember your poor child for his father's sake, that chose you and loved you in his happiest times. Get those letters (if it be possible) which I writ to the Lords, wherein I sued for my life, but God knoweth that it was for you and yours that I desired it, but it is true that I disdain myself for begging it. And know it (dear wife) that your son is the child of a true man, and who, in his own respect, despiseth Death, and all his misshapen and ugly forms.

I cannot write much. God know how hardly I stole this time, when all sleep; and it is time to separate my thoughts from this world. Beg my dead body, which living was denied you; and either lay it at Sherbourne if the land continue, or in Exeter church, by my father and mother. I can write no more. Time and Death call me away.

The everlasting, infinite, powerful and inscrutable God that is goodness itself, mercy itself, the true life and light, keep you and yours, and have mercy on me, and teach me to forgive my persecutors and false accusers; and send us to meet in His glorious kingdom. My true wife, farewell. Bless my poor boy; pray for me. My true God hold you both in His arms.

Written with the dying hand of sometime thy husband, but now (alas) overthrown. Your's that was; but now not my own,

W. RALEIGH

KING CHARLES I

Charles I is, I suppose, the epitome of the arrogant aristocrat. He became king at the age of 25. He lacked his father's (James I) shrewdness and tended to live in a world of his own. He was a weak child and it was thought, at one time, that he would not live. He was proud, obstinate and pious. One of the tenderest pictures of the King is when he visited Little Gidding, the religious house that Nicholas Ferrar set up, near Huntingdon, and, on an alarm, had to escape by lantern-light, across the fields to a near-by manor house. With his people he was out of sympathy though he was loved by his personal friends. Henrietta Maria had great influence over him. She was of an intriguing nature and frivolous—the reverse of Charles, sister to King Louis XIII and daughter of King Henry IV of France. Charles and Henrietta were married by proxy on 1st May 1625 and he received her at Canterbury on 13th June.

Clarendon, the historian, said of the King, 'He was the worthiest gentleman, the best master, the best friend, the best husband, the best father and the best Christian that the age in which he lived produced.'

Charles was executed on 30th January 1649, outside the Banqueting Hall of the Palace of Whitehall.

Oxford,
9th of April 1645

Dear Heart,

Though it be an uncomfortable thing to write by a slow messenger, yet all occasions of this which is now the only way of conversing with thee are so welcome to me as I shall be loth to lose any; but expect neither news nor public business from me by this way of conveyance. Yet, judging thee by myself, even these nothings will not be unwelcome to thee, though I chide thee—which if I could I would—for thy too sudden taking alarms.

I pray thee consider, since I love thee above all earthly things, and that my contentment is inseparably conjoined with thine, must not all my actions tend to serve and please thee? If thou knew what a life I lead (I speak not in respect of the common distractions), even in point of conversation, which in my mind is the chief joy or vexation of one's life, I dare say thou wouldest pity me. For some are too wise, others too foolish, some too busy, others too reserved, many fantastic. . . .

I confess thy company hath perhaps made me, in this, hard to be pleased, but not less to be pitied by thee, who art the only cure for this disease. The end of all is this, to desire thee to comfort me as often as thou canst with thy letters. And dost not thou think that to know particulars of thy health, and how thou spendest thy time, are pleasing subjects unto me, though thou hast no other business to write of?

Believe me, sweet heart, thy kindness is as necessary to comfort my heart as thy assistance is for my affairs.

Thine.

16   *King Charles I to the Queen-Consort, Henrietta Maria*

Oxford,
April 15th 1646

Dear Heart,

Since mine of the 13th to thee, not having heard anything

from Montreuil, I find myself like to be drawn into very great straits. And being absolutely resolved, God willing, never to fall into the rebels' hands as long as I can by any industry or danger prevent it, I have also resolved to expose myself to all the difficulties and hazards that can occur to my deliverance; and, not to flatter myself in this purpose, whether I be obliged to go to the Scotch—or what other course soever I shall be forced to take—they (the difficulties) will be great enough to invite me to think of those things which will be of essential necessity, in case I do not save myself. One which, though not only necessary in that case, is the having my son with thee in France.

I do therefore charge thee, as soon as thou shalt receive this, if then he shall not be with thee (which I would not willingly doubt), that thou send mine and thine own positive commands to him to come unto thee. And this I write to thee now without any scruple; for that in every event that my present purpose can possibly produce, this counsel is not to be disputed. For, whether I save myself, or be taken prisoner, my son can be no where so well, for all the reasons I have to look upon in consideration of thee, myself, and him, as that he should be now with thee in France.

Therefore, again I recommend to thee that, if he be not with thee, thou send immediately for him; assuring thee that most certainly, if God let me live, I will either privately or by force attempt very suddenly to get from hence. I have not now time to tell thee the rest of the particulars I have in my thoughts, in case I hear from Montreuil that things are prepared for my reception in the Scotch [*sic*] or that I be forced to take any other course; but shall send thee an express to inform thee at large. So I conjure thee to pray for him who is entirely thine.

CHARLES R.

DOROTHY OSBORNE

Anyone interested in the correspondence of the past will know and love the letters of Dorothy Osborne. So much has been written about them that they hardly need any introduction. When Thomas Peregrine Courtenay originally added, in an Appendix, extracts from forty-two of Dorothy's letters to his Life of *Sir William Temple*, Macaulay reviewing the book wrote, 'We find so much in the love letters which Mr. Courtenay has published, that we would gladly purchase equally interesting billets with ten times their weight in State papers taken at random.' He went on, 'The mutual relations of the two sexes seem to us to be at least as important as the mutual relations of any two Governments in the world; and a series of letters written by a virtuous, amiable, and sensible girl, and intended for the eye of her lover alone, can scarcely fail to throw some light on the relations of the sexes; whereas it is perfectly possible, as all who have made any historical researches can attest, to read bale after bale of despatches and protocols, without catching one glimpse of light about the relations of Governments.' It was Courtenay's book and Macaulay's review of it which excited Sir Edward Parry to research into Dorothy Osborne's life. Sir Edward's book *Letters from Dorothy Osborne to Sir William Temple, 1652–54*, is the standard edition.

Dorothy and William were Royalists and one of the interesting points from their letters is the fact that the Puritans made so little impact on life in the country. Yet it was not an easy engagement.

For one thing Dorothy was besieged by other admirers, amongst whom was Henry Cromwell, the Protector's son; for another William's father was against the match as he had far more wealthy and glamorous ladies whom he wished his son to marry. The courtship, then, went on for seven years until Christmas Day 1654 when they were married. A few days before Dorothy was stricken by smallpox. It made no difference to William's love for her, for this was 'a marriage of souls', and they enjoyed forty years of married life. One of Dorothy's most intimate friends was Queen Mary II, whose letters appear on pp. 52–59. It is possible that Dorothy died from her grief at the death of Mary.

17 *Dorothy Osborne to Sir William Temple*

[no date]

Sir,—Jane was so unlucky as to come out of town before your return, but she tells me she left my letter with Nan Stacy for you. I was in hope she would have brought me one from you; and because she did not I was resolv'd to punish her, and kept her up till one o'clock telling me all her stories. Sure, if there be any truth in the old observation, your cheeks glowed notably; and 'tis most certain that if I were with you, I should chide notably. What do you mean to be so melancholy? By her report your humour is grown insupportable. I can allow it not to be altogether what she says, and yet it may be very ill too; but if you loved me you would not give yourself over to that which will infallibly kill you, if it continue. I know too well that our fortunes have given us occasion enough to complain and to be weary of her tyranny; but, alas! would it be better if I had lost you or you me; unless we were sure to die both together, 'twould but increase our misery, and add to that which is more already than we can well tell how to bear. You are more cruel than she regarding a life that's dearer to me than that of the whole world besides, and which makes all the happiness I have or ever shall be capable of. Therefore, by all our friendship I conjure you and, by the power you have given me, command you, to preserve yourself with the same care that you would have me live. 'Tis all the obedience I require of you, and will be the greatest testimony you can give me of your faith. When you have promised me this, 'tis not impossible that I may promise you shall see me shortly; though my brother Peyton (who says he will come down to fetch his daughter) hinders me from making the journey in compliment to her. Yet I shall perhaps find business enough to carry me up to town. 'Tis all the service I expect from two girls whose friends have given me leave to provide for, that some order I must take for the disposal of them may serve for my pretence to see you; but then I must find you pleased and in good humour, merry as you were wont to be when we first met, if you will not have me show that I am nothing akin to my cousin Osborne's lady.

But what an age 'tis since we first met, and how great a change it has wrought in both of us; if there had been as great a one in my face, it could be either very handsome or very ugly. For God's sake, when we meet, let us design one day to remember old stories in, to ask one another by what degrees our friendship grew to this height 'tis at. In earnest, I am lost sometimes with thinking on't; and though I can never repent the share you have in my heart, I know not whether I gave it you willingly or not at first. No, to speak ingenuously, I think you got an interest there a good while before I thought you had any, and it grew so insensibly, and yet so fast, that all the traverses it has met with since has served rather to discover it to me than at all to hinder it. By this confession you will see that I am past all disguise with you, and that you have reason to be satisfied with knowing as much of my heart as I do myself. Will the kindness of this letter excuse the shortness on't? For I have twenty more, I think to write, and the hopes I had of receiving one from you last night kept me from writing this when I had more time; or if all this will not satisfy, make your own conditions, so you do not return it me by the shortness of yours. Your servant kisses your hands, and I am

Your faithful.

Sir—Why are you so sullen, and why am I the cause? Can you believe that I do willingly defer my journey? I know you do not. Why, then, should my absence now be less supportable to you than heretofore? Nay, it shall not be long (if I can help it), and I shall break through all inconveniences rather than deny you anything that lies in my power to grant. But by your own rules, then, may I not expect the same from you? Is it possible that all I have said cannot oblige you to a care of yourself? What a pleasant distinction you make when you say that 'tis not melancholy makes you do these things, but a careless forgetfulness. Did ever anybody forget themselves to that degree that was not melancholy in extremity? Good God! how you are altered; and what is it that has done it? I have known you when of all the things in the world you would not have been taken for a discontent; you were, as I thought, perfectly pleased with your condition; what has made it so much worse since? I know nothing you have lost, and am sure you have gained a friend that is capable of the highest degree of friendship you can propound, that has already given an entire heart for that which she received, and 'tis no more in her will than in her power ever to recall it or divide it; if this be not enough to satisfy you, tell me what I can do more?

There are a great many ingredients must go to the making me happy in a husband. First, as my cousin Franklin says, our humours must agree; and to do that he must have that kind of breeding that I have had, and used that kind of company. That is, he must not be so much a country gentleman as to understand nothing but hawks and dogs, and be fonder of either than his wife; nor of the next sort of them whose aim reaches no further than to be Justice of the Peace, and once in his life High Sheriff, who reads no book but Statutes, and studies nothing but how to make a speech interlarded with Latin that may amaze his disagreeing poor neighbours, and fright them rather than persuade them into quietness. He must not be a thing that began the world in a free school, was sent from thence to the university, and is at his furthest when he reaches the Inns of Court, has no acquaintance but those of his form in these places, speaks the French he has picked out of old laws, and admires nothing but the stories he has heard of the revels that were kept there before his time. He must not be a town gallant neither, that lives in a tavern and an ordinary, that cannot imagine how an hour should be spent without company unless it be in sleeping, that makes court to all the women he sees, thinks they believe him, and laughs and is laughed at equally. Nor a travelled Monsieur whose head is all feather inside and outside, that can talk of nothing but dances and duets, and has courage enough to wear slashes when every one else dies with cold to see him. He must not be a fool of no sort, nor peevish, nor ill-natured, nor proud, nor covetous; and to all this must be added, that he must love me and I him as much as we are capable of loving. Without all this, his fortune, though never so great, would not satisfy me; and with it, a very moderate one would keep me from ever repenting my disposal.

I have been as large and as particular in my descriptions as my cousin Molle is in his of Moor Park,—but that you know the place so well I would send it you,—nothing can come near his patience in writing it, but my reading on't. Would you had sent me your father's letter, it would not have been less welcome to me than to you; and you may safely believe that I am equally concerned with you in anything. I should be pleased to see something of my Lady Carlisle's writing, because she is so extraordinary a person. I have been thinking of sending you my picture till I could come myself; but a picture is but dull company, and that you need not; besides, I cannot tell whether it be very like me or not, though 'tis the best I ever had drawn for me, and Mr. Lilly [Lely] will have it that he never took more pains to make a good one in his life, and that was it I think that spoiled it. He was condemned for making the first he drew for me a little worse than I, and in making this better he has made it as unlike as t'other. He is now, I think, at my Lord Pagett's at Marloe [Marlow], where I am promised he shall draw a picture of my Lady for me, —she gives it me, she says, as the greatest testimony of her friendship to me, for by her own rule she is past the time of having pictures taken of her. After eighteen, she says, there is no face but decays apparently; I would fain have had her excepted such as had never been beauties, for my comfort, but she would not.

When you see your friend Mr. Heningham, you may tell him in his ear there is a willow garland coming towards him. He might have sped better in his suit if he had made court to me, as well as to my Lady Ruthin. She has been my wife this seven years, and whosoever pretends there must ask my leave. I have now given my consent that she shall marry a very pretty little gentleman, Sir Christopher Yelverton's son, and I think we shall have a wedding ere it be long. My Lady her mother, in great kindness, would have recommended Heningham to me, and told me in a compliment that I was fitter for him than her daughter, who was younger, and therefore did not understand the world so well; that she was certain if he knew me he would be extremely taken, for I would make just that kind of wife he looked for. I humbly thanked her, but said I was certain he would not make that kind of husband I looked for,—and so it went no further.

I expect my eldest brother here shortly, whose fortune is well mended by my other brother's death, so as if he were satisfied himself with what he has done, I know no reason why he might not be very happy; but I am afraid he is not. I have not seen my sister since I knew she was so; but, sure, she can have lost no beauty, for I never saw any that she had, but good black eyes, which cannot alter. He loves her, I think, at the ordinary rate of husbands, but not enough, I believe, to marry her so much to his disadvantage if it were to do again; and that would kill me were I as she, for I could be infinitely better satisfied with a husband that had never loved me in hopes he might, than with one that began to love me less than he had done.

I am yours.

19 *Dorothy Osborne to Sir William Temple*

[no date]

Sir,—I am extremely sorry that your letter miscarried, but I am confident my brother has it not. As cunning as he is, he could not hide from me, but that I should discover it some way or other. No; he was here, and both his men when this letter should have come, and not one of them stirred out that day; indeed, the next day they went all to London. The note you writ to Jane came in one of Nan's, by Collins, but nothing else; it must be lost by the porter that was sent with it, and 'twas very unhappy that there should be anything in it of more consequence than ordinary; it may be numbered amongst the rest of our misfortunes, all which an inconsiderate passion has occasioned. You must pardon me I cannot be reconciled to it, it has been the ruin of us both. 'Tis true that nobody must imagine to themselves ever to be absolute master on't, but there is a great difference betwixt that and yielding to it, between striving with it and soothing it up till it grows too strong for one. Can I remember how ignorantly and innocently I suffered it to steal upon me by degrees; how under a mask of friendship I cozened myself into that which, had it appeared to me at first in its true shape, I had feared and shunned? Can I discern that it has made the trouble of your life, and cast a cloud upon mine, that will help to cover me in my grave? Can I know that it wrought so upon us both as to make neither of us friends to one another, but agree in running wildly to our own destruction, and that perhaps of some innocent persons who might live to curse our folly that gave them so miserable a being? Ah! if you love yourself or me, you must confess that I have reason to condemn this senseless passion; that whereso'er it comes destroys all that entertain it; nothing of judgment or discretion can live with it, and it puts everything else out of order before it can find a place for itself. What has it brought my poor Lady Anne Blunt to? She is the talk of all the footmen and boys in the street, and will be company for them shortly, and yet is so blinded by her passion as not at all to perceive the misery she has brought herself to; and this fond love of hers has so rooted all sense of nature out of her heart, that, they say, she is no more moved than a statue with the affliction of a father and mother that doted on her, and had placed the comfort of their lives in her preferment. With all this is it not manifest to the whole world that Mr. Blunt could not consider anything in this action but his own interest, and that he makes her a very ill return for all her kindness; if he had loved her truly he would have died rather than have been the occasion of this misfortune to her. My cousin Franklin (as you observe very well) may say fine things now she is warm in Moor Park, but she is very much altered in her opinions since her marriage, if these be her own. She left a gentleman, that I could name, whom she had much more of kindness for than ever she had for Mr. Franklin, because his estate was less; and upon the discovery of some letters that her mother intercepted, suffered herself to be persuaded that twenty-three hundred pound a year was better than twelve hundred, though with a person she loved; and has recovered it so well, that you see she confesses there is nothing in her condition she desires to alter at the charge of a wish. She's happier by much than I shall ever be, but I do not envy her; may she long enjoy it, and I an early and a quiet grave, free from the trouble of this busy world, where all with passion pursue their own interests at their neighbour's charges; where nobody is pleased but somebody complains on't; and where 'tis impossible to be without giving and receiving injuries.

You would know what I would be at, and how I intend to dispose of myself. Alas! were I in my own disposal, you should come to my grave to be resolved; but grief alone will not kill. All that I can say, then, is that I resolve on nothing but to arm myself with patience, to resist nothing that is laid upon me, nor struggle for what I have no hope to get. I have no ends nor no designs, nor will my heart ever be capable of any; but like a country wasted by a civil war, where two opposing parties have disputed their right so long till they have made it worth neither of their conquests, 'tis ruined and desolated by the long strife within it to that degree as 'twill be useful to none,—nobody that knows the condition 'tis in will think it worth the gaining, and I shall not trouble anybody with it. No, really, if I may be permitted to desire anything, it shall be only that I may injure nobody but myself,—I can bear anything that reflects upon me; or if I cannot, I can die; but I would fain die innocent, that I might hope to be happy in the next world, though never in this. I take it a little ill that you should conjure me by anything, with a belief that 'tis more powerful with me than your kindness. No, assure yourself what that alone cannot gain will be denied to all the world. You would see me, you say? You may do so if you please, though I know not to what end. You deceive yourself if you think it would prevail upon me to alter my intentions; besides, I can make no contrivances; it must be here, and I must endure the noise it will make, and undergo the censures of a people that choose ever to give the worst interpretation that anything will bear. Yet if it can be any ease to you to make me more miserable than I am, never spare me; consider yourself only, and not me at all,—'tis no more than I deserve for not accepting what you offered me whilst 'twas in your power to make it good, as you say it then was. You were prepared, it seems, but I was surprised, I confess. 'Twas a kind fault though; and you may pardon it with more reason than I have to forgive it myself. And let me tell you this too, as lost and as wretched as I am, I have still some sense of my reputation left in me,—I find that to my cost,—I shall attempt to preserve it as clear as I can; and to do that, I must, if you see me thus, make it the last of our interviews. What can excuse me if I should entertain any person that is known to pretend to me, when I can have no hope of ever marrying him? And what hope can I have of that when the fortune that can only make it possible to me depends upon a thousand accidents and contingencies, the uncertainty of the place 'tis in, and the government it may fall under, your father's life or his success, his disposal of himself and of his fortune, besides the time that must necessarily be required to produce all this, and the changes that may probably bring with it, which 'tis impossible for us to foresee? All this considered, what have I to say for myself when people shall ask, what 'tis I expect? Can there by anything vainer than such a hope upon such grounds? You must needs see the folly on't yourself, and therefore examine your own heart what 'tis fit for me to do, and what you can do for a person you love, and that deserves your compassion if nothing else,—a person that will always have an inviolable friendship for you, a friendship that shall take up all the room my passion held in my heart, and govern there as master, till death come and take possession and turn it out.

Why should you make an impossibility where there is none? A thousand accidents might have taken me from you, and you must have borne it. Why would not your own resolution work as much upon you as necessity and time does infallibly upon people? Your father would take it very ill, I believe, if you should pretend to love me better than he did my Lady, yet she is dead and he lives, and perhaps may do to love again. There is a gentlewoman in this country that loved so passionately for six or seven years that her friends, who kept her from marrying, fearing her death, consented to it; and within half a year her husband died, which afflicted her so strongly nobody thought she would have

44

lived. She saw no light but candles in three years, nor came abroad in five; and now that 'tis some nine years past, she is passionately taken again with another, and how long she has been so nobody knows but herself. This is to let you see 'tis not impossible what I ask, nor unreasonable. Think on't, and attempt it at least; but do it sincerely, and do not help your passion to master you. As you have ever loved me do this.

The carrier shall bring your letters to Suffolk House to Jones. I shall long to hear from you; but if you should deny the only hope that's left me, I must beg you will defer it till Christmas Day be past; for, to deal freely with you, I have some devotions to perform then, which must not be disturbed with anything, and nothing is like to do it as so sensible an affliction. Adieu.

20   *Dorothy Osborne to Sir William Temple*

[no date]

Sir,—If you have ever loved me do not refuse the last request I shall ever make you; 'tis to preserve yourself from the violence of your passion. Vent it all upon me; call me and think me what you please; make me, if it be possible, more wretched than I am. I'll bear it all without the least murmur. Nay, I deserve it all, for had you never seen me you had certainly been happy. 'Tis my misfortunes only that have that infectious quality as to strike at the same time me and all that's dear to me. I am the most unfortunate woman breathing, but I was never false. No; I call heaven to witness that if my life could satisfy for the least injury my fortune has done you (I cannot say 'twas I that did them you), I would lay it down with greater joy than any person ever received a crown; and if I ever forgot what I owe you, or ever entertained a thought of kindness for any person in the world besides, may I live a long and miserable life. 'Tis the greatest curse I can invent; if there be a greater, may I feel it. This is all I can say. Tell me if it be possible I can do anything for you, and tell me how I may deserve your pardon for all the trouble I have given you. I would not die without it.

[no date]

. . . 'Twill be pleasinger to you, I am sure, to tell you how fond I am of your lock. Well, in earnest now, and setting aside all compliments, I never saw finer hair, nor of a better colour; but cut no more on't, I would not have it spoiled for the world. If you love me, be careful on't. I am combing, and curling, and kissing this lock all day, and dreaming on't all night. The ring, too, is very well, only a little of the biggest. Send me a tortoise one that is a little less than that I sent for a pattern. I would not have the rule so absolutely true without exception that hard hairs be ill-natured, for then I should be so. But I can allow that all soft hairs are good, and so are you, or I am deceived as much as you are if you think I do not love you enough. Tell me, my dearest, am I? You will not be if you think I am

Yours.

1619   1655

JOHN PENRUDDOCK

Nothing could be more tender than the few love letters we have from men about to die on the scaffold. They are true lovers' letters. They seem, as in this letter from John Penruddock to his wife the day before he died, to hold the essential essence of love, a culmination of love. In them the whole point of love seems to be crystallised and eternally held under a glass. If, at the moment of death, a man could still so love his wife, how much more idyllic must have been their young love!

John Penruddock was a Royalist 'who tried in vain to renew the exiled King's cause in arms; his force was quickly out-numbered and he was beheaded at Exeter'.

22   *John Penruddock to his wife*

4th May 1655

Dearest Best of Creatures!

I had taken leave of the world when I received yours; it did at once recall my fondness to life, and enable me to resign it. As I am sure I shall leave none behind me like you, which weakens my resolution to part from you, so when I reflect I am going to a place where there are none but such as you, I recover my courage. But fondness breaks in upon me; and as I would not have

47

my tears flow to-morrow, when your husband and the father of
our dear babes is a public spectacle, do not think meanly of me,
that I give way to grief now in private, when I see my sand run so
fast, and within a few hours I am to leave you helpless and exposed
to the merciless and insolent that have wrongfully put me to a
shameful death, and will object the shame to my poor children. I
thank you for all your goodness to me, and will endeavour so to
die as to do nothing unworthy that virtue in which we have
mutually supported each other, and for which I desire you not to
repine that I am first to be rewarded, since you ever preferred me
to yourself in all other things. Afford me, with cheerfulness, the
precedence of this. I desire your prayers in the article of death;
for my own will then be offered for you and yours.

SIR CHRISTOPHER WREN

The great fire of London had one excellent effect, at least. It gave Sir Christopher Wren his great opportunity. Old St Paul's, it is true, was in a ruinous state before the fire and Charles II had already asked Wren to prepare a plan for restoration which he did in May 1666. The building was destroyed in the following September and the first stone of the new cathedral was laid on 21st June 1675. Wren undertook to make designs for the rebuilding of fifty burnt London churches.

Wren was not only immortalised in stone. Who does not know the famous clerihew:

> Sir Christopher Wren
> Went to dine with some men,
> He said 'If anyone calls,
> Tell them I'm designing St Paul's.'

No doubt Faith Coghill, to whom Wren wrote the following exquisite love letter, would have appreciated the lines. He married her, the daughter of Sir John Coghill, in December 1669. There were two sons of the marriage.

[no date]

Madam,

The artificer having never before met with a drowned Watch, like an ignorant physician has been so long about the cure that he hath made me very unquiet that your commands should be so long deferred; however, I have sent the watch at last and envy the felicity of it, that it should be so near your side, and so often enjoy your Eye, and be consulted by you how your Time shall pass while you employ your hand in your excellent works. But have a care of it, for I put such a Spell into it that every Beating of the Ballance will tell you 'tis the pulse of my Heart which labours as much to serve you and more Truly than the watch; for the watch I believe will sometimes lie, and sometimes perhaps be idle and unwilling to go, having received so much injury by being drenched in that briny bath, that I despair it should ever be a True Servant to you more. But as for me (unless you drown me too in my Tears) you may be confident I shall never cease to be, Your most affectionate, humble servant,

CHR. WREN

QUEEN MARY II

These historical figures, the kings and queens of the past, are involved so completely in the events of their times that they become shadowy puppets who were influenced by their reaction to the plots, the religious tensions, even the scanty medical knowledge of the days they lived through. Their 'opinions' are identified by their 'history' which they helped to make. Indeed, in one sense, it is true that they matter only as 'historical figures', names to classify a period—the years of their reigning. It is not until we sit before their love letters (if any still survive) that they become real persons suffering from jealousies, passion, longings and anxieties.

Queen Mary was the wife of William III. She was the eldest daughter and heiress of James II by his first marriage with Anne Hyde, daughter of the Earl of Clarendon. She was married, at 15, to William Prince of Orange-Nassau and, from a spoilt girl, she developed into the mature woman who could renounce any claims to the throne that she possessed in favour of her husband. She adored William and clung tenaciously to the Protestant religion. In 1688 James fled to France and William landed and was welcomed in the West Country. He made his way from Exeter to London and, when Mary joined him in 1689, they were proclaimed King and Queen and crowned on 11th April.

Mary, whose unfulfilled longing for children induced in her a melancholy which undermined her spirit, died of smallpox, after a reign of six years, in 1694. Many years after her death her letters

51

were found in a box known as 'King William's Chest'. We have none of William's letters.

24 Queen Mary II to King William III

Whitehall, June $\frac{19}{29}$, 1690

You will be weary of seeing every day a letter from me, it may be; yet being apt to flatter myself, I will hope you will be as willing to read as I to write. And indeed it is the only comfort I have in this world, besides that of trust in God. I have nothing to say to you at present that is worth writing, and I think it unreasonable to trouble you with my grief, which I must continue while you are absent, though I trust every post to hear some good news or other from you; therefore, I shall make this very short, and only tell you I have got a swell'd face, though not quite so bad yet, as it was in Holland five years ago. I believe it came by standing too much at the window when I took the waters. I cannot enough thank God for your being so well past the dangers of the sea; I beseech him in his mercy still to preserve you so, and send us once more a happy meeting upon earth. I long to hear again from you how the air of Ireland agrees with you, for I must own I am not without fears for that, loving you so entirely as I do, and shall till death.

25 Queen Mary II to King William III
[Upon the arrival of the French fleet on the coast]

Whitehall, the $\frac{2\ \text{July}}{22\ \text{June}}$, 1690
Half 11 at night

The news which is come tonight of the French fleet being upon the coast, makes it thought necessary to write you both ways; and I, that you may see how matters stand in my heart, prepare a letter for each. I think lord Torrington has made no haste; And I cannot tell you whether his being sick, and staying for lord Pembroke's regiment, will be a sufficient excuse; but I will not take your time with my reasonings, I shall only tell you, that I am so little afraid, that I begin to fear I have not sense enough to apprehend the danger; for whether it threatens Ireland, or this place, to me 'tis much at one, as to the fear; for as much a coward as you think me, I fear more for your dear person than my poor carcass. I know who is the most necessary in the world. What I fear most at present is not hearing from you. Love me whatever happens, and be assured I am ever intirely yours till death.

26 *Queen Mary II to King William III*
[Upon the same subject]

2 July

Whitehall, the 22 June, 1690

As I was ready to go into my bed, lord Nott. came and brought me a letter, of which he is going to give you an account; for my own part, I shall say nothing to it, but that I trust God will preserve us, you where you are, and poor I here. Methinks lord Torrington has made no haste; they say he stays for lord Pembroke's regiment; he also has not been very quick, for he received it at 8 this evening, and kept it till now, that he has sent it open to lord Nott. I thank God I am not much afraid; I think too little; which makes me fear 'tis want of apprehending the danger. That which troubles me most in all things is your absence and the fear I am in. Something may be done to hinder us from hearing from you; in that case I don't know what will become of us. I still trust in God who is our only help. Farewell, I will trouble you with no more, but only desire you, whatsoever happens, to love me as I shall you to death.

[She writes a long letter about the coming of the French fleet and ends]

$$\frac{4 \text{ July}}{\text{Whitehall, June 24, 1690}}$$

Since I have writ this, I was called out to lord Nott. who brought me your dear letter of the $\frac{28\text{th}}{18\text{th}}$, which is so welcome that I cannot express it, especially because you pity me, which I like and desire from you, and you only. As for the building, I fear there will be many obstacles; for I spoke to sir J. Lowther this very day, and hear so much use for money, and find so little, that I cannot tell whether that of Hampton Court will not be a little the worse for it, especially since the French ar in the Channel, and at present between Portland and us, from whence the stone must come; but in a day or two, I hope to give you a more certain account, this being only my own conjecture. God be praised that you are so well, I hope in his mercy he will continue it. . . . It is now candle-light, and I dare say no more but that I am ever and entirely yours.

28 *Queen Mary II to King William III*

[She began the letter at eight in the morning]

$$\frac{\text{July 8}}{\text{Whitehall, June 28, 1690}}$$
10. at night

Since my writing this a great deal of news [which she reveals] but before I went out of the room, I received your dear letter from Lough-bricklin, but I cannot express what I then felt, and still feel, at the thoughts that now it may be you are ready to give battle, or have done it. My heart is ready to burst. I can say nothing, but pray to God for you. This has waked me who was almost asleep, and almost puts me out of any possibility of saying any more, yet I must strive with my heart to tell you, that this afternoon the ill news of the battle of Fleury came; I had a letter from the Prince of Waldec, with a copy of the account he sent you, so that I can say nothing, but that God, in whose hands all events only are, knows best why he has ordered it so, and to him we must submit. . . . I must end my letter, for my eyes are at present in somewhat a worse condition than before I received your letter; my impatience for another from you is as great as my love, which will not end but with my life, which is very uneasy to me at present; but I trust in God, who alone can preserve you and comfort me.

29 *Queen Mary II to King William III*
[On his being wounded]

16
Whitehall, July 6, 1690

I can never give God thanks enough as long as I live for your preservation; I hope in his mercy this is a sign he preserves you to finish the work he has begun by you; but I hope it may be a warning to you, to let you see you are exposed to as many accidents as others; and though it has pleased God to keep you once in so visible a manner, yet you must forgive me if I tell you that I should think it a tempting God to venture again without great necessity; I know what I say of this kind will be attributed to fear; I own I have a great deal for your dear person, yet I hope I am not unreasonable upon the subject, for I do trust in God, and he is pleased every day to confirm me more and more in the confidence I have in him; yet my fears are not less, since I cannot tell, if it should be his will to suffer you to come to harm for our sins, and when that might happen; For though God is able, yet many times he punishes the sins of a nation as it seems good in his sight. Your writing me word how soon you hoped to send me good news, shews me how soon you thought there might be some action, and that thought put me in perpetual pain. This morning when I heard the express was come, before lord Nott. came up, I was taken with a trembling for fear, which has hardly left me yet, and I really don't know what I do. Your letter came just before I went to chapell; and though the first thing lord Notting. told me was, that you were very well, yet the thoughts that you expose yourself thus to danger, fright me out of my wits, and make me not able to keep my trouble to myself; but for God's sake let me beg you to take more care for the time to come; consider what depends upon your safety; there are so many more important things than myself, that I think I am not worthy naming them. But it may be the worst will be over before this time, so that I will say no more. . . .

It is now past 10 o'clock; I don't tell it you for an excuse, for I am not sleepy; my impatience is too great to hear from you again, that I am not master of it, nor indeed of myself, so that you must excuse me from saying more than is just necessary. Lord Nott. will give you an account of all that has been done. [Here follows a paragraph on who shall command the Fleet, Lord Monmouth or the Queen's choice, Shovell, who 'They tell me is the best officer of his age'. She ends her letter] I hope you will forgive me if I forget half what I have to say, for really my concern for you has got the mastery, and I am not able to think of anything else but that I love you in more abundance than my own life.

30   *Queen Mary II to King William III*

$$\frac{27}{\text{Whitehall, July 17, 1690}}$$

Every hour makes me more impatient to hear from you, and every-thing I hear stir, I think brings me a letter. I shall not go about to excuse myself; I know 'tis a folly to a great degree, to be so uneasy as I am at present, when I have no reason to apprehend any ill cause, but only might attribute your silence to your marching farther from Dublin, which makes the way longer. I have stay'd till I am almost asleep in hopes; but they are vaine, and I must once more go to bed, and wish to be waked with a letter from you, which I shall at last get, I hope. Till I know whether you come or no, I can not resolve to write you all that has past this day, till which time I thought you had given me wrong characters of men, but now I see they answer my expectation of being as little of a mind as of a body. Adieu, do but love me, and I can bear any thing.

31 *Queen Mary II to King William III*

Aug. 9
Whitehall, July 30, 1690

You will not wonder that I did not write last night, when you know that at noon I received yours, by Mr Butler, whose face I shall love to see ever hereafter, since he has come twice with such good news. That he brought yesterday was so welcome to me, that I won't go about expressing it, since 'tis impossible; but for my misfortune I have another reason to be glad of your coming, and a very strong one, if compared to any thing but the kindness I have for your dear self, and that is the divisions which, to my thinking, encrease here daily, or at least appear more and more to me. The business of the commission is again put off by Mr Russell. At my coming from the Council, I was told of Mr Butler's being come, who soon brought me your letter, and tho' I was in hourly expectation, yet being sure you were coming did really transport me so, that yet I hardly have recovered it, and there is such joy every where, that 'tis not to be exprest.

I have one thing to beg, which is, that if it be possible, I may come and meet you upon the road, either where you dine, or anywhere else, for I do so long to see you, that I am sure had you as much mind to see your poor wife again, you would propose it; but do as you please; I will say no more, but that I love you so much it cannot encrease, else I am sure it would.

Sept 5
Whitehall, Aug. 26, 1690

I believe you will be glad for your cousin's sake, that she will
be disposed of before her mother dies; and I ever heard it at the
Hague that this man was good-natured, which will make him use
her well, though she is so much older; and for his good fortune,
she has enough I believe, to govern him more gently than another
cousin of yours does her spouse. I can't help laughing at this wedding, though my poor heart is ready to break every time I think in
what perpetual danger you are; I am in greater fears than can be
imagined by any who loves less than myself. I count the hours and
the moments, and have only reason enough left to think, as long
as I have no letters all is well. I believe, by what you write, that
you got your cannon Friday at farthest, and then Saturday I suppose you began to make use of them; judge then what cruel
thoughts they are to me to think what you may be exposed to all
this while. I never do anything without thinking now, it may be,
you are in the greatest dangers, and yet I must see company upon
my sett days; I must play twice a week; nay, I must laugh and talk,
tho' never so much against my will; I believe I dissemble very ill
to those who know me, at least 'tis a great constraint to myself, yet
I must endure it; all my motions are so watch'd, and all I do so
observed, that I eat less, or speak less, or look more grave, all is lost
in the opinion of the world; so that I have this misery added to
that of your absence and my fears for your dear person, that I must
grin when my heart is ready to break, and talk when my heart is
so oppress'd I can scarce breathe. In this I don't know what I
should do, were it not for the grace of God which supports me; I
am sure I have great reason to praise the Lord while I live for this
great mercy, that I don't sink under this affliction; nay, that I
keep my health; for I can neither sleep nor eat. I go to Kensington
as often as I can for air, but then I can never be quite alone;
neither can I complain, that would be some ease; but I have
nobody whose humour and circumstances agrees with mine
enough to speak my mind freely to; besides, I must hear of business, which being a thing I am so new in, and so unfit for, does but
break my brains the more, and not ease my heart. I see I have

insensibly made my letter too long upon my own self, but I am confident you love enough to bear with it for once; I don't remember that I have been guilty of the like fault before, since you went; and that is now three months, for which time of almost perpetual fear and trouble, this is but a short account, and so I hope may pass; 'Tis some ease to me to write my pain, and 'tis a great satisfaction to believe you will pity me, it will be yet more when I hear it from yourself in a letter, as I am sure you must if it were but out of common good nature; how much more then out of kindness, if you love me as well as you make me believe, and as I endeavour to deserve a little by that sincere and lasting kindness I have for you. . . .

LORD PETERBOROUGH

Charles Mordaunt, 3rd Earl of Peterborough, was celebrated as 'one of those men of careless wit and negligent grace who scatter a thousand *bons mots* and idle verses' which, on inspection, often turn out to be profoundly dull. He was a small, fierce man who, politically something of a firebrand, was a keen opponent of James II. He suggested to William of Orange the idea of an invasion of England and, later, when William was King, he was made a Privy Councillor.

His first wife died in 1709. She was Carey, daughter of Sir Alexander Frazer of Dores. In 1722 Charles secretly married Anastasia Robinson, a famous singer. They did not live together and it was only a few days before his death that she was acknowledged the Countess of Peterborough. Though there are no dates to the letters he wrote to Mrs. Howard, later Countess of Suffolk and mistress of George II, they were probably written during the time of his marriage. The poet Gay is supposed to have helped Mrs. Howard compose her replies.

33   Lord Peterborough to Mrs. Howard (later Countess of Suffolk)

[172–?]

Change of air, the common remedy has no effect; and flight,

60

the refuge of all who fear, gives me no manner of security or ease; a fair devil haunts me wherever I go, though perhaps not so malicious as the black ones, yet more tormenting. How much more tormenting is the beauteous devil than the ugly one! The first I am always thinking of, the other seldom comes in my thoughts; the terrors of the ugly devil very often diminish upon consideration, but the oppressions of the fair one become more intolerable every time she comes into my mind.

The chief attribute of the devil is tormenting. Who could look upon you and give you that title? Who can feel what I do and give you any other?

But, most certainly I have more to lay to the charge of the fair one that can be objected to Satan or Beelzebub. We may believe that they only have a mind to torment because they are tormented; if they endeavour to procure us misery it is because they are in pain: they must be our companions in suffering; but my white devil partakes none of my torments.

In a word, give me heaven, for it is in your power, or you may have an equal hell! Judge of the disease by the extravagant symptoms; one moment I curse you, the next I pray for you.

Oh! hear my prayers or I am miserable. Forgive me if I threaten you; take this for a proof as well as punishment. If you can prove inhuman you shall have reproaches from Moscow, China, or the barbarous quarters of Tartary.

Believe me, for I think I am in earnest: this I am sure of, I could not endure my ungrateful country but for your sake.

34 *Mrs. Howard to Lord Peterborough*

[172–?]

I have carefully perused your lordship's letter about your fair devil and your black devil, your hell and tortures, your heaven and happiness—those sublime expressions which ladies and gentlemen use in their gallantries and distresses.

I suppose by your fair devil you mean nothing less than an angel. If so, my lord, I beg leave to give some reasons why I

61

think a woman is neither like an angel nor a devil, and why successful and unhappy love do not in the least resemble heaven and hell. It is true, you may quote these thousand gallant letters and precedents for the use of these love terms, which have a mighty captivating sound in the ears of a woman, and have been with equal propriety applied to all women in all ages.

In the first place, my lord, an angel pretends to be nothing else but a *spirit*. If, then, a woman was no more than an angel what could a lover get by the pursuit?

The black devil is a spirit too, but one that has lost her beauty and retained her pride. Tell a woman this and ask how she likes the simile.

The pleasure of an angel is offering praise; the pleasure of a woman is receiving it.

Successful love is very unlike heaven, because you may have success one hour, and lose it the next. Heaven is unchangeable. Who can say so of love letters? In love there are as many heavens as there are women; so that, if a man be so unhappy as to lose one heaven, he need not throw himself headlong into hell.

This thought might be carried further. But perhaps you will ask me, if a woman be neither like angel or devil, what is she like? I answer, that the only thing that is like a woman is—*another woman*.

How often has your lordship persuaded foreign ladies that nothing but them could make you forsake your dear country. But at present I find it is more to your purpose to tell me that I am the only woman that could prevail with you to stay in your ungrateful country.

35 *Mrs. Howard to Lord Peterborough*

[no date]

I cannot much wonder that men are always so liberal in making presents of their hearts, yet I cannot help admiring the women who are so very fond of these acquisitions. Let us consider the ingredients that make up the heart of man.

It is composed of dissimulation, self-love, vanity, inconstancy, equivocation, and such fine qualities. Who then would make that a present to a lady, when they have one of their own so very like it?

A man's heart never wants the outward appearance of truth and sincerity. Every lover's heart is so finely varnished with them, that it is almost impossible to distinguish the true from the false ones. According to my observations the false ones have generally the finest gloss.

When your lordship asks a heart for a heart you seem to reckon them all of equal value. I fancy you think them all false ones, which is the surest way not to be often imposed upon. I beg your lordship, in this severe opinion of hearts, to except mine as well as your own.

If you were so happy as to be the owner of a false heart, you would esteem it as the most perfect present for a lady; for should you make her a present of such a one as yours was before you parted with it, it is fifty to one whether you would receive a true one in return.

Therefore, let everyone who expects an equivalent for his heart be provided with a false one, which is equally fit for the most professed lover. It will burn, flame, bleed, pant, sigh, and receive as many darts, and appear altogether as charming as a true one. Besides, it does not in the least embarrass the bearer, and I think your lordship was always a lover of liberty.

JONATHAN SWIFT

Jonathan Swift is one of the most tragic figures in English literature. His latest biographer, William Kean Seymour, says: 'Beyond question Swift is one of the greatest figures in English or any other literature. He wrote in a variety of modes and styles, his subjects ranging from personal wit and whimsy to the profound consideration of the state of mankind as he saw and diagnosed it during the span of his active writing life.'

While he was a young man at his parish in Kilroot, Belfast, he met and fell in love with a friend's cousin, Jane Waring, a daughter of the Archdeacon of Dromore. He called her 'Varina' and offered her 'his hand and his fortune'. But before she would accept him (it appears that she could not make up her mind to marry him), Sir William Temple asked Swift to come back to Moor Park (where he had acted as Temple's secretary before going to Kilroot) with an offer of 'a better prospect of interest'. Swift wrote to Varina one of the strangest of all love letters. It was, indeed, farewell.

Swift knew Stella, Esther Johnson, from his earlier days at Moor Park where she had been his pupil. He gives her various pet names, such as M.D. in his letters. None of Stella's letters to Swift have been preserved, though Dr. Madden told Dr. Johnson that they were privately married in the garden by Dr. Asge, Bishop of Clogher. Stella died in 1727.

While Swift was living in London he met Hester Vanhomrigh. She became the celebrated 'Vanessa' and he was already writing to

64

her in 1712 at about the time he apologises to Stella for not writing to her.

Hester Vanhomrigh was of Dutch descent. Swift encouraged her with the idea of marriage but his constant delay threw her into a state of nervous exhaustion. In the end Swift turned on her and the disappointment killed her.

Swift has been described as a 'monster' but it must be remembered that he was struggling against the disease which had been his constant companion since college days. Vanessa, who must have heard of Swift's relations with Stella, wrote to her and asked her to explain their exact relationship. Stella, it is said, gave Vanessa's letter to Swift who rode at once to Cellbridge, where Vanessa lived, threw the letter on a table and, without a word, returned to Dublin. It is the cruelty of this visit which is supposed to have caused her death. Certainly she did not live for long after it.

36   Jonathan Swift to Jane Waring (Varina)

April 29, 1696

Madam—Impatience is the most inseparable quality of a lover. . . . That dearest object upon which all my prospect of happiness entirely depends, is in perpetual danger to be removed for ever from my sight. Varina's life is daily wasting, and though one just and honourable action would furnish health to her and unspeakable happiness to us both, yet some power that aspires at human felicity has that influence to hold her continually doting upon her cruelty, and me on the cause of it. This fully convinces me of what we are told, that the miseries of man's life are all beaten out on his own anvil.

Why was I so foolish to put my hopes and fears into the power and management of another? Liberty is doubtless the most valuable blessing of life, yet we are fond to fling it away on those who have been these 5000 years using us ill.

. . . I am a villain if I have not been poring this half-hour over the paper merely for want of something to say to you—or is it rather that I have so much to say to you that I know not where to begin, though at best it is all very likely to be arrant repetition.

. . . You have now had time enough to consider my last letter, and to form your own resolutions upon it. I wait your answer with a world of impatience . . . and how far you will stretch the point of your unreasonable scruples to keep me here will depend upon the strength of the love you pretend for me. In short, madam, I am once more offer'd the advantage to have the same acquaintance with greatness that I formerly enjoyed, and with better prospect of interest. I here solemnly offer to forego it all for your sake. I desire nothing of your fortune, you shall live where and with whom you please till my affairs are settled to your desire; and in the meantime I will push my advancement with all the eagerness and courage imaginable, and do not doubt to succeed.

Study seven years for objections against all this, and, by Heaven, they will at last be no more than trifles and puts off. It is true you have known sickness longer than you have me, and therefore you are more loth to part with it as an older acquaintance. But listen to what I here solemnly protest by all that can be witness to an oath, that if I leave this kingdom before you are mine, I will endure the utmost indignities of fortune rather than ever return again, though the King would send me back his deputy. And if it must be so, preserve yourself in God's name, for the next lover who has those qualities you love so much beyond any of mine, and who will highly admire you for the advantage which shall never share any esteem from me.

Would to Heaven you were but awhile sensible of the thoughts into which my present distractions plunge me; they hale me a thousand ways and I am not able to bear them. It is so, by Heaven! the love of Varina is of more tragical consequence than her cruelty. Would to God you had hated and scorned me from the beginning! It was your pity opened the first way to my misfortune, and now your love is finishing my ruin; and is it so then? In a fortnight I must take eternal farewell of Varina, and (I wonder) will she weep at parting, just a little to justify her poor pretence of some affection for me? and will my friends still continue reproaching me for the want of gallantry and neglecting a close siege? How comes it that they all wish us married together, they knowing my circumstances and yours extremely well, and I am sure love you too much, if it be only for my sake, to wish

66

you anything that might cross your interest or your happiness?

Surely, Varina, you have but a very mean opinion of the joys that accompany a true, honourable, unlimited love; yet either nature and our ancestors have highly deceived us or else all other sublunary things are dross in comparison. Is it possible you can yet be insensible to the prospect of a rapture and delight so innocent and so exalted? Trust me, Varina, Heaven has given us nothing else worth the loss of a thought. . . . The only felicity permitted to human life we clog with tedious circumstances and barbarous formality. By Heaven, Varina, you are more experienced and have less virgin innocence than I. Would not your conduct make one think you were hugely skilled in all the little politic methods of intrigue? Love with the gall of too much discretion is a thousand times worse than with none at all. It is a peculiar part of nature which art debauches but cannot improve. . . . And 'tis as possible to err in the excess of piety as of love.

These are the rules I have long followed with you, Varina; and had you pleased to imitate them we should both have been infinitely happy. The little disguises and affected contradictions of your sex were all (to say the truth) infinitely beneath persons of your pride and mine; paltry maxims that they are, calculated for the rabble of humanity. O Varina, how imagination leads me beyond myself and all my sorrows! It is sunk, and a thousand graves lie open! No, madam, I will give you no more of my unhappy temper, though I derive it all from you.

Farewell, madam, and may love make you awhile forget your temper to do me justice. Only remember that if you still refuse to be mine you will quickly lose, for ever lose, him that has resolved to die as he has lived all yours.

JON. SWIFT

37 *Hester Vanhomrigh (Vanessa) to Jonathan Swift*
[Endorsed: 1st]

London, Sept. ye 1st, 1712

Had I a correspondent in China, I might have had an answer by this time. I never could think till now that London was so far off in your thoughts and that twenty miles were by your computation equal to some thousands. I thought it a piece of charity to undeceive you in this point and to let you know, if you'll give yourself the trouble to write, I may probably receive your letter in a day. 'Twas that made me venture to take pen in hand the third time. Sure you'll not let it be to no purpose. You must needs be extremely happy where you are, to forget your absent friends; and I believe you have formed a new system and think there is no more of this world, passing your sensible horizon. If this be your notion I must excuse you; if not, you can plead no other excuse; and if it be so, I must reckon myself of another world; but I shall have much ado to be persuaded till you send me some convincing arguments of it. Don't dally in a thing of this consequence, but demonstrate that 'tis possible to keep up a correspondence between friends, though in different worlds, and assure one another, as I do you, that

I am

Your most obedient & humble servant

E. VAN HOMRIGH

38   *Vanessa to Jonathan Swift*
    [Endorsed: 3rd]

London, June, 1713

'Tis unexpressible the concern I am in ever since I heard from Mr. Lewis that your head is so much out of order. Who is your physician? For God sake don't be persuaded to take many slops. Satisfy me so much as to tell me what medicines you have taken and do take. How did you find yourself whilst a shipboard? I fear 'tis your voyage has discomposed you, and then so much business following so immediately, before you had time to recruit —'twas too much. I beg, make all haste imaginable to the country for I firmly believe that air and rest will do you more good than anything in the world besides. If I talk impertinently, I know you have goodness enough to forgive me when you consider how great

68

an ease 'tis for me to ask these questions, though I know it will be a great while before I can be answered—I am sure I shall think it so. Oh! what would I give to know how you do at this instant. My fortune is too hard: your absence was enough, without this cruel addition.

Sure the powers above are envious of your thinking so well, which makes them at some times strive to interrupt you. But I must confine my thoughts, or at least stop from telling them to you, or you'll chide, which will still add to my uneasiness. I have done all that was possible to hinder myself from writing to you till I heard you were better, for fear of breaking my promise, but 'twas all in vain; for had [I] vowed neither to touch pen, ink or paper, I certainly should have some other invention. Therefore I beg you won't be angry with me for doing what is not in my power to avoid.

Pray make Parvisol write me word what I desire to know, for I would not for the world have you hold down your head. I am impatient to the last degree to hear how you are. I hope I shall soon have you here.

39   *Jonathan Swift to Vanessa*
     [Addressed: To Miss Hessy. Endorsed: 3rd]

Laracor, July 8th, 1713

I stayed but a fortnight in Dublin, very sick, and returned not one visit of a hundred that were made me—but all to the Dean, and none to the Doctor. I am riding here for life, and think I am something better, and hate the thoughts of Dublin, and prefer a field-bed and earthen floor before the great house there, which they say is mine. I had your last spleenatic letter. I told you when I left England, I would endeavour to forget everything there, and would write as seldom as I could. I did indeed design one general round of letters to my friends, but my health has not yet suffered me. I design to pass the greatest part of the time I stay in Ireland here in the cabin where I am now writing, neither will I leave the kingdom till I am sent for; and if they have no further service for me I will never see England again. At my first coming I thought I should have died with discontent, and was horribly melancholy while they were installing me; but it begins to wear off, and change to dulness. My river walk is extremely pretty, and my canal in great beauty, and I see trouts playing in it.

I know not any one thing in Dublin; but Mr. Ford is very kind, and writes to me constantly what passes among you. I find you are likewise a good politician; and I will say so much to you, that I verily think, if the thing you know of had been published just upon the Peace, the Ministry might have avoided what hath since happened. But I am now fitter to look after willows, and to cut hedges, than meddle with affairs of state. I must order one of the workmen to drive those cows out of my Island, and make up the ditch again; a work much more proper for a country vicar than driving out factions and fencing against them. And I must go and take my bitter draught to cure my head, which is spoilt by the bitter draughts the public hath given me.

How does Davila go on? Johnny Clark is chosen portreeve of our town of Trim; and we shall have the assizes there next week, and fine doings; and I must go and borrow a horse to meet the judges, and Joe Beaumont and all the boys that can get horses will go too. Mr. Warburton has but a thin school. Mr. Percival has built up the other side of his house, but people whisper that it is but scurvily built. Mr. Steers is come to live in Mr. Melthorp's house, and 'tis thought the widow Melthorp will remove to Dublin.

Nay, if you do not like this sort of news, I have no better. So go to your Dukes and Duchesses, and leave me to Goodman Bumford and Patrick Dolan of Clonduggan.

Adieu.

40 *Jonathan Swift to Vanessa*

[Addressed: To Mrs. Hessy Van. Endorsed: 4th]

[? End of 1714]

I will see you in a day or two, and believe me, it goes to my soul not to see you oftener. I will give you the best advice, countenance and assistance I can. I would have been with you sooner if a thousand impediments had not prevented me. I did not imagine you had been under difficulties: I am sure my whole fortune should go to remove them. I cannot see you, I fear, to-day, having affairs of my place to do; but pray think it not want of friendship or tenderness, which I will always continue to the utmost.

Monday morn.

41 *Vanessa to Jonathan Swift*
[Endorsed: 4th]

Dublin, 1714

You cannot but be sensible, at least in some degree, of the many uneasinesses I am slave to—a wretch of a brother, cunning executors and importunate creditors of my mother's—things I can no way avoid being subject to at present, and weighty enough to sink greater spirits than mine without some support. Once I had a friend that would see me sometimes, and either commend what I did or advise me what to do, which banished all my uneasiness. But now, when my misfortunes are increased by being in a disagreeable place, amongst strange, prying, deceitful people, whose company is so far from an amusement that it is a very great punishment, you fly me, and give me no reason but that we are amongst fools and must submit. I am very well satisfied that we are amongst such, but know no reason for having my happiness sacrificed to their caprice. You once had a maxim, which was to act what was right and not mind what the world said. I wish you would keep to it now. Pray what can be wrong in seeing and advising an unhappy young woman? I can't imagine. You can't but know that your frowns make my life insupportable. You have taught me to distinguish, and then you leave me miserable. Now all I beg is that you will for once counterfeit (since you can't otherwise) that indulge[nt] friend you once were till I get the better of these difficulties, for my sister's sake; for were not she involved (who I know is not so able to manage them as I am), I have a nobler soul then sit struggling with misfortunes, when at the end I can't promise myself any real happiness. Forgive me; and

I beg you'd believe it is not in my power to avoid complaining as I do.

[Endorsed: 6th]

Dublin, 1714

Well, now I plainly see how great a regard you have for me. You bid me be easy, and you'd see me as often as you could. You had better said, as often as you could get the better of your inclinations so much, or as often as you remembered there was such a one in the world. If you continue to treat me as you do you will not be made uneasy by me long. 'Tis impossible to describe what I have suffered since I saw you last; I am sure I could have bore the rack much better than those killing, killing words of yours. Sometimes I have resolved to die without seeing you more; but those resolves, to your misfortune, did not last long. For there is something in human nature that prompts one so to find relief in this world, I must give way to it, and beg you'd see me and speak kindly to me; for I am sure you'd not condemn anyone to suffer what I have done, could you but know it. The reason I write to you is because I cannot tell i[t] you, should I see you; for when I begin to complain, then you are angry, and there is something in your look so awful, that it strikes me dumb. Oh! that you may but have so much regard for me left, that this complaint may touch your soul with pity. I say as little as ever I can: did you but know what I thought, I am sure it would move you. Forgive me, and believe I cannot help telling you this, and live.

43 *Vanessa to Jonathan Swift*

Celbridge, 1720

Believe me 'tis with the utmost regret that I now complain to you, because I know your good nature such, that you cannot see

72

any human creature miserable without being sensibly touched. Yet what can I do? I must either unload my heart and tell you all its griefs, or sink under the unexpressible distress I now suffer by your prodigious neglect of me. 'Tis now ten long, long weeks since I saw you, and in all that time I have never received but one letter from you, and a little note with an excuse. Oh—how have you forgot me! You endeavour by severities to force me from you; nor can I blame you, for with the utmost distress and confusion I behold myself the cause of uneasy reflections to you. Yet I cannot comfort you, but here declare that 'tis not in the power of art, time or accident to lessen the unexpressible passion which I have for—. Put my passion under the utmost restraint, send me as distant from you as the earth will allow, yet you cannot banish those charming ideas, which will ever stick by me whilst I have the use of memory. Nor is the love I bear you only seated in my soul, for there is not a single atom of my frame that is not blended with it. Therefore don't flatter yourself that separation will ever change my sentiments, for I find myself unquiet in the midst of silence, and my heart is at once pierced with sorrow and love. For Heaven's sake tell me what has caused this prodigious change in you, which I have found of late. If you have the least remains of pity for me left, tell me tenderly. No, don't tell it, so that it may cause my present death; and don't suffer me to live a life like a languishing death, which is the only life I can lead if you have lost any of your tenderness for me.

44   *Vanessa to Jonathan Swift*

Celbridge, 1720

Tell me sincerely if you have once wished with earnestness to see me since I wrote to you. No, so far from that, you have not once pitied me, though I told you how I was distressed. Solitude is insupportable to a mind which is not easy. I have worn out my days in sighing, and my nights with watching and thinking of —, —, —, —, who thinks not of me. How many letters must I send you before I shall receive an answer? Can you deny me in my

73

misery the only comfort which I can expect at present? Oh! that I could hope to see you here, or that I could go to you. I was born with violent passions, which terminate all in one—that unexpressible passion I have for you. Consider the killing emotions which I feel from your neglect of me, and shew some tenderness for me, or I shall lose my senses. Sure, you cannot possibly be so much taken up but you might command a moment to write to me and force your inclinations to do so great a charity.

I firmly believe, could I know your thoughts, (which no human creature is capable of guessing at, because never anyone living thought like you), I should find that you have often in a rage wished me religious, hoping then I should have paid my devotions to Heaven. But that would not spare you, for was I an enthusiast, still you'd be the deity I should worship. What marks are there of a deity but what you are to be known by? You are present everywhere; your dear image is always before my eyes; sometimes you strike me with that prodigious awe, I tremble with fear; at other times a charming compassion shines through your countenance, which revives my soul. Is it not more reasonable to adore a radiant form one has seen, than one only described?

WILLIAM CONGREVE

The greatest English master of comedy was educated at Kilkenny and Dublin where he was a contemporary and friend of Swift. His family moved to Staffordshire at the Revolution and William was entered as a student of law at the Middle Temple in 1691. A first novel *Incognito* is only remembered because Dr. Johnson said of it 'he would rather praise it than read it'.

Congreve had a large number of women friends or, as they were called at this period, 'reigning charmers'. At one time it was Arabella Hunt, a singer; at another a 'Madame Berenger', but his most longstanding love affairs were with Mrs. Bracegirdle, who acted in all his plays, and Henrietta, Duchesss of Marlborough. When Congreve died Henrietta erected a splendid tomb to him in Westminster Abbey and a rumour got about that she had him 'done' in wax, dressed in his own clothes and had the 'puppet' sit with her while she supped. He left her £10,000. As for Mrs. Bracegirdle, she inherited no more than £200 and Arabella Hunt, dying before Congreve, received an epigram,

> Were there on earth another voice like thine,
> Another hand so blessed with skill divine,
> The late afflicted world some hopes might have,
> And harmony retrieve thee from the grave.

The following love letters were, however, written to her.

[1690?]

Dear Madam—Not believe that I love you? You cannot pretend to be so incredulous. If you do not believe my tongue, consult my eyes, consult your own. You will find by yours that they have charms; by mine that I have a heart which feels them. Recall to mind what happened last night. That at least was a lover's kiss. Its eagerness, its fierceness, its warmth, expressed the God its parent. But oh! its sweetness, and its melting softness expressed him more. With trembling in my limbs, and fevers in my soul I ravish'd it. Convulsions, pantings, murmurings shew'd the mighty disorder within me: the mighty disorder increased by it. For those dear lips shot through my heart, and thro' my bleeding vitals, delicious poison, and an avoidless but yet a charming ruin.

What cannot a day produce? The night before I thought myself a happy man, in want of nothing, and in fairest expectation of fortune; approved of by men of wit, and applauded by others. Pleased, nay charmed with my friends, my then dearest friends, sensible of every delicate pleasure, and in their turns possessing all.

But Love, almighty Love, seems in a moment to have removed me to a prodigious distance from every object but you alone. In the midst of crowds I remain in solitude. Nothing but you can lay hold of my mind, and that can lay hold of nothing but you. I appear transported to some foreign desert with you (oh, that I were really thus transported!), where, abundantly supplied with everything, in thee, I might live out an age of uninterrupted extasy.

The scene of the world's great stage seems suddenly and sadly chang'd. Unlovely objects are all around me, excepting thee; the charms of all the world appear to be translated to thee. Thus in this said [*sic* sad?] but oh, too pleasing state! my soul can fix upon nothing but thee; thee it contemplates, admires, adores, nay depends on, trusts on you alone.

If you and hope forsake it, despair and endless misery attend it.

[no date]

Dear Madam—May I presume to beg pardon for the fault I committed. So foolish a fault that it was below not only a man of sense but a man; and of which nothing could ever have made me guilty but the fury of a passion with which none but your lovely self could inspire me. May I presume to beg pardon for a fault which I can never forgive myself? To purchase that pardon what would I not endure? You shall see me prostrate before you, and use me like a slave while I kiss the dear feet that trample upon me. But if my crime be too great for forgiveness, as indeed it is very great, deny me not one dear parting look, let me see you once before I must never see you more.

Christ! I want patience to support that accursed thought, I have nothing in the world that is dear to me but you. You have made everything else indifferent; and can I resolve never to see you more? In spight of myself I must always see you. Your form is fixed by fate in my mind and is never to be remov'd. I see those lovely piercing eyes continually, I see each moment those ravishing lips which I have gazed on still with desire, and still have touch'd with transport, and at which I have so often flown with all the fury of the most violent love.

Jesus! from whence and whither am I fallen? From the hopes of blissful extasies to black despair! From the expectation of immortal transports, which none but your dear self can give me, and which none but he who loves like me could ever so much as think of, to a complication of cruel passions and the most dreadful condition of human life.

My fault indeed has been very great, and cries aloud for the severest vengeance. See it inflicted on me: see me despair and die for that fault. But let me not die unpardon'd, madam; I die for you, but die in the most cruel and dreadful manner. The wretch that lies broken on the wheel alive feels not a quarter of what I endure. Yet boundless love has been all my crime; unjust, ungrateful, barbarous return for it!

Suffer me to take my eternal leave of you; when I have done that how easy will it be to bid all the rest of the world adieu.

SIR RICHARD STEELE

The marriage of Richard Steele and his 'dear Prue' is one of the happiest. It was like an eternal love affair. Richard was an honest man with a deep sense of honour where things like worldly advancement and success were concerned. We can see him walking in the parks and streets of London dressed in the period clothes, the periwig, gold lace, scarlet coat, Mechlin lace and silk sash, very much the man of his time. The letters he wrote to Prue (hers are lost) run to over 400 and are masterpieces of tender passion (they are preserved in the British Museum).

Richard Steele was, as he said, 'an Englishman born in Dublin'. His father was an attorney. Richard began by writing plays and a small book, *The Christian Hero*, to keep him safe, he said, 'from unwarrantable pleasures'. When his first wife, a wealthy widow, died, leaving him a rich man, he fell in love with and married, in 1709, Mary Scurlock. He nicknamed her 'Prue' because she was always trying to defeat his extravagance by her prudence. In 1709, also, he founded the *Tatler*, replacing it, in 1711, by the *Spectator*. He was knighted in 1715. Richard was a witty, brilliant, extravagant man, full of enthusiasm, impetuous and delightful. On one of his letters Prue wrote, 'He was, when he wrote the following letter, as agreeable and pleasant a man as any in England. October 1716.' Prue died, in Carmarthen, on 20th September 1717.

[Saturday, 9th August] 1707

Madam,

Your wit and beauty are suggestions which may easily lead you into the intention of my writing to you. You may be sure that I cannot be cold to so many good qualities as all that see you must observe in you. You are a woman of a very good understanding, and will not measure [my] thoughts by any ardour in my expressions, which is the ordinary language on these occasions.

I have reasons for hiding from my nearest relation any purpose I may have resolv'd upon of waiting on you if you permit it; and I hope you have confidence from mine, as well as your own character, that such a condescension should not be ill us'd by, Madam, yr most obedient ser'nt.

48   *Richard Steele to Mary Scurlock*

9 August, 1707

Madam,—I writ you on Saturday, by Mrs. Warren, and give you this trouble to urge the same request I made then; which was, that I may be admitted to wait upon you. I should be very far from desiring this if it were a transgression of the most severe rules to allow it. I know you are very much above the little arts which are frequent in your sex, of giving unnecessary torment to their admirers; I therefore hope you will do so much justice to the generous passion I have for you, as to let me have an opportunity of acquainting you upon what motives I pretend to your good opinion. I shall not trouble you with my sentiments till I know how they will be received; and as I know no reason why the difference of sex should make our language to each other differ from the ordinary rules of right reason, I shall affect plainness and sincerity in my discourse to you, as much as other lovers do perplexity and rapture. Instead of saying 'I shall die for you', I profess I should be glad to lead my life with you. You are as beautiful, as witty, as prudent, and as good-humoured as any woman breathing; but, I must confess to you, I regard all these excellences as you will please to direct them for my happiness or misery. With me, madam, the only lasting motive to love, is the hope of its becoming mutual. I beg of you to let Mrs. Warren send me word when I may attend you. I promise you I will talk of nothing but indifferent things; though, at the same time, I know not how I shall approach you in the tender moment of first seeing you after this declaration which has been made by, madam,

Your most obedient and most faithful humble
servant.

49 Richard Steele to Mary Scurlock

[14th August] 1707

Madam,

I came to your house this night to wait on you; but you have commanded me to expect the happiness of seeing you at another time of more leisure. I am now under your own roof while I write; and that imaginary satisfaction of being so near you, tho' not in your presence, has in it something that touches me with so tender ideas, that it is impossible for me to describe their force. All great passion makes us dumb; and the highest happiness, as well as highest grief, seizes us too violently to be expressed by our words.

You are so good as to let me know I shall have the honour of seeing you when I next come here. I will live upon that expectation, and meditate on your perfections till that happy hour. The vainest woman upon earth never saw in her glasse half the attractions which I view in you. Your air, your shape, your every glance, motion, and gesture, have such peculiar graces, that you possess my whole soul, and I know no life but in the hopes of your approbation: I know not what to say, but that I love you with the sincerest passion that ever entered the heart of man. I will make it the business of my life to find out means of convincing you that I prefer you to all that's pleasing upon earth. I am, Madam, your most obedient, most faithful humble ser'nt.

Saturday Night [30th August, 1707]

Dear, Lovely Mrs. Scurlock,

I have been in very good company, where your unknown name, under the character of the woman I lov'd best, has been often drunk; so that I may say I am dead drunk for your sake, which is more than 'I dye for you.'

St. James's Coffee House,
1 September, 1707

Madam—It is the hardest thing in the world to be in love, and yet attend to business. As for me, all who speak to me to find out, and I must lock myself up, or other people will do it for me.

A gentleman asked me this morning, 'What news from Lisbon?' and I answered, 'She is exquisitely handsome.' Another desired to know 'when I had been last at Hampton Court?' I replied, 'It will be on Tuesday come se'nnight.' Pr'ythee allow me at least to kiss your hand before that day, that my mind may be in some composure. O love!

> A thousand torments dwell about thee,
> Yet who would live, to live without thee?

Methinks I could write a volume to you; but all the language on earth would fail in saying how much, and with what disinterested passion, I am ever yours.

GEORGE FARQUHAR

George Farquhar was born in Londonderry, the son of a clergyman and is chiefly remembered for his play *The Beaux' Stratagem* during the writing of which he was taken mortally ill. He survived long enough, however, not only to finish the play but to take an extra benefit on the third night.

Farquhar called himself 'the most amorous of his sex'. The real love of his life was 'Penelope', the famous actress Mrs Oldfield. Farquhar was responsible for her first stage appearance at the age of 16. None of his letters have a date, only the day of the week.

52   George Farquhar to Anne Oldfield (actress)

Sunday, after Sermon [1699?]

I came, I saw, and was conquered; never had man more to say, yet can I say nothing; where others go to save their souls, there have I lost mine; but I hope that Divinity which has the justest title to its service has received it; but I will endeavour to suspend these raptures for a moment, and talk calmly.—

Nothing on earth, madam, can charm, beyond your wit but

your beauty: after this not to love you would proclaim me a fool; and to say I did when I thought otherwise would pronounce me a knave; if anybody called me either I should resent it; and if you but think me either I shall break my heart.

You have already, madam, seen enough of me to create a liking or an aversion; your sense is above your sex, then let your proceeding be so likewise, and tell me plainly what I have to hope for. Were I to consult my merits my humility would chide any shadow of hope; but after a sight of such a face whose whole composition is a smile of good nature, why should I be so unjust as to suspect you of cruelty. Let me either live in *London* and be happy or retire again to my desert to check my vanity that drew me thence; but let me beg you to receive my sentence from your own mouth, that I may hear you speak and see you look at the same time; then let me be unfortunate if I can.

If you are not the lady in mourning that sat upon my right hand at church, you may go to the devil, for I'm sure you're a witch.

53 *George Farquhar to Anne Oldfield*

[1699?]

Madam,—If I haven't begun thrice to write and as often thrown away my pen, may I never take it up again; my head and my heart have been at cuffs about you two long hours,—says my head, you're a coxcomb for troubling your noddle with a lady whose beauty is as much above your pretensions as your merit is below her love.

Then answers my heart,—Good Mr. Head, you're a block-head. I know Mr. F——r's merit better than you; as for your part, I know you to be as whimsical as the devil, and changing with every new notion that offers, but for my share I am fixt, and can stick to my opinion of a lady's merit for ever, and if the fair she can secure an interest in me, Monsieur Head, you may go whistle.

Come, come, (answered my head) you, Mr. Heart, are always leading the gentleman into some inconvenience or other; was it not you that first enticed him to talk to this lady? Your damn'd confounded warmth made him like this lady, and your busy impertinence has made him write to her; your leaping and skipping disturbs his sleep by night and his good humour by day; in short, sir, I will hear no more on't; I am head, and will be obeyed.

You lie, sir, replied my heart (being very angry), I am head in matters of love, and if you don't give your consent, you shall be forced, for I am sure that in this case all the members will be on my side. What say you, gentlemen Hands!

Oh (say the hands), we would not forego the tickling pleasure of touching a delicious white soft skin for the world.

Well, what say you, Mr. Tongue?

Zounds, says the linguist, there is more extasy in speaking three soft words of Mr. Heart's suggesting than whole orations of Signior Head's, so I am for the lady, and here's my honest neighbour, Lips, will stick to't.

By the sweet power of kisses, that we will, (replied the lips) and presently some other worthy members, standing up for the Heart, they laid violent hands (*nemine contradicente*) on poor Head, and knocked out his brains. So now, madam, behold me, as perfect a lover as any in Christendom, my heart firmly dictating every word I say. The little rebel throws itself into your power, and if you don't support it in the cause it has taken up for your sake, think what will be the condition of the headless and heartless

FARQUHAR

54   *George Farquhar to Anne Oldfield*

Monday, Twelve o'clock at night. [1699?]

Give me leave to call you dear madam, and tell you that I am now stepping into bed, and that I speak with as much sincerity as if I were stepping into my grave. Sleep is so great an emblem of death that my words ought to be as real as if I were sure never to awaken; then may I never again be blest with the light of the sun and the joys of *Wednesday* if you are not as dear to me as my hopes of waking in health to-morrow morning. Your charms lead me, my inclinations prompt me, and my reason confirms me.—Madam, your faithful and humble servant.

My humble service to the lady who must be the chief mediator for my happiness.

55 *George Farquhar to Anne Oldfield*

Friday Night, Eleven o'clock [1699?]

If you find no more rest from your thoughts in bed than I do, I could wish you, madam, to be always there, for there I am most in love. I went to the play this evening and the music roused my soul to such a pitch of passion that I was almost mad with melancholy. I flew thence to *Spring Garden* where with envious eyes I saw every man pick up his mate, whilst I alone walked like solitary *Adam* before the creation of *Eve*, but the place was no paradise to me, nothing I found entertaining but the nightingale which methought in sweet notes like your own pronounced the name of my dear *Penelope*—*as the fool thinketh the bell clinketh.* From hence I retired to the tavern where methought the shining glass represented your fair person, and the sparkling wine within it looked like your lovely wit and spirit. I met my dear mistress in everything, and I propose presently to see her in a lively dream, since the last thing I do is to kiss her dear letter, clasp her charming ideal in my arms, and so fall asleep—

My morning songs, my evening prayers,
My daily musings, nightly cares.

Adieu!

ALEXANDER POPE

Alexander Pope was born in Lombard Street, London, on 21st May 1688. 'Ever since his infancy' he was, he said, 'in love with one after the other of them, week by week.' He was referring to the daughters of Lister Blount, a Roman Catholic clergyman, who lived with their father in an Elizabethan mansion by the Thames near Reading. Teresa was born on 15th October; Martha on 15th June 1690. Pope seems to have been attracted to Teresa at first, but Martha, afterwards, became his confidant and companion. In the latter part of his life he depended on her for care and sympathy. He speaks of her as 'a woman friend . . . with whom I have spent three or four hours a day for the last fifteen years'.

Pope's correspondence with Lady Mary Wortley Montagu was carried on while she was with her husband on an embassy to Constantinople. When she returned she settled at Twickenham where Pope lived. They quarrelled and it has been suggested that the reason for the quarrel was that Pope, forgetting she was married, made serious love to her. Lady Mary laughed at him; Pope was deeply wounded and the affair (if it had ever existed in anyone's mind but Pope's) was at an end.

Bath, September [1714]

Madam,—I write to you for two reasons, one is because you commanded it, which will be always a reason to me in anything; the other, because I sit at home to take physic, and they tell me that I must do nothing that costs me great application or great pains, therefore I can neither say my prayers nor write verses. I am ordered to think but slightly of anything, and I am practising, if I can think so of you, which, if I can bring about, I shall be above regarding anything in nature for the future; I may then think of the world as a hazel nut, the sun as a spangle, and the king's coronation as a puppet show. When my physic makes me remember those I love, may it not be said to work kindly? Hide, I beseech you, this pun from Miss Patty, who hates them in compliance to the taste of a noble earl, whose modesty makes him detest double meanings. . . .

Let me tell her she will never look so finely while she is upon the earth as she would in the water. It is not here, as in most instances, but those ladies that would please extremely must go out of their own element. She does not make half so good a figure on horseback as Christina, Queen of Sweden; but were she once seen in Bath, no man would part with her for the best mermaid in Christendom.

Ladies, I have you so often, I perfectly know how you look in black and white. I have experienced the utmost you can do in any colours; but all your movements, all your graceful steps, all your attitudes and postures, deserve not half the glory you might here attain of a moving and easy behaviour in buckram; something betwixt swimming and walking; free enough, yet more modestly half-naked than you appear anywhere elsewhere.

You have conquered enough already by land; show your ambition, and vanquish also by water. We have no pretty admirers on these seas, but must strike sail to your white flags were they once hoisted up. The buckram I mention is a dress particularly useful at this time, when the Princess is bringing over the fashion of German ruffs. You ought to dress yourself to some degree of stiffness beforehand; and when our ladies' chins have been tickled awhile with a starched muslin and wires, they may possibly bear the brush of a German beard and whisker.

87

You are to understand, madam, that my *violent* passion for your fair self and your sister has been divided, and with the most wonderful regularity in the world. Even from my infancy I have been in love with one after the other of you week by week, and my journey to Bath fell out in the three hundred seventh-sixth week of the reign of my sovereign lady Martha. At the present writing hereof it is the three hundred and eighty-ninth week of the reign of your most serene majesty, in whose service I was listed some weeks before I beheld her. This information will account for my writing to either of you hereafter, as she shall happen to be queen regent at that time.

I could tell you a most delightful story of Dr. Parnelle, but want room to display it in all its shining circumstances. He had heard it was an excellent cure for love, to kiss the aunt of the person beloved, who is generally of years and experience enough to damp the fiercest flame. He tried this course in his passion for you, and kissed Mrs. Englefield at Mrs. Dancaster's [Duncastle]. This recipe he hath left written in the style of a divine as follows:—

'Whoso loveth Miss Blount shall kiss her aunt and be healed; for he kisseth her not as her husband, who kisseth and is enslaved for ever as one of the foolish ones; but as a passenger who passeth away and forgetteth the kiss of her mouth, even as the wind saluteth a flower in his passage, and knoweth not the odour thereof.'

57 *Alexander Pope to Martha Blount*

[no date]

Most Divine—It is some proof of my sincerity towards you, that I write when I am prepared by drinking to speak truth; and sure a letter after twelve at night must abound with that noble ingredient. That heart must have abundance of flames, which is at once warmed by wine and you: wine awakens and expresses the lurking passions of the mind, as varnish does the colours that are sunk in a picture, and brings them out in all their natural

88

glowings. My good qualities have been so frozen and locked up in a dull constitution at all my former sober hours, that it is very astonishing to me, now I am drunk, to find so much virtue in me.

In these overflowings of my heart I pay you my thanks for these two obliging letters you favoured me with of the 18th and 24th instant. That which begins with 'My charming Mr Pope!' was a delight to me beyond all expression; you have at last entirely gained the conquest over your fair sister. It is true you are not handsome, for you are a woman, and think you are not: but this good humour and tenderness for me has a charm that cannot be resisted. That face must needs be irresistible which was adorned with smiles, even when it could not see the coronation! [of George I, September 1714] I do suppose you will not show this epistle out of vanity, as I doubt not your sister does all I write to her. . . .

58 Alexander Pope to Teresa Blount

Aug. 7 [1716]

Madam,—I have so much esteem for you, and so much of the other thing, that, were I a handsome fellow, I should do you a vast deal of good: but as it is, all I am good for, is to write a civil letter, or to make a fine speech. The truth is, that considering how often and how openly I have declared love to you, I am astonished (and a little affronted) that you have not forbid my correspondence, and directly said, *See my face no more!*

It is not enough, madam, for your reputation, that you have your hands pure from the stain of such ink as might be shed to gratify a male correspondent. Alas! while your heart consents to encourage him in this lewd liberty of writing, you are not (indeed you are not) what you would so fain have me think you—a prude! I am vain enough to conclude that (like most young fellows) a fine lady's silence is consent, and so I write on—

But, in order to be as innocent as possible in this epistle, I will tell you news. You have asked me news a thousand times, at the first word you spoke to me; which some would interpret as if

89

you expected nothing from my lips: and truly it is not a sign two lovers are together, when they can be so impertinent as to inquire what the world does. All I mean by this is, that either you or I cannot be in love with the other: I leave you to guess which of the two is that stupid and insensible creature, so blind to the other's excellences and charms.

59 Alexander Pope to Lady Mary Wortley Montagu

Aug. 18, 1716

Madam,—I can say little to recommend the letters I am beginning to write to you, but that they will be the most impartial representations of a free heart, and the truest copies you ever saw, though of a very mean original.—You will do me an injustice if you look upon anything I shall say from this instant, as a compliment either to you or to myself. Whatever I write will be the real thought of that hour, and I know you will no more expect it of me to persevere till death, in every sentiment or notion I now set down, than you could imagine a man's face should never change after his picture was once drawn. . . .

I think I love you as well as King Herod could Herodias (though I never had so much as one dance with you), and would as freely give you my heart in a dish as he did another's head.

But since Jupiter will not have it so, I must be content to show my taste in life, as I do my taste in painting, by loving to have as little drapery as possible, 'not that I think everybody naked altogether so fine a sight as yourself and a few more would be;' but because it is good to use people to what they must be acquainted with; and there will certainly come some day of judgment to uncover every soul of us. We shall then see how the prudes of this world owed all their fine figure only to their being a little straiter laced and that they were naturally as arrant squabs as those that went more loose, nay, as those that never girded their loins at all.

But a particular reason to engage you to write your thoughts the most freely to me, is, that I am confident no one knows you better. For I find, when others express their opinion of you, it falls very short of mine and I am sure at the same time theirs is such as you would think sufficiently in your favour.

You may easily imagine how desirous I must be of corresponding with a person who had taught me long ago that it was as possible to esteem at first sight, as to love: and who have since ruined me for all the conversation of one sex, and almost all the friendship of the other.

How often have I been quietly going to take possession of that tranquillity and indolence I had so long found in the country, when one evening of your conversation has spoiled me for a *solitaire* too. Books have lost their effect upon me, and I was convinced since I saw you, that there is something more powerful than philosophy, and, since I heard you, that there is one alive wiser than all the sages. A plague of female wisdom! it makes a man ten times more uneasy than his own.

What is very strange, Virtue herself, when you have the dressing her, is too amiable for one's repose. What a world of good might you have done in your time, if you had allowed half the fine gentlemen who have seen you to have but conversed with you! They would have been strangely caught,[1] while they thought only to fall in love with a fair face, and you had bewitched them with reason and virtue; two beauties that the very fops pretend to have an acquaintance with.

The unhappy distance at which we correspond removes a great many of those punctilious restrictions and decorums that oftentimes in nearer conversation prejudice truth to save good breeding. I may now hear of my faults, and you of your good qualities, without a blush on either side. We converse upon such unfortunate generous terms as exclude the regards of fear, shame or design in either of us. . . .

Let me begin then, madam, by asking you a question which may enable me to judge better of my own conduct than most instances of my life. In what manner did I behave the last hour I saw you? What degree of concern did I discover when I felt a misfortune, which I hope you will never feel, that of parting from what one most esteems? For if my parting looked but like

[1] In this passage when first published, the word 'bit' was substituted for 'caught'.

that of your common acquaintance, I am the greatest of all the hypocrites that ever decency made.

I never since pass by the house but with the same sort of melancholy that we feel upon seeing the tomb of a friend, which only serves to put us in mind of what we have lost. I reflect upon the circumstances of your departure, your behaviour in what I may call your last moments, and I indulge a gloomy kind of satisfaction in thinking that you gave some of those last moments to me. I would fain imagine this was not accidental, but proceeded from a penetration, which I know you have in finding out the truth of people's sentiments, and that you were not unwilling the last man that would have parted with you, should be the last that did.

I really looked upon you then as the friends of Curtius might have done upon that hero in the instant he was devoting himself to glory, and running to be lost out of generosity . . . I am with all unalterable esteem and sincerity, Madam, your most faithful, obedient, humble servant.

60   *Alexander Pope to Lady Mary Wortley Montagu*

Oct. 1717

Madam,—I write as if I were drunk; the pleasure I take in thinking of your return transports me beyond the bounds of common sense and decency. . . . I have been made enough to make all the inquiry I could at what time you set out, and what route you were to take. If Italy run yet in your thoughts, I hope you will see it in your return. If I but knew you intended it, I would meet you there, and travel back with you.

I would fain behold the best and brightest thing I know, in the scene of ancient virtue and glory; I would fain see how you look on the very spot where Curtius sacrificed himself for his country; and observe what difference there would be in your eyes, when you ogled the statue of Julius Caesar, and a Marcus Aurelius.

Allow me but to sneak after you in your train, to fill my

pockets with coins, or to lug an old busto behind you, and I shall be proud beyond expression. Let people think, if they will, that I did all this for the pleasure of treading on classic ground; I would whisper other reasons in your ear. The joy of following your footsteps would as soon carry me to Mecca as to Rome; and let me tell you as a friend if you are really disposed to embrace the Mahometan religion, I will fly on pilgrimage with you thither, with as good a heart, and as sound devotion, as every Jeffery Rudel, the Provençal poet, went after the fine Countess of Tripoly to Jerusalem. . . . When people speak most highly of you, I think them sparing: when I try myself to speak of you, I think I am cold and stupid. I think my letters have nothing in them, but I am sure my heart has so much, that I am vexed to find no better name for your friend and admirer, than your friend and admirer.

LADY MARY WORTLEY MONTAGU

Lady Mary Wortley Montagu, the eldest daughter of Evelyn Pierrepoint, later Duke of Kingston, was baptised at Covent Garden on 26th May 1689. When she was 8 years old she is reputed to have been, on account of her wit and beauty, the toast of the Kit-Kat Club. Her fame rests on her enormous correspondence on all subjects, written either in England or during her stay on the Continent.

She corresponded with Anne Wortley Montagu, champion of women's rights. Anne's replies were often drafted by her brother Edward. When Anne died, in 1709, Mary and Edward continued to write to each other. However, Mary's father, now Marquess of Dorchester, would not allow the marriage because Wortley refused to entail his estate on a possible heir. The couple eloped at the beginning of September 1712. Certain of the letters suggest that this elopement held an element of comedy. The actual courtship was prolonged throughout by a fluctuation of mixed emotions on both sides. For Mary, material considerations such as the question of dowry, Wortley's settlement and her father's opposition to him, weighed heavily. She also favoured the country, solitude and limited society. Edward however was just the reverse, he liked the town, social attractions and, where Mary was concerned, he was extremely jealous. The result of two such opposites was a love/hate relationship eloquently expressed in the courtship letters.

After the elopement Mary went with her husband to Constantinople where he had been appointed ambassador.

Horace Walpole, whom she visited in Florence in 1740, took a dislike to her and spread unwarranted scandal about her and the son of the Countess Palazzo. Edward became a miser in his last years and died in 1761, a millionaire. Mary only outlived him by a year.

61 *Lady Mary to Edward Wortley Montagu*
[28th March 1710]

Perhaps you'l be surprizd at this Letter. I have had manny debates with my selfe before I could resolve on it. I know it is not Acting in Form, but I do not look upon you as I do upon the rest of the world, and by what I do for you, you are not to judge my manner of acting with others. You are Brother to a Woman I tenderly lov'd.[1] My protestations of freindship are not like other people's. I never speak but what I mean, and when I say love, it is for ever. I had that real concern for Mrs. Wortley I look with some regard on every one that is related to her. This and my long Acquaintance with you may in some measure excuse what I am now doing.

I am surprizd at one of the Tatlers you sent me.[2] Is it possible to have any sort of Esteem for a person one beleives capable of having such triffling Inclinations? Mr. Bickerstaff has very wrong notions of our sex. I can say there are some of us that dispises charms of show, and all the pageantry of Greatnesse, perhaps with more ease than any of the Philosophers. In contemning the world they seem to take pains to contemn it. We dispise it, without takeing the pains to read lessons of Morrality to make us do it. At least I know I have allwaies look'd upon it with contempt without being at the Expence of one serious refflection to oblige me to it. I carry the matter yet farther. Was I to chuse of £2,000 a year or twenty thousand, the first would be my choice.

[1] Anne Wortley died in autumn 1709.
[2] No. 143 (9th March 1710) by Steele.

There is something of an unavoidable embarras in makeing what is calld a great figure in the world, [that] takes off from the happynesse of Life. I hate the noise and hurry inseparable from great Estates and Titles, and look upon both as blessings that ought only to be given to Fools, for tis only to them that they are blessings.

The pritty Fellows you speak of, I own entertain me sometimes, but is it impossible to be diverted with what one dispises? I can laugh at a puppet shew, at the same time I know there is nothing in it worth my attention or regard. General Notions are generally wrong. Ignorance and Folly are thought the best foundations for Virtue, as if not knowing what a Good Wife is was necessary to make one so. I confess that can never be my way of reasoning. As I allwaies forgive an Injury when I think it not done out of malice, I can never think my selfe oblig'd by what is done without design. Give me leave to say it (I know it sounds Vain): I know how to make a Man of sense happy, but then that man must resolve to contribute something towards it himselfe. I have so much Esteem for you I should be very sorry to hear you was unhappy, but for the world I would not be the Instrument of makeing you so, which (of the humour you are) is hardly to be avoided if I am your Wife. You distrust me. I can neither be easy nor lov'd where I am distrusted, nor do I beleive your passion for me is what you pretend it; at least I'm sure, was I in love I could not talk as you do.

Few Women would have spoke so plainly as I have done, but to dissemble [is] among the things I never do. I take more pains to approve my conduct to my selfe than to the world, and would not have to accuse my selfe of a minute's deceit. I wish I lov'd you enough to devote my selfe to be for Ever miserable for the pleasure of a day or two's happynesse. I cannot resolve upon it— You must think otherwise of me or not at all.

I don't injoin you to burn this Letter. I know you will.[1] Tis the first I ever writ to one of your sex and shall be the last. You must never expect another. I resolve against all correspondance of this kind. My resolutions are seldom made and never broken.

[1] Wortley did not burn the letter; in fact he made a careful copy.

8 April [1710]

'In the Humour You are'—'If I am distrusted'—that is in other words, if you Love me—if You have any Apprehension of Losing me. My Dearest Lady M[ary], you had wrong'd me had you taken me to be of another Humour, had you thought otherwise of me or believ'd I coud Think Otherwise of you. Do you Imagine any one that is able to set a just Value on You can under a Passion be less uneasy or insecure? I appeal even to your Experience, which to my great Grief is so much less than mine, whether any one that Loves is free from Fear. [Passage omitted.] It requires an uncommon greatness of Mind to chose to be reduc'd to less than a third part of your present Attendance, your Apartments, your Table, and be quite stript of what glitters more than all the rest of those Ornaments that are not part of You, the Train of Admirers. Did I to gain You quit the same Proportion of my small Trappings, I own my happiness would not arise from a selfe denial, and therefore you will think me ungenerous in recommending it to you. It would be the highest improvement of that Model of life I always took to be the best. I coud almost come up to the Rules you laid down when you said your letter shoud have bin dated from another world.[1] I ever believ'd the compleatest Plan of Felicity that we are acquainted with, was to enjoy one woman friend, one Man, and to think it of little moment whether those that were made use of to fill up some idle hours were Princes or Peasants, wise or foolish, but rather to seek the Lower as less likely to work any change in mind thoroughly satisfi'd that knew no want nor so much as a wish. Had I you, I shoud have at one view before me all the Charms of either sex met together. I shoud enjoy a perpetual succession of new Pleasures, a constant Variety in One. This is far beyond what I thought sufficient to make life Happy. . . .

[1] Refers to her letter of 8th August 1709 to Anne Wortley.

[April 1710]

I can't account for my fears that you do not love me but from a dispondence in my temper which disposes me this moment to dispeare of ever seeing you againe. If I were to finde myself described in any writings I shud believe the author had strain'd a carrictor beyond nature, and yet there appears no extravagance to me, since I consider you come the neerest notion of a fine gentleman of any I ever saw. . . .

64   Edward Wortley Montagu to Lady Mary

20 April [1710]

Tho last night I was perfectly well till I saw the letter sign'd by you, I am this morning downright sick. Had there bin any such thing as Sympathy that is occasion'd by Griefe, I shou'd have bin sensible of it when you first fell ill. I had griev'd at your Illness, tho I had bin sure you hated me. An Aversion may possibly be remov'd, but the loss of you woud be irretrievable; there has not yet bin, there never will be, another L.M. You see how far a man's passion carries [his] reflexions. It makes him uneasy because the [wor]st may possibly happen from the least dangerous Distempers. I take yours to be so, and think a thousand to one that I hear of your recovery when I hear of you next. I am not the least concern'd to fancy your Colour may receive some Alteration. I shoud be overjoy'd to hear your Beauty was very much impair'd, cou'd I be pleas'd with any thing that wou'd give you displeasure, for it woud lessen the number of your Admirers, but even the loss of a feature, nay of your Eyes themselves, wou'd not make you seem less beautifull to—[Passage omitted.]

I have this minute receivd your 2 Letters. I know not how to direct to you, whether to London or the country, or if in the country to Durham or Wortley. Tis very likely you'l never receive this. I hazard a great deal if it falls into other hands, and I write for all that—

I wish with all my soul I thought as you do. I endeavor to convince my selfe by your Arguments, and am sorry my reason is so obstinate not to be deluded into an Opinion that tis impossible a Man can esteem a Woman. I suppose I should then be very easy at your thoughts of me. I should thank you for the wit and Beauty you give me and not be angry at the follys and weaknesses, but to my Infinite affliction I can beleive neither one nor tother. One part of my Character is not so good nor th'other so bad as you fancy it. Should we ever live together you would be disapointed both ways; you would find an easy equality of temper you do not expect, and a thousand faults you do not imagine. You think if you marry'd me I should be passionately fond of you one month and of some body else the next. Neither would happen. I can esteem, I can be a freind, but I don't know whether I can Love. Expect all that is complaisant and easy, but never what is fond in me. You Judge very wrong of my Heart when you suppose me capable of veiws of Interest, and that any thing could oblige me to flatter any body. Was I the most indigent Creature in the world I should answer you as I do now, without adding or deminishing. I am incapable of Art, and 'tis because I will not be capable of it. Could I deceive one minute, I should never regain my own good Opinion, and who could bear to live with one they despis'd?

If you can resolve to live with a Companion that will have all the deference due to your superiority of good sense, and that your proposals can be agreable to those on whom I depend—I have nothing to say against them.

As to travelling, tis what I should doe with great pleasure, and could easily quit London upon your account, but a retirement in the country is not so disagreable to me, as I know a few months would make it tiresome to you. Where people are ty'd for Life, tis their mutual Interest not to grow weary of one Another. If I had all the personal charms that I want, a Face is too slight a foundation for happynesse. You would be soon tir'd with seeing every day the same thing, where you saw nothing else. You would have leisure to remark all the defects, which would encrease in proportion as the novelty lessend, which is allwaies a great charm. I should have the displeasure of seeing a coldnesse, which tho' I could not reasonably blame you for, being involuntary, yet it would render me uneasy, and the more because I know a Love may be reviv'd which Absence, Inconstancy, or even Infidelity has extinguish'd, but there is no returning from a degout given by Satiety.

I should not chuse to live in a croud. I could be very well pleasd to be in London without makeing a great Figure or seeing above 8 or 9 agreable people. Apartments, Table, etc. are things that never come into my head. But [I] will never think of any thing without the consent of my Family, and advise you not to fancy a happynesse in entire solitude, which you would find only Fancy.

Make no an[swer t]o this. If you can like me on my own terms, tis not to me you must make your proposals. If not, to what purpose is our Correspondance?

However, preserve me your Freindship, which I think of with a great deal of pleasure and some Vanity. If ever you see me marry'd, I flatter my selfe you'l see a Conduct you would not be sorry your Wife should Imitate.

66   *Edward Wortley Montagu to Lady Mary*

[5th May 1710]

The letter you sent into the Country came this evening.[1] It is in every part of it a Contradiction to the Compliment you make me and proves that no one is superior to you in good sense. However, I heartily thank you for it as well as for your saying you can bring your selfe to be easy and Complaisant. I wish you had bin able to stop there and forbear telling me you cou'd be nothing more. Had you, immediatly after you said you might be easy, gone to the mention of settlements, I might only have taken you to be very prudent and still have hop'd for something above easi-

[1] Her letter of 25th April.

ness and Complaisance. But to say there cou'd be nothing more and then be so exact about the method of proposing, I refer it to yourselfe whether this does not look as if you were studying how to put yourselfe in the road to happiness and not preparing to enter upon the Possession of it. [Passage omitted] The satiety you speak of never happens where there is not a want of understanding on the side of t'other. A very small share of Reason with a great deal of kindness will secure a Passion longer than the perfection of it with your sort of Return. If you say a man is not satiated when he has got rid of such an Attachment, I will not say he is, nor quarrel with you about a word, but this I must beg leave to say, that I had much rather be cur'd, and that I shoud be much longer in curing by what you call satiety than such a Coldness as yours. If you woud keep a man a slave for a long time that you dont value, I can't say you are in the wrong or that he woud be less serviceable to you than if you did value him. But for my part I can have no such Ambition. I shoud be sorry to be ti'd to one to whom I coud take my selfe to be superiour, or whom I coud live with as if I had any power. For this reason, as much as I desir'd to have you, I woud not think of it without first letting you know all I knew my selfe of my temper, that if it did not suit with yours it might give you no trouble. Most others woud have first secur'd you and then seem'd surpriz'd you should not be satisfid in any place or Company that pleas'd them most. That I have chose rather to love you than govern you will, I hope, give me some title to that Friendship you promise me.

I am not sure a retirement woud agree with me better than with others, but a man shoud never run the hazard of hearing one he loves find fault with a Place where she may not only have as much as she pleases of his Company, but know she has his heart wholly to herselfe.

67   *Lady Mary to Edward Wortley Montagu*

[15th August 1712]
Friday night

I tremble for what we are doing. Are you sure you will love me for ever? Shall we never repent? I fear, and I hope. I foresee all that will happen on this Occassion. I shall incense my Familly [to] the highest degree. The gennerallity of the World will blame my conduct, and the Relations and freinds of —— will invent a thousand storyes of me, yet—tis possible you may recompense every thing to me. In this Letter (which I am fond of) you promise me all that I wish.—Since I writ so far, I receiv'd your friday Letter. I will be only yours, and I will do what you please. (Postscript) You shall hear from me again to morrow, not to contradict but to give Some directions. My resolution is taken— Love me and use me well.

68   Lady Mary to Edward Wortley Montagu

[16th August 1712]
Satterday Morning

I writ you a Letter last night in some passion. I begin to fear again; I own my selfe a coward.—You made no reply to one part of my Letter concerning my Fortune. I am afraid you flatter your selfe that my F[ather] may be at length reconcile'd and brought to reasonable terms. I am convince'd by what I have often heard him say, speaking of other cases like this, he never will. The fortune he has engag'd to give with me was settle'd, on my B[rother's] marriage, on my sister and my selfe, but in such a manner that it was left in his power to give it all to either of us, or divide it as he thought fit. He has given it all to me. Nothing remains for my sister but the free bounty of my F[ather] from what he can save, which notwithstanding the greatnesse of his Estate may be very little. Possibly after I have disoblig'd him so much, he may be glad to have her so easily provided for, with Money allready rais'd, especially if he has a design to marry him selfe, as I hear.

I do not speak this that you should not endeavor to come to terms with him, if you please, but I am fully perswaded it will be to no purpose. He will have a very good Answer to make, that I suffer'd this Match to proceed, that I made him a very silly figure in it, that I have let him spend £400 in wedding cloaths, all which I saw without saying any thing. When I first pretended to oppose this Match, he told me he was sure I had some other design in my head. I deny'd it with truth, but you see how little appearance there is of that Truth. He proceeded with telling me that he would never enter into treaty with another Man, etc., and that I should be sent immediately into the North, to stay there, and when he dy'd he would only leave me an Annuity of £400.

I had not courrage to stand this Vein, and I submitted to what he pleas'd. He will now object against me, why, since I intended to marry in this Manner, I did not persist in my first resolution? that it would have been as easy for me to run away from T[horesby] as from hence, and to what purpose did I put him and the Gentleman I was to marry for Expense etc.? He will have a thousand plausible reasons for being irreconcilable, and tis very probable the World will be on his Side.—Refflect now for the last time in what manner you must take me. I shall come to you with only a Nightgown[1] and petticoat, and this is all you will get with me.

I have told a Lady of my Freinds what I intend to do. You will think her a very good Freind when I tell you she has proffer'd to lend us her house, if we would come there the first Night. I did not accept of this, till I had let you know it. If you think it more convenient to carry me to your Lodging, make no scrupule of it. Let it be what it will; if I am your Wife, I shall think no place unfit for me where you are. I beg we may leave London next morning, where ever you intend to go. I should wish to go out of England if it suits with your Affairs. You are the best Judge of your father's temper. If you think it would be obliging to him, or necessary for you, I will go with you immediately to ask his pardon and his blessing. If that is not proper at first, [I] think the best Scheme is going to the Spaw. When you come back you may endeavor to Make your Father admit of seeing me, and treat with mine (tho' I persist in thinking it will be to no purpose). But I cannot think of living in the midst of my Relations and Acquaintance after so unjustifiable a step—unjustifiable to the World.—But I think I can justify my selfe to my selfe.—

I again beg you to hire a Coach to be at the door early Monday morning to carry us some part of our way, wherever you

[1] Formal evening dress.

resolve our Journey shall be. If you determine to go to the Lady's house, you had better come with a coach and 6 at 7 a clock to morrow. She and I will be in the balconey that looks on the road; you have nothing to do but to stop under it, and we will come down to you. Do in this what you like best. After all, think very seriously. Your [letter], which will be waited for, is to determine every thing. I forgive you a coarse Expression[1] in your last, which however I wish had not been there. You might have said something like it without expressing it in that Manner, but there was so much complaisance in the rest of it, I ought to be satisfy'd. You can shew me no goodnesse I shall not be sensible of. However, think again, and resolve never to think of me if you have the least doubt, or that it is likely to make you uneasy in your Fortune. I beleive to travell is the most likely way to make a Solitude agreable, and not tiresome. Remember you have promis'd it.

Tis something Odd for a Woman that brings nothing to expect any thing, but after the way of my Education I dare not pretend to live but in some degree suitable to [it]. I had rather die than return to a dependancy upon Relations I have disoblig'd. Save me from that fear if you Love me. If you cannot, or think I ought not to expect it, be sincere and tell me so. Tis better I should not be yours at all, than for a short happynesse involve my selfe in Ages of Misery. I hope there will never be Occasion for this precaution but however tis necessary to make it. I depend entirely on your honnour, and I cannot suspect you of any way doing wrong. Do not imagine I shall be angry at anything you can tell me. Let it be sincere. Do not impose on a Woman that leaves all things for you.

[1] Cuckoldom.

LAURENCE STERNE

Laurence Sterne was born at Clonmel, Ireland, on 24th November 1713. His father was an army officer and, for the first ten years of his life, Laurence followed the regiment from place to place in England and Ireland. After school in Halifax and Jesus College, Cambridge, he obtained the living of Sutton-in-the-Forest, near York, in 1738. His literary reputation is, of course, based on the novel *Tristram Shandy*.

He was undoubtedly, on paper at least, something of a Casanova. He had three principal love affairs. The first with Elizabeth Lumley, who became his wife; the second with Catherine de Fourmantel; the third with Eliza or Elizabeth Draper. However, he was something of a charlatan, in that he was driven to copying from his original love letters to his wife, to send to later conquests! Eliza Draper was the wife of a Bombay lawyer. Through ill-health she came back to England.

Sterne died in his lodgings, 41 Old Bond Street on 18th March 1768, three weeks after the publication of his book *A Sentimental Journey through France and Italy*.

[1740]

You bid me tell you, my dear L., how I bore your departure for S——, and whether the valley where D'Estella stands, retains still its looks—or, if I think the roses or jessamines smell as sweet as when you left it. Alas! every thing has now lost its relish and look! The hour you left D'Estella, I took to my bed. I was worn out by fevers of all kinds, but most by that fever of the heart with which thou knowest well I have been wasting these two years—and shall continue wasting till you quit S——. The good Miss S——, from the forebodings of the best of hearts, thinking I was ill, insisted upon my going to her. What can be the cause, my dear L., that I never have been able to see the face of this mutual friend, but I feel myself rent to pieces? She made me stay an hour with her, and in that short space I burst into tears a dozen different times—and in such affectionate gusts of passion, that she was constrained to leave the room, and sympathize in her dressing-room. I have been weeping for you both, said she, in a tone of the sweetest pity—for poor L.'s heart, I have long known it—her anguish is as sharp as yours—her heart as tender—her constancy as great—her virtues as heroic. Heaven brought you not together to be tormented. I could only answer her with a kind look, and a heavy sigh—and returned home to your lodgings (which I have hired till your return) to resign myself to misery. Fanny had prepared me a supper—she is all attention to me—but I sat over it with tears; a bitter sauce, my L., but I could eat it with no other—for the moment she began to spread my little table, my heart fainted within me. One solitary plate, one knife, one fork, one glass! I gave a thousand pensive penetrating looks at the chair thou hadst so often graced, in those quiet and sentimental repasts—then laid down my knife and fork, and took out my handkerchief, and clapped it across my face, and wept like a child. I do so this very moment, my L.; for, as I take up my pen, my poor pulse quickens, my pale face glows, and tears are trickling down upon the paper as I trace the word L——. O thou, blessed in thyself, and in thy virtues—blessed to all that know thee—to me most so, because more do I know of thee than all thy sex. This is the philtre, my L., by which thou hast charmed me, and by which thou wilt hold me thine, whilst virtue and faith hold this world together. This, my friend, is the plain and simple magic, by which I told Miss —— I have won a place in that heart of thine, on which I depend so satisfied, that time, or distance, or change of every thing which might alarm the hearts of little men, create no uneasy suspence in mine. Wast thou to stay in S—— these seven years, thy friend, though he would grieve, scorns to doubt or to be doubted—'tis the only exception where security is not the parent of danger. I told you poor Fanny was all attention to me since your departure—contrives every day bringing in the name of L. She told me last night (upon giving me some hartshorn) she had observed my illness began the very day of your departure for S——; that I had never held up my head; had seldom, or scarce ever smiled; had fled from all society—that she verily believed I was broken-hearted, for she had never entered the room, or passed by the door, but she heard me sigh heavily— that I neither ate, or slept, or took pleasure in any thing as before. Judge then, my L., can the valley look so well—or the roses and jessamines smell so sweet as heretofore? Ah me!— But adieu—the vesper bell calls me from thee to my God!

L. STERNE

70   *Laurence Sterne to Catherine de Fourmantel*
[York, 1759?]

My dear Kitty,
    If this billet catches you in bed, you are a lazy sleepy little slut, and I am a giddy, foolish, unthinking fellow for keeping you so late up; but this Sabbath is a day of sorrow—for I shall not see my dear creature, unless you meet me at Taylor's half an hour after twelve; but in this, do as you like. I have ordered Matthew to turn thief and steal you a quart of Honey. What is Honey to the sweetness of thee who are sweeter than all the flowers it comes from? I love you to distraction, Kitty, and will love you to eternity, so adieu! and believe what time only will prove me, that I am y^{rs}.

London, 176[0]

My dear Kitty,

I have arrived here safe & sound, except for the Hole in my
Heart, which you have made like a dear enchanting Slut as you
are. I shall take Lodgings this morning in Picadilly or the Hay-
market, & before I seal this letter, will let you know where to
direct a Letter to me, which Letter I shall wait for by the return of
the Post with great impatience; so write, my dear Love, without
fail. I have the greatest honors paid me & most civilities shewn
me, that were ever known from the Great; and am engaged all
ready to ten Noble Men & Men of fashion to dine. Mr. Garrick
pays me all & more honour than I could look for. I dined with
him to-day, & he has promised Numbers of great People to carry
me to dine with 'em. He has given me an Order for the Liberty
of his Boxes, and of every part of his House for the whole
Season; & indeed leaves nothing undone that can do me either
Service or Credit; he has undertaken the management of the Book-
sellers, & will procure me a great price—but more of this in my next.

And now my dear, dear Girl! let me assure you of the truest
friendship for you, that ever man bore towards a woman. Where
ever I am, my heart is warm towards you, & ever shall be till it is
cold for ever. I thank you for the kind proof you gave me of your
Love, and of y^r desire to make my heart easy, in ordering y^r
self to be denied to you know who;—whilst I am so miserable to be
separated from my dear, dear Kitty, it would have stabb'd my soul
to have thought such a fellow could have the Liberty of comeing
near you. I therefore take this proof of your Love & good principles most kindly, & have as much faith & dependence upon
you in it, as if I was at y^r Elbow;—would to God I was at it this
moment! but I am sitting solitary & alone in my bed Chamber
(ten o'clock at night, after the Play), & would give a Guinea for a
squeeze of y^r hand. I send my Soul perpetually out to see what
you are adoing;—wish I could send my Body with it. Adieu,
dear & kind Girl! and believe me ever y^r kind friend & most aff^te
Admirer. I go to the Oratorio this night.

Adieu! Adieu!

P.S. My service to yr Mama.

Mount Coffee-House, Tuesday, 3 o'Clock [1765?]

There is a strange mechanical effect produced in writing a billet-doux within a stonecast of the lady who engrosses the heart and soul of an inamorato—for this cause (but mostly because I am to dine in this neighbourhood) have I, Tristram Shandy, come forth from my lodgings to a coffee-house the nearest I could find to my dear Lady ——'s house, and have called for a sheet of gilt paper, to try the truth of this article of my creed. Now for it—

O my dear lady—what a dishclout of a soul hast thou made of me? I think, by the bye, this is a little too familiar an introduction, for so unfamiliar a situation as I stand in with you—where heaven knows, I am kept at a distance—and despair of getting one inch nearer you, with all the steps and windings I can think of to recommend myself to you. Would not any man in his senses run diametrically from you—and as far as his legs would carry him, rather than thus causelessly, foolishly, and foolhardily expose himself afresh—and afresh, where his heart and reason tells him he shall be sure to come off loser, if not totally undone? Why would you tell me you would be glad to see me? Does it give you pleasure to make me more unhappy—or does it add to your triumph, that your eyes and lips have turned a man into a fool, whom the rest of the town is courting as a wit? I am a fool—the weakest, the most ductile, the most tender fool that ever woman tried the weakness of—and the most unsettled in my purposes and resolutions of recovering my right mind. It is but an hour ago, that I kneeled down and swore I never would come near you—and after saying my Lord's Prayer for the sake of the close, *of not being led into temptation*—out I sallied like any Christian hero, ready to take the field against the world, the flesh, and the devil; not doubting but I should finally trample them all down under my feet. And now I am got so near you—within this vile stone's cast of your house—I feel myself drawn into a vortex, that has turned my brain upside downwards; and though I had purchased a box ticket to carry me to Miss *******'s benefit, yet I know very well, that was a single line directed to me to let me know Lady —— would be alone at seven, and suffer me to spend the evening with her, she would infallibly see every thing verified I have told her. I dine at Mr. C——r's in Wigmore-street, in this neighbourhood, where I shall stay till seven, in hopes you purpose to put me to this proof. If I hear nothing by that time, I shall conclude you are better disposed of—and shall take a sorry hack, and sorrily jog on to the play. Curse on the word. I know nothing but sorrow—except this one thing, that I love you (perhaps foolishly, but)

most sincerely,

L. STERNE

73   *Laurence Sterne to Mrs. H.*

Coxwould, October 12, 1767

Ever since my dear H. wrote me word she was mine, more than ever woman was, I have been racking my memory to inform me where it was that you and I had that affair together. People think that I have had many, some in body, some in mind, but as I told you before, you have had me more than any woman—therefore you must have had me, [Hannah], both in mind, and in body. Now I cannot recollect where it was, nor exactly when—it could not be the lady in Bond-street, or Grosvenor-street, or —— Square, or Pall Mall. We shall make it out, H., when we meet. I impatiently long for it—'tis no matter. I cannot now stand writing to you to-day. I will make it up next post—for dinner is upon table, and if I make Lord F—— stay, he will not frank this. How do you do.? Which parts of *Tristram* do you like best? God bless you.

Yours,

L. STERNE

HORACE WALPOLE

Horace Walpole, 4th Earl of Orford, was the youngest son of Sir Robert Walpole by Catherine Shorter, though scandal has it that Lord Hervey was really his father. One of the great friends of his youth was the poet Gray with whom he did the Grand Tour. Unfortunately they quarrelled before the Tour was over. Later Walpole apologised to Gray for his behaviour. He has been called 'the best letter writer in the English language'.

It was in Lady Herries's drawing-room that Walpole first met the charming sisters Mary and Agnes Berry. They were educated and intelligent women. 'Mr Berry,' wrote Walpole to Lady Ossory 'carried his daughters for two or three years to France and Italy, and they are returned the best informed and the most perfect creatures I ever saw at their age. They are exceedingly sensible, entirely natural and unaffected, frank, and being qualified to talk on every subject. Nothing is so easy and agreeable as their conversation. . . . They are of pleasing figures; Mary, the eldest, sweet, with fine dark eyes that are very lively when she speaks, with a symmetry of face that is the more interesting from being pale. Agnes, the younger, has an agreeable, sensible countenance, hardly to be called handsome, but almost. She is less animated than Mary, but seems, out of deference to her sister, to speak seldomer, for they dote on each other, and Mary is always praising her sister's talents.'

Three years later Walpole again wrote to Lady Ossory. 'In short they are extraordinary beings. and I am proud of my partiality for them; and since the ridicule can only fall on me, and not on them, I care not a straw for its being said that I am in love with one of them; people shall choose which, it is as much with both as either.' He was only really happy when the sisters were at home, near him, either in London or Twickenham. But, from the large correspondence, it seems obvious that he was most in love with Mary.

74 *Horace Walpole to the Misses Mary and Agnes Berry*

Strawberry Hill, June 30, 1789

I am more of an old fondle-wife than I suspected when I could put myself into such a fright on not hearing from you exactly on the day when I had settled I should; but you had promised to write on the road, and though you did, your letter was not sent to the post at the first stage, as Almighty Love concluded it would be, and as Almighty Love would have done, and so he imagined some dreadful calamity must have happened to you. But you are safe under grand maternal wings, and I will say no more on what has happened. Pray present my duty to grand-mama, and let her know what a promising young grandson she has got.

Were there any such thing as sympathy at a distance of two hundred miles, you would have been in a mightier panic than I was, for on Saturday se'ennight, going to open the glass case in the tribune, my foot caught in the carpet, and I fell with my whole weight against the corner of the marble altar on my side, and bruised the muscle so badly that for ten days I could not move without screaming. I am convinced that I should have broken a rib, but I fell on the cavity whence two of my ribs had been removed that are gone to Yorkshire. I am much better both of my bruise and of my lameness, and shall be ready to dance at my own wedding when my wives return. . . .

You are not the first Eurydice that has sent her husband to the devil, as you have kindly proposed to me; but I will not undertake the jaunt; for if old Nicholas Pluto should enjoin me not to look back to you, I should certainly forget the prohibition, like my predecessor. Besides, I am a little too old to take a voyage twice, which I am so soon to repeat, and should be laughed at by the good folks on the other side of the water, if I proposed coming back for a twinkling only. No, I chuse as long as I can

Still with my fav'rite Berrier to remain.

  *   *   *   *   *   *   *

I am delighted that my next letter is to come from wife the second. I love her as much as you, and I am sure you like that I should. I should not love either so much, if your affection for each other were not so mutual; I observe and watch all your ways and doings, and the more I observe you, the more virtues I discover in both. Nay, depend upon it, if I discover a fault you shall hear of it.

You came too perfect into my hands, to let you be spoilt by indulgence. All the world admires you, yet you have contracted no vanity, advertised no pretensions, are simple and good as nature made you, in spite of all your improvements. Mind *you* and *yours* are always, from my lips and pen, of what grammarians call the *common of two*, and signify *both*, so I shall repeat that memorandum no more. . . .

75 *Horace Walpole to the Misses Mary and Agnes Berry*
  [Extract]

               July 15, 1789

I have scarce left myself any room for conjugal douceurs; but as you see how very constantly you are in my thoughts, I am at least not fickle, on the contrary, I am rather disposed to jealousy. You have written to Mr. Pepys, and he will have anticipated my history of his being established in Palazzo Dudley; and that will make this letter more and more wrinkled. Well! he cannot send you 'Bonner's Ghost,' and I shall have the satisfaction of tantalizing you four or five days longer—if this is not love—the deuce is in it. Does one grudge that the beloved object should be pleased by anyone but oneself, unless beloved object there be?

Do not be terrified however; jealousy most impartially divided between Two can never come to great violence. Wife Agnes has indeed given me no cause, but my affection for both is so compounded into one love that I can think of neither separately. Frenchmen often call their mistress *mes Amours*, which would be no wish in me. A propos, Lady Lucas told me t'other day of two young Irish couples who ran away from Dublin, and landed in Wales, and were much surprised to find that Holyhead was not Gretna Green. Adieu! mes Amours.

76 *Horace Walpole to the Misses Mary and Agnes Berry*

Ex Officina Arbutiana, July 19, 1789

Such unwriting wives I never knew! and a shame it is for an author, and what is more, for a printer, to have a Couple so unlettered. I can find time amidst all the hurry of my shop to write small quartos to them continually. In France, where nuptiality is not the virtue the most in request, a wife will write to her consort, tho' the doux billet should contain but two sentences, of which I will give you a precedent: A Lady sent the following to her spouse: 'Je vous ecrit, parceque je n'ai rien a faire; et je finis, parceque je n'ai rien a vous dire.' I do not wish for quite so laconic a poulet; besides, your ladyships *can* write.

77 *Horace Walpole to the Misses Mary and Agnes Berry*

Strawberry Hill, August 13, 1789

I have received at once most kind letters from you both, too kind, for which you both talk of gratitude. Mercy on me! which

114

is the obliged, and which is the gainer? Two charming beings, whom everybody likes and approves, and who yet can be pleased with the company and conversation and old stories of a Methusalem? or I, who at the end of my days have fallen into more agreeable society than ever I knew at any period of my life? I will say nothing of your persons, sense, or accomplishments, but where, united with all those, could I find so much simplicity, void of pretensions and affectation? This from any other man would sound like compliment and flattery; but in me, who have appointed myself your guardian, it is a duty to tell you of your merits, that you may preserve and persevere in them. If ever I descry any faults, I will tell you as freely of them. Be just what you are, and you may dare my reproofs.

I will restrain even reproaches, tho' in jest, if it puts my sweet Agnes to the trouble of writing when she does not care for it. It is the extreme quality of my affection for both that makes me jealous if I do not receive equal tokens of friendship from both; and though nothing is more just than the observation of two sisters repeating the same ideas, yet never was that remark so ill applied. Tho' your minds are so congenial, I have long observed how originally each of you expresses her thoughts. I could repeat to you expressions of both, which I remember as distinctly as if I had only known either of you.

For the future there shall be perfect liberty among us. Either of you shall write when she pleases; while my letters are inseparably meant to both, tho' the direction may contain but one name, lest the postman should not comprehend a double address. . . .

78   *At the close of 1789 Horace Walpole inscribed his Catalogue of Strawberry Hill to the Misses Berry:*

To
The Dear Sisters

MARY and AGNES BERRY

This description
of
His Villa at Strawberry Hill
Which they often made delightfull
By their Company, Conversation, and Talents,
is offered
by

HORACE WALPOLE

From a heart overflowing with
Admiration, Esteem, and Friendship
Hoping
That long after he shall be no more,
It may, while amusing them
Recall some kind thoughts
Of a most devoted
And affectionate humble friend

December 1789.

79 *Horace Walpole to the Misses Mary and Agnes Berry*

Strawberry Hill, Sunday Night,
April 3, 1791

Oh! what a shocking accident! oh! how I detest your going abroad more than I have done yet in my crossest mood! You escaped the storm on the 10th October that gave me such an alarm; you passed unhurt through the cannibals of France and their republic of Ladrones and Poissardes, who terrified me sufficiently—but I never expected that you would dash yourself to pieces at Pisa. You say I love truth, and that you have told me the exact truth, but how can fear believe?

You say you slept *part* of the night after your fall. Oh! but the other part. Was not you feverish? How can I wait above a month for answers to an hundred questions I want to ask; and
116

how a week for another letter! A little comfort I have had since I received that horrid account; I have met Mrs Lockart at Lady Hesketh's, and she has assured me that there is a very good surgeon at Pisa—if he is, he must have blooded you directly. How could you be well enough to write the next day? Why did not Miss Agnes for you? But I conclude she was not recovered enough by your fall.

When I am satisfied that you have not hurt yourself more than you own, I will indulge my concern about the outside of your nose, about which I shall not have your indifference. I am not in love with you, yet fully in love enough not to bear any damage done to that perfect nose, or to any of all your beautiful features; then, too, I shall scold your thoughtlessness.

How I hate a party of pleasure! it never turns out well; fools fall out, and sensible people fall down. Still I thank you a million of times for writing yourself; if Miss Agnes had written for you, I confess I should have been ten times more alarmed than I am, and yet I am alarmed enough.

My sweet Agnes, I feel for you too, tho' you have not the misery of being a thousand miles from your wounded sister, nor are waiting for a second account. The quantity of blood she lost, has, I trust, prevented any fever. I would ask for every tiny circumstances, but alas! I must wait above a month for an answer. . . .

80   *Horace Walpole to Miss Mary Berry*

Strawberry Hill. Aug. 3, 1791

How cruel to know you ill at such distance! how shocking to just have patience, when one has none! . . . Your fever I am persuaded was no light one. Your fêtes and balls and the heat have occasioned your illness, you both left England in search of health, and yet have done as much as you could have performed in London, where at least the cold can tolerate crowds and fatigue . . . I longed to see Agnes's writing, and she never could have it sent more apropros, since there was occasion for it—you yourself were both kind and unkind to write so much—but burn the French! Why write so much about them? For heaven's sake be more careful; you are both of you delicate and far from strong. You bid me take care of myself, to what purpose do I cocker myself against November, if you two fling away your healths, nay, I will not look so early as to November.

Do not I implore you set out in great heats. Fatigue and hot bad inns may lay you up where there is no assistance. Oh! I now feel again all the aversion I felt last year to your journey. Travel slowly, I beseech you; I had rather wait months for you, than have you run any risk. Surely you will keep very quiet till you begin your journey, and perfectly recruit your health.

81   *Horace Walpole (now Lord Orford) to Miss Mary Berry*

1791

You have hurt me excessively! We had passed a most agreeable evening, and then you poisoned all by one cruel word. I see you are too proud to like to be obliged by me, tho' you see that my greatest, and the only pleasure I have left is to make you and your sister a little happier if I can; and *now*, when it is a little more in my power, you cross me *in trifles even*, that would compensate for the troubles that are fallen on me. I thought my age would have allowed me to have a friendship that consisted in nothing but distinguishing merit. You allow the vilest of tribunals, the newspapers, to decide how short a way friendship may go. Where is your good sense in this conduct? And will you punish me, because, what you nor mortal being can prevent, a low anonymous scribbler pertly takes a liberty with your name? I cannot help repeating that you have hurt me.

Dec. 13, 1791

My dearest Angel,—I had two persons talking law to me, and was forced to give an immediate answer, so that I could not even read your note till I had done. And now I do read it, it breaks my heart.

If my most pure affection has brought grief and mortification on you, I shall be the most miserable of men. . . . You know I scarce wish to live but to carry you to Cliveden! . . . Is all your felicity to be in the power of a newspaper? Are your virtue and purity, and my innocence about you; are our consciences no shield against anonymous folly or envy? Would you only condescend to be my friend if I were a beggar. . . . For your own sake, for poor mine, combat such extravagant delicacy, and do not poison the few days of a life which you, and you only, can sweeten. . . . How could you say you wish you had not returned.

To Miss Mary Berry.

WILLIAM COWPER

William Cowper's letters are, with Lamb's and Edward Fitz-Gerald's, the best in the language. They describe life in the country, at Olney where he lived for so many years, the transla-tion of Homer which engaged much of his time and the writing of his other poems; his devoted relations both with Mrs. Unwin who looked after him all his life, after he left London, and with his cousin Lady Hesketh.

However, in 1757, he was in London at the Inner Temple and there he met and fell in love with Theodora Jane, second daughter of his uncle, Ashley Cowper. Charles Cowden Clarke says, 'She is described as a person of beauty, accomplishments, and more than ordinary understanding. The attachment was warmly returned, and would have been consummated in marriage had not, first, his circumstances been so precarious, and had not, in the second place, the father objected to the match, on the ostensible ground that the parties were too nearly related in blood. Probably his real reason was, that he knew Cowper's hereditary tendency to insanity. The cousins, however, continued to love, although the father's will forbade any farther intercourse, and the after incidents in Cow-per's sad story put their marriage entirely out of the question. Theodora cherished his memory—long and carefully preserved the copies of poems he had given her, and is suspected of having done him effective pecuniary service at a future period of his life. That this disappointment produced Cowper's malady, is not true—for that unquestionably lay in the system—that it, along with many other untoward circumstances, increased its virulence, seems certain.' He wrote his poems to her under the name of 'Delia'.

83   *William Cowper to his cousin Theodora Jane Cowper (Delia)*

Would my Delia know if I love, let her take
My last thought at night, and the first when I wake;
With my prayers and best wishes preferr'd for her sake.

Let her guess what I muse on, when rambling alone
I stride o'er the stubble each day with my gun,
Never ready to shoot till the covey is flown.

Let her think what odd whimsies I have in my brain,
When I read one page over and over again,
And discover at last that I read it in vain.

Let her say why so fix'd and so steady my look,
Without ever regarding the person who spoke,
Still affecting to laugh, without hearing the joke.

Or why then with pleasure her praises I hear
(That sweetest of melody sure to my ear),
I attend, and at once inattentive appear.

And lastly, when summon'd to drink to my flame,
Let her guess why I never once mention her name,
Though herself and the woman I love are the same.

84   *William Cowper to his cousin Theodora Jane Cowper*

Bid adieu, my sad heart, bid adieu to thy peace!
Thy pleasure is past, and thy sorrows increase;
See the shadows of evening how far they extend,
And a long night is coming that never may end;

For the sun is now set that enliven'd the scene,
And an age must be past e'er it rises again.

Already deprived of its splendour and heat,
I feel thee more slowly, more heavily beat;
Perhaps over strain'd with the quick pulse of pleasure,
Thou art glad of this respite to beat at thy leisure;
But the sigh of distress shall now weary thee more,
Than the flutter and tumult of passion before.

The heart of a lover is never at rest,
With joy overwhelm'd or with sorrow oppress'd;
When Delia is near, all is ecstacy then,
And I even forget I must lose her again.
When absent, as wretched, as happy before,
Despairing I cry, I shall see her no more!

SIR JOSHUA REYNOLDS

The most eminent figure in the English School of painting was born at Plympton Earl, Devonshire, on 16th July 1723. Reynolds's great wish was to visit Rome. This was made possible by Lord Edgcumbe who knew Captain (later Viscount) Keppel. Keppel had just been appointed to command the Mediterranean Squadron and he invited the artist to sail with him in the *Centurion*. Reynolds stayed at Port Mahon, the guest of the Governor of Minorca, while Keppel had 'conversations' with the Bey of Algiers who was charged with piracy. From here he wrote to Miss Weston whom he met when he was living in London, in Lincoln's Inn Fields, where he was a pupil of Thomas Hudson, the leading portrait painter of his time. The love affair, it appears, came to nothing.

85 Joshua Reynolds to Miss Weston

(Port Mahon) December O.S. 10th 1749

Dear Miss Weston,—My memory is so bad that I vow I dont remember whether or no I writ you about my expedition before I left England, since, I am sure I have not, for I have writ to nobody. I sailed from Plimouth so long agone as May 11th and am got no further yet than Port Mahon, but before you shall receive this expect to be on tother side of the water.

I have been kept here near two months by an odd accident, I dont know whether to call it a lucky one or not, a fall from a horse down a precipice, which cut my face in such a manner as confined me to my room, so that I was forced to have recourse to painting as an amusement at first i have now finished as many portraits as will come to a hundred pounds the unlucky part of the Question is my lips are spoiled for kissing for my upper lip was so bruised that a great peice was cut off and the rest — that I have but a — to look at, but in — won't perceive the defect.[1]

So far it has been — tour to me that can — When we were at sea I amused myself with reading. . . . When I am settled at Rome I will write to you again to let you know how to direct to me in the meantime I shall be much obliged to you if you will call and see that my goods are safe and not spoiling I would write to him who has them could I think of his name I should be glad if you had a spare place in your garret that they could be at your house From your slave

J. REYNOLDS

[1] The dashes are hiatuses in the original.

1732   *1818*

WARREN HASTINGS

In the spring of 1769, says Macaulay, Warren Hastings embarked on board the *Duke of Grafton* for India and began a voyage distinguished by incidents with might furnish matter for a novel. It was on this voyage that the future Governor General of India met his second wife, the Baroness Imhoff. It may have been a shipboard romance but it was not until eight years later that 'Marian', as he called her, was able to obtain a divorce from the Baron.

To read Warren Hastings's life is to be taken back to the 'great' days of the British Raj in India. When his wife had to return to England because of bad health, he fitted up a cabin for her on the ship with a profusion of sandal wood and carved ivory, and went to enormous expense to engage a female companion for her on the voyage.

Marian was forty when Warren Hastings married her and had a family of grown-up children. The impeachment of Hastings was decided upon in 1786. The actual trial did not begin until 1788. For seven years Hastings defended himself with great dignity against a charge of 'high crimes and misdemeanours'. Finally, in 1795, his wealth dissipated by the trial, the House of Lords acquitted him.

Calcutta, December 26, 1784

My beloved Marian,—I have received your letter of the 3rd August. I received it on my return from the play. I could not go to bed, but sat reading it till past two, and afterwards lay long after counting three, without being able to close my eyes. Whether I was happy or unhappy in reading it I cannot tell you. I fear my disappointment on one subject equalled my joy for your safety, the close of your perils, and the promise that you would soon be as well as you ever had been at any period of your life. I have since thought only on the good, and I thank God for it. The attentions shown to you on your arrival, though what I expected, made no small part of my rejoicing. Something might at the first have been yielded to you on my account; more surely to your character which had preceded you; and your character is marked with virtues all original, and such as would naturally excite curiosity and respect; but I am certain that they who were your first visitors would have wished to repeat their visits early and stimulate others with the same desire to see you.

I read much in your letter to admire, to be delighted with. . . . They have given me my freedom and opened the road to my happiness. Yet my Marian forgive me—I do not feel the joy which I ought. I am too much attached to my public character and its relations, and dread the ruin which I see impending over them. . . . May Heaven prosper my design, bless my Marian, and speedily reunite us with every necessary means of happiness within our possession! If I have enough for a decent subsistence I want no pensions and despise titles. At this instant I have but one wish and a *little one* annexed to it, and O God grant them! Amen.

JAMES BOSWELL

James Boswell was born in Edinburgh, eldest son of Alexander Boswell, who, when he was raised to the bench, took the title of Lord Auckinleck.

Boswell met William Johnson Temple at Edinburgh University. They became lifelong friends and Boswell suggested that they write to each other. Temple was vicar of St Gluvias, Penryn in Cornwall and the correspondence went on for thirty-seven years. In his letters Boswell discussed every possible topic, from the violence of his passion for Miss W, through his own health and spirits, to the study of the law. In 1763 Boswell met Johnson. Of recent years a large number of books both by and on Boswell have been published. This letter to Temple can hardly be described as a love letter in the strict sense. It is nevertheless very much about love and is of the essence of Bozzy, as his friends called him.

87   James Boswell to The Reverend William Temple

Edinburgh, 8 February, 1768

My dear friend,

All is over between Miss Blair and me. I have delayed writing till I could give you some final account. About a fortnight

127

after she went to the country, a report went that she was going to be married to Sir Alexander Gilmour, Member of Parliament for the county of Midlothian, a young man about thirty, who has £1,600 a year of estate, was formerly an officer in the Guards, and is now one of the clerks of the Board of Green Cloth, £1,000 a year—in short a noble match, though a man of expence and obliged to lead a London life. After the fair agreement between her and me, which I gave you fully in my last, I had a title to know the truth. I wrote to her seriously and told her that if she did not write me an answer I should believe the report to be true. After three days, I concluded from her silence that she was at last engaged. I endeavoured to laugh off my passion, and I got Sir Alexander Gilmour to frank a letter to her, which I wrote in a pleasant strain, and amused myself with the whim. Still, however, I was not absolutely certain, as her conduct has been so prudent all along. At last she comes to town, and who comes too but my old rival, the Nabob? I got acquainted with Mr. Fullarton, and he and I joked a good deal about our heiress. Last night he proposed that he and I should go together and pay her a visit for the first time after her return from the country. Accordingly we went and I give you my word, Temple, it was a curious scene. However, the Princess behaved exceedingly well, though with a reserve more than ordinary. When we left her we both exclaimed, 'Upon my soul, a fine woman!' I began to like the Nabob much; so I said to him, 'I do believe, Mr. Fullarton, you and I are in same situation here. Is it possible to be upon honour, and generous in an affair of this kind?' We agreed it was. Each then declared he was serious in his love for Miss B. and each protested he never before believed the other in earnest. We agreed to deal by one another in a fair and candid manner. I carried him to sup at a lady's, a cousin of mine, where we stayed till half an hour past eleven. We then went to a tavern and the good old claret was set before us. He told me that he had been most assiduous in attending Miss Blair; but she never gave him the least encouragement and declared he was convinced she loved me as much as a woman could love a man. With equal honesty I told all that has past between her and me, and your observation on the *wary mother*. 'What,' said he, 'did Temple say so? If he had lived twenty years in the country with them, he could not have said a better thing.' I then told him Dempster's humorous saying that all Miss B's connections were in an absolute confederacy to lay hold of every man who has a £1,000 a year, and how I called their system a *Salmond Fishing*. 'You have hit it,' said he, 'we're all kept in play; but I am positive you are the fish and Sir Alexander is only a mock salmon to force you to jump more expeditiously at the bait.' We sat till two this morning. We gave our words as men of honour that we would be honest to each other: so that neither should suffer needlessly and, to satisfy ourselves of our real situation, we gave our words that we should both ask her this morning, and I should go first. Could there be anything better than this? The Nabob talked to me with the warmth of the Indies, and professed the greatest pleasure on being acquainted with me.

Well, Temple, I went this morning and she made tea to me alone. I then asked her seriously if she was to be married to Sir Alexander. She said it was odd to believe every thing people said, and why did I put such question? &c. I said that she knew very well I was much in love with her, and that if I had any chance I would take a great deal of trouble to make myself agreeable to her. She said I need not take the trouble, and I must not be angry, for she thought it best to tell me honestly. 'What then', said I, 'have I no chance?' 'No,' said she. I asked her to say so upon her word and upon honour. She fairly repeated the words. So I think, Temple, I had enough.

She would not tell me whether she was engaged to the knight. She said she would not satisfy an idle curiosity. But I own I had no doubt of it. What amazed me was that she and I were as easy and as good friends as ever. I told her I have great animal spirits and bear it wonderfully well. But this is really hard: I am thrown upon the wide world again. I don't know what will become of me.

Before dinner, the Nabob and I met, and he told me that he went and, in the most serious and submissive manner, begged to know if she was engaged. She would give him no satisfaction and treated him with a degree of coldness that overpowered him quite, poor man!

Such is the history of the lovers of this cruel Princess, who certainly is a lucky woman to have had a sovereign sway over so many admirers. I have endeavoured to make merry on my misfortune.

A Crambo Song on losing my Mistress

Although I be an honest *Laird*,
In person rather strong and brawny,
For me the Heiress never car'd,
For she would have the Knight, Sir Sawney.

And when with ardent vows, I swore
Loud as Sir Jonathan Trelawney,
The Heiress shewed me to the door,
And said, she'd have the Knight, Sir Sawney.

She told me, with a scornful look,
I was ugly as a Tawney;
For she a better fish could hook,
The rich and gallant Knight, Sir Sawney.

N.B. I can find no more rhymes to Sawney.

Now that all is over, I see many faults in her, which I did not see before. Do you not think she has not feeling enough, nor that ingenuous spirit which your friend requires? The Nabob and many other people are still of opinion that she has not made sure of Sir Sawney, and that all this may be finesse. But I cannot suspect so young a creature of so much artifice and whatever may be in it, I am honourably off, and you may wonder at it, but I assure you I am very easy and cheerful. I am, however, resolved to look out for a good wife, either here or in England. I intend to be in London in March. My address will be at Mr. Dilly's, Bookseller. But I expect to hear from you before I set out, which will not be till the 14th of March. I rejoice to hear that Mrs. Temple is in a good way. My best wishes ever attend you and her.

I am your most affectionate friend,

JAMES BOSWELL

11 February. I have allowed my letter to lie by till this day. The heiress is a good Scots lass. But I must have an English woman. My mind is now twice as enlarged as it has been for some months. You cannot say how fine a woman I may marry, perhaps a Howard or some other of the noblest in the kingdom.

MRS. PIOZZI

As Mrs. Thrale she was the friend of Dr. Johnson and Fanny
Burney. She married Gabriele Piozzi in 1784. Dr. Johnson 'drove
the memory of Mrs. Thrale from his mind, burning every letter of
hers on which he could lay a hand'.

When Piozzi himself died, his wife retired to Bath. She was
close on seventy. She met a young actor there, William Augustus
Conway who, although not much of an actor, was handsome and
elegant. Mrs. Piozzi was infatuated by him. Her letters to him
begin in 1819, when she was close on seventy-three.

88   *Mrs. Piozzi (formerly Mrs. Thrale) to William Augustus Conway*

Weston Super Mare, Sept. 1, 1819

Three Sundays have now elapsed since James brought me
dearest Mr. Conway's promise to write to me the very next—
and were it not for the newspaper which came on Tuesday, the
24th August—sending me to rest comfortable, tho' sick enough,
and under the influence of laudanum, I should relapse into my
former state of agonizing apprehension on your account, but that
little darling autograph round the paper was written so steady,

and so completely in the old way,—whenever I look at it, my spirits revive, and Hope (true Pulse of Life) ceases to intermit, for a while at least,—and bids me be assured we soon shall meet again. I really was very ill three or four days; but the jury of matrons, who sat on my complaint, acquitted the apricots which I accused, and said they all, but two, proved *an alibi*.

Did I not once predict that dear Mr Conway would live to an extreme old age? Your Sibyl has always been right, and it was natural I should think so. The oak and cedar are said by naturalists to take the deepest root of all the trees; when these fancies cross your memory three-score years hence, do not forget the old friend of your young days, should you live to those of Methuselah; none more true, none more tender, none more disinterested will you ever find than H. L. Piozzi. Good night! and God bless my dearest and most valued friend! for whose perfect recovery and long-continued happiness I will pray till the post comes in.—Yes; and till life goes out from poor H.L.P. I would keep up my spirits —as you wish me—and your spirits too. But how can I? Send a newspaper at least. Oh, for a breath of intelligence, however short, respecting health and engagements.

89 Mrs. Piozzi to William Augustus Conway

7 Oct. 1819

I write—like my dearest friend—a brief communication; not to beg letters; the last half broke my heart, but to tell you that having directed mine to Mrs. Rudd, I fear it will not be received safely. I wish my beloved friend to keep his spirits up, but have enough to do on his dear account—to keep up my own. Yet shall not the one alleviating drop of comfort, as you kindly call my letters,—ever fail.

Your being shut out by ill health from fortune and from fame is very affecting indeed. Suffer nothing that you are not obliged to suffer; however, we shall get through the dusky night and enjoy a bright morning after all. Your youth and strength are full in perfection, but 'tis on God's favour I depend for your recovery. Here am I, however, praying most fervently for your restoration to all that makes life desirable, and giving God thanks for the power he lends me of affording solace to the finest soul, the fairest emanation of its celestial origin that ever was inclosed in human clay—such clay! But we must all be contented to bear our cross—the Paschal Lamb—type of our blessed Saviour, was ordered to be eaten with bitter herbs, and have I then been all the while complaining? Let us take things as God sends them, and be thankful—Dear Hope,—

> A cordial innocent as strong—
> Man's heart at once inspirits—and serenes.

She sweetens pain and sorrows into joy, and sends me smiling through my tears to rest. Good-night—God send His angel to watch over you, and grant us yet a happy meeting by the 20th of October.

H.L.P.

90 *Mrs. Piozzi to William Augustus Conway*

Midnight, Feb. 2, 1820

I would not hurry you for the world. . . . Take your own time, and do it in your own way; or rather suffer Nature to do it —that has done so much for you; more, I do think, than for any mortal man. See what a scar the surgeon, however, skilful, would have made in that beautiful neck, while Nature's preparation, thro' previous agony, made suppurating ease come on unfelt; and the wound heals almost without a cicatrix—does it not??? So will it be with the mind. My own hasty folly—and my *'violent love outran the Pauser Reason.'*

Morning, Feb. 3.—I have had some sleep, and am now on my knees giving thanks to God for the power he has lent to you, to resolve against sinful dissipation. Oh spare the soul which He thus deigns to preserve; oh keep that person pure which His good

133

spirit will one day inhabit—throwing a Radiance round. Accept my best acknowledgments for having promised me so sweetly that you would try to rise superior to all low desires. . . . Do not stir out; do not tempt Heaven, or Heaven's king, who by your abscess has saved your precious life, so prayed for by poor H.L.P.

91   *Mrs. Piozzi to William Augustus Conway*
     [Extract]

Feb. 3, 1820

'Tis not a year and quarter since dear Conway, accepting of my portrait sent to Birmingham, said to the bringer—'oh if *your lady* but retains her friendship; oh if I can but keep *her* patronage —I care not for the rest.' . . . And now, when that friendship follows you through sickness and through sorrow, now that her patronage is daily rising in importance—upon a lock of hair given . . . or refused by une petite traitresse—hangs all the happiness of my once high-spirited and high-blooded friend. Let it not be so. Exalt Thy Love-Dejected Heart, and rise superior to such narrow minds. Do not however fancy she will be ever punished in the way you mention; no, no. She'll wither on the thorny stem, dropping the faded and ungathered leaves—a China rose, of no good scent or flavour—false in apparent sweetness, deceitful when depended on. Unlike the flower produced in colder climates, which is sought for in old age, preserved even after death, a lasting and an elegant perfume—a medicine, too, for those whose shattered nerves require astringent remedies.

Let me request of you . . . to love yourself, . . . and to reflect on the necessity of not dwelling on any particular subject too long or too intensely. . . .

This is preaching, but remember how the sermon is written at three, four, and five o'clock by an octogenarian pen, a heart twenty-six years old, and as H.L.P. feels it to be all your own.

HENRY FREDERICK, DUKE OF CUMBERLAND

The letters of Henry Frederick to Lady Grosvenor are, in their childish simplicity, their lack of punctuation, their bad spelling, some of the most delightful love letters in existence.

Henry was the son of Frederick, Prince of Wales and brother to George III. Henry was known as a great lover. His most famous 'affair' was with Henrietta Vernon, Lady Grosvenor, whose husband was unfaithful to her. Henry Frederick's life, at this time, was like something from the stage. He pursued Henrietta into Cheshire, following her about in disguise which was not always successful. They were discovered. Lord Grosvenor, unable to bring an action for divorce on account of his own conduct, brought one for criminal conversation at which, for the first time, a Prince of the Blood appeared as defendant. 'The verdict of a British jury,' says Merydew, 'in whose charge is female chastity, sanctity of marriage, and the general custody of morals was of course against him, and damages were awarded to the amount of £10,000.' Henry was not put off by the verdict, although he deserted Henrietta for an intrigue with the wife of a wealthy timber merchant. Following this affair Henry fell in love with a Mrs. Horton, the daughter of an Irish peer and the widow of a Derbyshire gentleman. She insisted on marriage and in October 1771 they were married in Calais. The King forbade them both to come to Court.

My own dearest Love,—How sorry I am that I am deprived the pleasure of seeing you this evening but especially as you are in pain God grant it over upon my knees I beg it altho' it may go off for a few days it must return and then you will be easy my only Joy will be happy, how shall I thank you for your very kind note your tender manner of expressing yourself calling me your dear friend and at this time that you should recollect me.

I wish I dare lye all the while by your bed and nurse you— for you will have nobody near you that loves you as I do thou dearest Angel of my Soul o' that I could but bear your pain for you I should be happy what grieves me most that they who *ought to feel* don't know inestimable Prize the Treasure they have in you— thank God if it should happen now Mr Croper is out of town and you may be quiet for a few days—I shall go out of town to-night but shall stay just for an answer pray if you can just write me word how you find yourself, I shall be in Town by eight To-morrow Evening in hopes of hearing again.

I am sure my angel is not in greater pain than what my heart feels for my adorable angel—I sent this by D—— [Countess of Dunhoff] servant she is gone to Renelagh so if you write direct it to her the Boy has my orders and will bring it to me—Adieu God bless you and I hope before morning your dear little one.
                    Directed to Lady Grosvenor.

93   *Henry Frederick, Duke of Cumberland to Harriet, Lady Grosvenor*

[17—?]

My dear little Angel,—I am this instant going out of Town ten thousand thanks for your kind note I am sure nothing could make my aking heart to night bearable to me than when you say you are sensible how much I love you pray God it may be over before morning or that you may be better I shall be in Town at eight o'clock for I shall long to know how you are don't mention to D that I wrote by her servant to you for I have ordered him not to tell—

Adieu Good night God bless the Angel of my Soul Joy and Happiness without whom I have no comfort and with whom all happiness alive au revoir I hope very soon.

Directed to Lady Grosvenor.

94   *Henry Frederick, Duke of Cumberland to Harriet, Lady Grosvenor*
[Extract]
$$[17—?]$$

My dear little Angel,—I wrote my last letter to you yesterday at eleven o'clock just when we sailed I dined at two o'clock and as for the afternoon I had some music I have my own servant a-board that plays . . . and so got to bed about 10—I then prayed for you *my dearest love kissed your dearest little hair* and laye down and dreamt of you had you on the dear little *couch* ten thousand times in my arms kissing you and telling you how much I loved and adored you and you seem pleased but alas when I woke it found it all dillusion *nobody by me but myself at sea.* . . . I am sure the account of this days duty can be no pleasure to you my love yet it is exactly what I have done and as I promised you always to let you know my motions and thoughts I have now performed my promise this day to you and always will untill the very last letter you shall have from me.

When I shall return to you that instant O' my love mad and happy beyond myself to tell you how I love you and have thought of you ever since I have been separated from you. . . . I hope you are well I am sure I need not tell you I have had nothing in my thoughts but your dearself and long for the time to come back again to you will all the while take care of myself because you desire *my dear little Friend* does the angel of my heart pray do you take care of your dearself for the sake of your faithful servant who lives but to love you to adore you, and to bless the moment that

137

has made you generous enough to own it to him I hope my dear nay I will dare to say you never will have reason to repent it. . . .

Indeed my dear angel I need not tell you I know you read the reason too well that made me do so it was to write to you for God knows I wrote to no one else nor shall I at any other but to the King God bless you most amiable and dearest little creature living—

95   Harriet, Lady Grosvenor to the Duke of Cumberland

[17—?]

My dearest Soul,—I'm in constant hopes of C—— sending me a letter from you and I'm very anxious to hear you are arrived safe I imagine and hope it will come to-morrow thank God I've some delightful news to tell you my Ld setts out for London next Wednesday. . . . I feer you cannot read this but I'm writing foast as I feer this will be too late for the poast—Everything goes on well and he is in very tollerable— . . . I feer this letter will be certainly too late so must conclude my dear Soul I do love you most sincerely indeed I'm out of my wits with joy at the thought of seeing you my Dear Friend believe me ever most sincerely and affectionately Yrs.

What a scrawl I always write to you I'm really ashamed to a degree of myself my Dear Soul . . . you may write in ink safely as he is sure to go on Wednesday shd any unforseen Accident keep him which is totally improbable I would meet the Post Boy in the Lane once more dearest Soul Farewell.

96   Harriet, Lady Grosvenor to the Duke of Cumberland

Friday Night [17—?]

My dearest Soul,—How happy you made me by your letter it seems ages to me since I heard from you tho' in reality not many

138

days, but minutes count for years with those that love, but I don't
like to hear that you have still a little cough you don't take care
of yourself I wish I could take care of you indeed. . . . Mr G——
is just gone out for an hour, so I take this favourable time to write
to you and shall send it off soon in the morning, I long most
heartily for the time I shall see you again your letter came perfectly safe I was so happy to get it, I hope you will have received
my last safe where I sent you the Acct. of Hollywell, only think of
your having lost to Tarpolley I should have been so miserable if
I'd known it at the time I'm so sorry, how dreadful at that
time of night its a horrible intricket road, I'd a very odd discourse
with Mr G—— to-day about my Lord he first begun by saying
he was very uneasy about his health and did not think he was so
well as he used to be and he ought to take great care, he after
that said he thought he gave up his whole time attention &
fortune to horses and was worse and worse infatuated than ever
about them & that he never could talk upon any other subject
therefore he could never have any discourse with him and that he
would lose all his acquaintance but Jockeys, I could not help
laughing at his description of him which was very just for he sais he
will set for half an hour with his eyes fixed on a Table or a Chair
and then apply to Tomm or anybody that is by, do you know what
Mare such a Filly was got out of, or can you tell what Horse such
a Colt was got out of by Gd I've got the best stud in England
nobody will have any horses to run but me very soon, then if he or
anybody that dont understand that subject offers to mention
anything else he is as cross as anything for half an hour, and then
fast asleep, so says Mr G—— . . . this was as you may imagine a
Tete a Tete subject but its so exact a picture of him I was resolved
you should have it— . . . . in bed before eleven when I always
dream of you my Dearest Friend—I hope soon to have a letter
from Carry with some writing from you in milk . . . how I long
for the 1st and 2nd of Decr yet it is being too selfish for what a
situation for you but I'll say no more of that as you are so kind
to say you don't mind it, today is my Birth day I think it has
turned out quite lucky to me as I've such an opportunity of
writing to you.

Mr Gro——r is come home which obliges me to shorten it
vexes me tho' I've nothing but nonsense to talk off—I dont like
to be interrupted & prevented & I must write to Carry a line as

I inclose this to her, I see Almacks begins the 1st Decr do take a Dance there, and tell me how it looks it will make but two days difference & I cant bear to prevent you from everything O' dear I am always teazing you I think I'm quite provoked at myself, I wish to God I was the only one to suffer in an uncomfortable situation and I'd bear everything with pleasure but the thoughts of my dearest Friend being unhappy is ten times more to me than anything I could ever suffer, indeed my dearest life it is believe me that is my greatest anxiety and concern, I can never make you amends but my sincerest love you shall ever have from the bottom of my soul that you are kind enough to say you value and as long as you esteem it and give me yours it will be our mutual comfort, God bless you my dearest soul—I'm glad the time is fixed for the Parliament meeting which I hope will bring up to Town

Farewell a thousand times most sincerely till we meet My Dearest Soul ever most faithfully and affectionately

Yrs. H. . . .

1754   1832

GEORGE CRABBE

George Crabbe is considered, by those who do not read him, to be a poet of gloom and depression. It is true that he wrote against the abuses of his time but he could frequently paint very comic pictures as when he wrote of the curate who 'sometimes saved his cash, By interlinear days of frugal hash'. He falls between the eighteenth and nineteenth centuries with his Augustan couplets and his 'revolutionary' choice of subject. The truth was he was a reformer.

He was born at Aldeburgh, in Suffolk, and was apprenticed to a doctor. While working for a surgeon at Woodbridge he met Sarah Elmy. They were engaged for a long time, indeed, until Crabbe gave up his 'doctoring' job, came to London and, in a famous letter, appealed to Edmund Burke for help, which was not refused. Sarah Elmy was the 'Mira' of Crabbe's early poems and they were married in 1783. Mira died in 1813 and Crabbe, on a visit to Sidmouth, again met one of his lady friends, Charlotte Ridout. Charlotte had recently rejected a suitor of her own age and Crabbe, so much the older, proposed marriage. She accepted. However, away from her, Crabbe had second thoughts, perhaps influenced by his children and the disparity in their ages—and as René Huchon, his biographer says, 'he sacrificed his passion to his misgivings and preserved his freedom'.

97   *The 'Lucy' of the eighth tale from* Tales of the Hall *by George Crabbe was undoubtedly inspired by Mira. . . .*

> There was such goodness, such pure nature seen
> In Lucy's looks, a manner so serene;
> Such harmony in motion, speech, and air,
> That without fairness she was more than fair,
> Had more than beauty in each speaking grace,
> That lent their cloudless glory to the face;
> Where mild good sense in placid looks was shown,
> And felt in every bosom but her own. . . .
> A tender spirit, freed from all pretence
> Of wit, and pleased in mild benevolence.

98   *After one of his visits to Parham, Suffolk—Mira's home—George Crabbe wrote . . .*

> Oh! days remember'd well! remember'd all!
> The bitter-sweet, the honey, and the gall;
> Those garden rambles in the silent night,
> Those trees so shady, and that moon so bright;
> That thick-set alley by the arbour closed,
> That woodbine seat where we at last reposed;
> And then the hopes that came and then were gone,
> Quick as the clouds beneath the moon pass'd on:
> 'Now in this instant shall my love be shown,'
> I said. Oh! no, the happy time is flown!

99   *In the early days of meeting Mira, George Crabbe further immortalised her. . . .*

> Then Mira came! be ever blest the hour
> That drew my thoughts half-way from folly's power.
> She first my soul with loftier notions fired;
> I saw their truth, and as I saw admired;

With greater force returning reason moved,
And as returning reason urged, I loved;
Till pain, reflection, hope, and love allied
My bliss precarious to a surer guide,
To Him who gives pain, reason, hope, and love. . . .
One beam of light He gave my mind to see,
And gave that light, my heavenly fair, by thee;
That beam shall raise my thoughts, and mend my strain,
Nor shall my vows, nor prayers, nor verse be vain.

100   *George Crabbe's poem on departing from Charlotte Ridout to whom*
      he had offered marriage

September 1814

    Yes! I must go—it is a part
That cruel Fortune has assign'd me,—
    Must go, and leave, with aching heart,
What most that heart adores behind me.

    Still I shall see thee on the sand
Till o'er the space the water rises,
    Still shall in thought behind thee stand.
And watch the look affection prizes.

    But ah! what youth attends thy side
With eyes that speak his soul's devotion—
    To thee as constant as the tide
That gives the restless wave its motion?

    Still in thy train must he appear,
For ever gazing, smiling, talking?
    Ah! would that he were sighing here,
And I were there beside thee walking!

    Wilt thou to him that arm resign,
Who is to that dear heart a stranger,
    And with those matchless looks of thine
The peace of this poor youth endanger?

Away this fear that fancy makes
When night and death's dull image hide thee:
　In sleep, to thee my mind awakes;
Awake, it sleeps to all beside thee.

　Who could in absence bear the pain
Of all this fierce and jealous feeling,
　But for the hope to meet again
And see those smiles all sorrow healing?

　Then shall we meet, and, heart to heart,
Lament that fate such friends should sever,
　And I shall say—'We must not part';
And thou wilt answer—'Never, never!'

MARY WOLLSTONECRAFT
GODWIN

This unhappy, brilliant woman, twice tried to commit suicide. Her childhood in the house of her drunken father was miserable. She went out to work as a governess, a companion and a book-writer for Joseph Johnson, the bookseller and publisher. She published, in 1792, *A Vindication of the Rights of Women* for which she is chiefly known. Then, over 30, she went to Paris to study 'liberty at its source' and fell in love with an American, Captain Gilbert Imlay. She lived with him as his wife. Soon after the birth of their child Imlay began to tire of her and, returning to London, Mary tried to poison herself. A sort of reconciliation was brought about but Mary, after her return from Norway, discovered that Imlay was having an affair with an actress. This time she threw herself off Putney Bridge, after waiting 'for her clothes to be so saturated that they might the more easily drag her down to muddy death'. She was rescued and, later, married the philosopher, William Godwin. Oddly enough Imlay returned her love letters. She gave them to Godwin, who published them after her death, remarking that they were as good as *The Sorrows of Werther*. She died on the birth of her second daughter Mary, Shelley's wife. She was buried in St Pancras Churchyard. It was by her grave, where Mary, her daughter, used to sit and read, that Shelley first asked Mary to become his wife.

Paris, August 1793
Past twelve o'clock Monday night

I obey an emotion of my heart, which made me think of wishing thee, my love, good night! before I go to rest, with more tenderness than I can to-morrow, when writing a hasty line or two under Colonel ——'s eye. You can scarcely imagine with what pleasure I anticipate the day, when we are to begin almost to live together; and you would smile to hear how many plans of employment I have in my head, now that I am confident my heart has found peace in your bosom. Cherish me with that dignified tenderness, which I have only found in you; and your own dear girl will try to keep under a quickness of feeling, that has sometimes given you pain. Yes, I will be good, that I may deserve to be happy; and whilst you love me, I cannot again fall into the miserable state which rendered life a burthen almost too heavy to be borne.

But, good night! God bless you! Sterne says that is equal to a kiss—yet I would rather give you the kiss into the bargain, glowing with gratitude to Heaven, and affection to you. I like the word affection, because it signifies something habitual; and we are soon to meet, to try whether we have mind enough to keep our hearts warm. I will be at the barrier a little after ten o'clock to-morrow.

Yours

102   *Mary Wollstonecraft to Gilbert Imlay*

Paris, 1794
Evening, September 23

I have been playing and laughing with the little girl so long, that I cannot take up my pen to address you without emotion. Pressing her to my bosom, she looked so like you (entre nous, your best looks, for I do not admire your commercial face), every nerve seemed to vibrate to the touch, and I began to think that there was something in the assertion of man and wife being one—for you seemed to pervade my whole frame, quickening the beat of my heart, and lending me the sympathetic tears you excited.

Have I anything more to say to you? No; not for the present —the rest is all flown away; and indulging tenderness for you, I cannot now complain of some people here, who have ruffled my temper for two or three days past.

103 *Mary Wollstonecraft to Gilbert Imlay*

Paris, 1795
January 9

I just now received one of your hasty *notes*; for business so entirely occupies you, that you have not time, or sufficient command of thought, to write letters. Beware! you seem to be got into a whirl of projects and schemes, which are drawing you into a gulph that, if it do not absorb your happiness, will infallibly destroy mine.

Fatigued during my youth by the most arduous struggles, not only to obtain independence, but to render myself useful, not merely pleasure, for which I had the most lively taste—I mean the simple pleasures that flow from passion and affection—escaped me, but the most melancholy views of life were impressed by a disappointed heart on my mind. Since I knew you I have been endeavouring to go back to my former nature, and have allowed some time to glide away, winged with the delight which only spontaneous enjoyment can give. Why have you so soon dissolved the charm?

I am really unable to bear the continual inquietude which you and ——'s never-ending plans produce. This you may term want of firmness, but you are mistaken; I have still sufficient firmness to pursue my principle of action. The present misery, I cannot find a softer word to do justice to my feelings, appears to me unnecessary, and therefore I have not firmness to support it as you may think I ought. I should have been content, and still wish, to retire with you to a farm. My God! anything but these continual anxieties, anything but commerce, which debases the mind, and roots out affection from the heart.

I do not mean to complain of subordinate inconveniences; yet I will simply observe that, led to expect you every week, I did not make the arrangements required by the present circumstances, to procure the necessaries of life. In order to have them, a servant, for that purpose only, is indispensable. The want of wood has made me catch the most violent cold I ever had; and my head is so disturbed by continual coughing, that I am unable to write without stopping frequently to recollect myself. This, however, is one of the common evils which must be borne with— bodily pain does not touch the heart, though it fatigues the spirits.

Still, as you talk of your return, even in February, doubtingly, I have determined, the moment the weather changes, to wean my child. It is too soon for her to begin to divide sorrow! And as one has well said, 'despair is a freeman', we will go and seek our fortune together.

This is not a caprice of the moment, for your absence has given new weight to some conclusions that I was very reluctantly forming before you left me. I do not choose to be a secondary object. If your feelings were in unison with mine, you would not sacrifice so much to visionary prospects of future advantage.

104 Mary Wollstonecraft to Gilbert Imlay

London, November 1795
Sunday morning

I have only to lament, that, when the bitterness of death was past, I was inhumanly brought back to life and misery. But a fixed determination is not to be baffled by disappointment; nor will I allow that to be a frantic attempt which was one of the calmest acts of reason. In this respect, I am only accountable to myself. Did I care for what is termed reputation, it is by other circumstances that I should be dishonoured.

You say, 'that you know not how to extricate ourselves out

of the wretchedness into which we have been plunged.' You are extricated long since. But I forbear to comment. If I am condemned to live longer, it is a living death.

It appears to me that you lay much more stress on delicacy than on principle; for I am unable to discover what sentiment of delicacy would have been violated by your visiting a wretched friend, if indeed you have any friendship for me. But since your new attachment is the only sacred thing in your eyes, I am silent —Be happy! My complaints shall never more damp your enjoyment; perhaps I am mistaken in supposing that even my death could, for more than a moment. This is what you call magnanimity. It is happy for yourself, that you possess this quality in the highest degree.

Your continually asserting that you will do all in your power to contribute to my comfort, when you only allude to pecuniary assistance, appears to me a flagrant breach of delicacy. I want not such vulgar comfort, nor will I accept it. I never wanted but your heart—That gone, you have nothing more to give. Had I only poverty to fear, I should not shrink from life. Forgive me then, if I say, that I shall consider any direct or indirect attempt to supply my necessities, as an insult which I have not merited, and as rather done out of tenderness for your own reputation, than for me. Do not mistake me; I do not think that you value money, therefore I will not accept what you do not care for, though I do much less, because certain privations are not painful to me. When I am dead, respect for yourself will make you take care of the child.

I write with difficulty—probably I shall never write to you again. Adieu!

God bless you!

ROBERT BURNS

Burns was born on 25th January 1759, in a cottage about two miles from Ayr. He was the eldest son of a small farmer, William Burness. Carlyle said of Burns 'that he was fortunate in his father—a man of thoughtful, intense character, as the best of our peasants are, valuing knowledge, possessing some and open-minded for more, of keen insight and devout heart, friendly and fearless; a fully unfolded man seldom found in any rank of society, and worth descending far into society to seek . . .'.

Burns's love affairs were numerous. At 14 'handsome Nell' also 14, a fellow field labourer, initiated him into the 'sweet passion' which he said, in spite of 'acid disappointment, ginhouse prudence and bookworm philosophy I hold to be the first of human joys, and our dearest blessing here below'.

Towards the end of 1787 Burns met Mrs M'Lehose, the celebrated 'Clarinda', at the house of Miss Nimmo. Agnes M'Lehose was born in Glasgow, well educated and well connected, her maiden name being Craig (Burns said she was 'the first cousin of Lord Craig') and married to James M'Lehose in 1776. They separated by 1780. Agnes was then only 21. She returned to her father's house. Later she joined 'a social circle in Edinburgh of which she became an ornament' and 'at this period she began cultivating the muses'. From the moment Burns met her at Miss Nimmo's, the correspondence began, he calling himself 'Sylvander' and she 'Clarinda'. It may be added that her husband had gone off to Jamaica and taken a black mistress. Burns was, at the time of the letters, engaged to Jean Armour whom he subsequently married.

[1773]

MY HANDSOME NELL

O once I lov'd a bonie lass,
 An' ay I love her still,
An' whilst that virtue warms my breast,
 I'll love my handsome Nell.

As bonie lasses I hae seen,
 And money full as braw, [fine]
But, for a modest, gracefu' mien,
 The like I never saw.

A bonie lass, I will confess,
 Is pleasant to the e'e; [eye]
But without some better qualities,
 She's no' a lass for me.

But Nelly's looks are blythe and sweet,
 And what is best of a',
Her reputation is complete,
 And fair without a flaw.

She dresses ay sae clean and neat,
 Both decent and genteel;
And then there's something in her gait
 Gars ony dress look weel. [makes]

A gaudy dress and gentle air,
 May slightly touch the heart,
But it's innocence and modesty
 That polishes the dart.

'Tis this in Nelly pleases me,
 'Tis this enchants my soul,
For absolutely in my breast
 She reigns without control.

[21st December] 1787

I beg your pardon, my dear 'Clarinda', for the fragment scrawl I sent you yesterday. I really don't know what I wrote. A gentleman for whose character, abilities, and critical knowledge, I have the highest veneration, called in just as I had begun the second sentence, and I would not make the porter wait. I read to my much-respected friend several of my own bagatelles, and, among others, your lines, which I had copied out. He began some criticisms on them, as on the other pieces, when I informed him they were the work of a young lady in this town; which I assure you, made him stare. My learned friend seriously protested, that he did not believe any young woman in Edinburgh was capable of such lines; and if you know anything of Professor Gregory, you will neither doubt of his abilities nor his sincerity. I do love you, if possible, still better for having so fine a taste and turn for poesy. I have again gone wrong in my usual unguarded way; but you may erase the word, and put esteem, respect, or any other tame Dutch expression you please in its place. I believe there is no holding converse, or carrying on correspondence with an amiable woman, much less a gloriously-amiable fine woman, without some mixture of that delicious passion, whose most devoted slave I have more than once had the honour of being. But why be hurt or offended on that account? Can no honest man have a prepossession for a fine woman, but he must run his head against an intrigue? Take a little of the tender witchcraft of love, and add it to the generous, the honourable sentiments of manly friendship, and I know but one more delightful morsel, which few, few in any rank ever taste. Such a composition is like adding a cream to strawberries; it not only gives the fruit a more elegant richness, but has a peculiar deliciousness of its own.

I enclose you a few lines I composed on a late melancholy occasion. I will not give above five or six copies of it at all; and I would be hurt if any friend should give any copies without my consent.

You cannot imagine, Clarinda (I like the idea of Arcadian names in a commerce of this kind), how much store I have set by the hopes of your future friendship. I don't know if you have a just idea of my character, but I wish you to see me as I am. I am, as most people of my trade are, a strange will-o'-wisp being; the victim, too frequently of much imprudence, and many follies. My great constituent elements are pride and passion; the first I have endeavoured to humanise into integrity and honour; the last makes me a devotee, to the warmest degree of enthusiasm, in love, religion, or friendship; either of them, or altogether, as I happen to be inspired. 'Tis true I never saw you but once; but how much acquaintance did I form with you at that once? Do not think I flatter you, or have a design upon you, Clarinda; I have too much pride for the one, and too little cold contrivance for the other; but of all God's creatures I ever could approach in the beaten way of acquaintance, you struck me with the deepest, the strongest, the most permanent impression. I say the most permanent, because I know myself well, and how far I can promise either on my prepossessions or powers. Why are you unhappy?— and why are so many of our fellow-creatures, unworthy to belong to the same species with you, blest with all they can wish? You have a hand all-benevolent to give,—why were you denied the pleasure? You have a heart formed, gloriously formed, for all the most refined luxuries of love,—why was that heart ever wrung? O Clarinda! shall we not meet in a state, some yet unknown state of being, where the lavish hand of Plenty shall minister to the highest wish of Benevolence, and where the chill north-wind of Prudence shall never blow over the flowery fields of enjoyment? If we do not, man was made in vain! I deserved most of the unhappy hours that have lingered over my head: they were the wages of my labour. But what unprovoked demon, malignant as hell, stole upon the confidence of un-mistrusting, busy fate, and dashed your cup of life with undeserved sorrow?

Let me know how long your stay will be out of town: I shall count the hours till you inform me of your return. Cursed etiquette forbids your seeing me, just now; and as soon as I can walk I must bid Edinburgh adieu. Lord, why was I born to see misery which I cannot relieve, and to meet with friends whom I can't enjoy! I look back with the pangs of unavailing avarice on my loss in not knowing you sooner. All last winter,—these three months past,—what luxury of intercourse have I not lost! Perhaps, though, 'twas better for my peace. You see I am either above, or incapable of dissimulation. I believe it is want of that particular

153

genius. I despise design, because I want either coolness or wisdom to be capable of it. I am interrupted. Adieu my dear Clarinda!

SYLVANDER

Friday Evening.

107 *Clarinda to Sylvander*

Friday evening [21st December] 1788

I go to the country early to-morrow morning, but will be home by Tuesday—sooner than I expected. I have not time to answer yours as it deserves; nor, had I the age of Methuselem, could I answer it in kind. I shall grow vain. Your praises were enough—but those of a Dr. Gregory superadded! Take care: many a 'glorious' woman has been undone by having her head turned. 'Know you!' I know you far better than you do me. Like yourself, I am a bit of an enthusiast. In religion and friendship quite a bigot—perhaps I could be so in love too; but everything dear to me in heaven and earth forbids! This is my fixed principle; and the person who would dare to endeavour to remove it I would hold as my chief enemy. Like you, I am incapable of dissimulation; nor am I, as you suppose, unhappy. I have been unfortunate; but guilt alone could make me unhappy. Possessed of fine children—competence,—fame,—friends, kind and attentive, —what a monster of ingratitude should I be in the eye of Heaven were I to style myself unhappy! True, I have met with scenes horrible to recollection—even at six years' distance; but adversity, my friend, is allowed to be the school of virtue. It oft confers that chastened softness which is unknown among the favourites of Fortune! Even a mind possessed of natural sensibility, without this, never feels that exquisite pleasure which nature has annexed to our sympathetic sorrows. Religion, the only refuge of the unfortunate, has been my balm in every woe. O! could I make her appear to you as she has done to me! Instead of ridiculing her tenets, you would fall down and worship her very semblance wherever you found it!

154

I will write you again at more leisure, and notice other parts of yours. I send you a simile upon a character I don't know if you are acquainted with. I am confounded at your admiring lines. I shall begin to question your taste, but Dr. G.! When I am low-spirited (which I am at times) I shall think of this as a restorative. Now for the simile:

> The morning sun shines glorious and bright,
> And fills the heart with wonder and delight!
> He dazzles in meridian splendour seen,
> Without a blackening cloud to intervene.
> So, at a distance viewed, your genius bright,
> Your wit, your flowing numbers give delight.
> But ah! when error's dark'ning clouds arise,
> When passion's thunder, folly's lightning flies,
> More safe we gaze, but admiration dies.
> And as the tempting brightness snares the moth,
> Sure ruin marks too near approach to both.

Good night; for Clarinda's 'heavenly eyes' need the earthly aid of sleep.

Adieu CLARINDA

P.S.—I entreat you not to mention our corresponding to one on earth. Though I've conscious innocence, my situation is a delicate one.

108 *Sylvander to Clarinda*

[12th January] 1788

You talk of weeping, Clarinda: some involuntary drops wet your lines as I read them. Offend me, my dearest angel! You cannot offend me,—you never offended me. If you had ever given me the least shadow of offence, so pardon me my God as I forgive Clarinda. I have read yours again: it had blotted my paper. Though I find your letter has agitated me into a violent head-ache, I shall take a chair and be with you about eight. A friend is to be with us at tea, on my account, which hinders me from coming sooner. Forgive, my dearest Clarinda, my unguarded expressions! For Heaven's sake, forgive me, or I shall never be able to bear my own mind.

Your unhappy,

SYLVANDER

109 *Clarinda to Sylvander*

Sunday Evening [13th January] 1788

I will not deny it, Sylvander, last night was one of the most exquisite I ever experienced. Few such fall to the lot of mortals! Few, extremely few, are formed to relish such refined enjoyment. That it should be so, vindicates the wisdom of Heaven. But, though our enjoyment did not lead beyond the limits of virtue, yet to-day's reflections have not been altogether unmixed with regret. The idea of the pain it would have given, were it known to a friend to whom I am bound by the sacred ties of gratitude (no more), the opinion Sylvander may have formed from my unreservedness; and, above all, some secret misgivings that Heaven may not approve, situated as I am—these procured me a sleepless night; and, though at church, I am not at all well.

Sylvander, you saw Clarinda last night, behind the scenes! Now, you'll be convinced she has faults. If she knows herself, her intention is always good; but she is too often the victim of sensibility, and, hence, is seldom pleased with herself.

[The long letter continues with a discourse on religion. She concludes]

Tuesday. Noon

Just returned from the Dean, where I dined and supped with fourteen of both sexes; all stupid. My Mary and I alone under-

156

stood each other. However, we were joyous, and I sung in spite of my cold; but no wit. 'Twould have been pearls before swine literalized. I recollect promising to write to you. Sylvander, you'll never find me worse than my word. If you have written me, (which I hope) send it to me when convenient, either at nine in the morning or evening. I fear your limb may be worse from staying so late. I have other fears too; guess them! Oh! my friend, I wish ardently to maintain your esteem; rather than forfeit one iota of it, I'd be content never to be wiser than now. Our last interview has raised you very high in mine. I have met with few, indeed, of your sex who understood delicacy in such circumstances; yet 'tis that only which gives relish to such delightful intercourse. Do you wish to preserve my esteem, Sylvander? do not be proud to Clarinda! She deserves it not. I subscribe to Lord B's sentiment to Swift; yet some faults I shall still sigh over, though you style it reproach even to hint them. Adieu! You have much in your power to add to the happiness or unhappiness of

CLARINDA

110 Sylvander to Clarinda

[4th February 1788]

. . . I am a discontented ghost, a perturbed spirit. Clarinda, if ever you forget Sylvander, may you be happy, but he will be miserable.

Oh, what a fool I am in love!—what an extravagant prodigal of affection! Why are your sex called the tender sex, when I never have met with one who can repay me in passion? They are either not so rich in love as I am, or they are niggards where I am lavish.

O, Thou, whose I am, and whose are all my ways! Thou see'st me here, the hapless wreck of tides and tempests in my own bosom: do Thou direct to thyself that ardent love, for which I have so often sought a return, in vain, from my fellow-creatures! If Thy goodness has yet such a gift in store for me, as an equal return of affection from her who, Thou knowest, is dearer to me than life, do Thou bless and hallow our band of love and

157

friendship; watch over us, in all our outgoings and incomings, for good; and may the tie that unites our hearts be strong and indissoluble as the thread of man's immortal life!

I am just going to take your Blackbird,[1] the sweetest I am sure, that ever sung, and prune its wings a little.

SYLVANDER

[1] The verses on a blackbird, by Clarinda.

GEORGE, PRINCE OF WALES
(later GEORGE IV)

George Augustus Frederick, said his tutor, Bishop Hurd, 'would be either the most polished gentleman or the most accomplished blackguard in Europe—possibly both'. He was handsome and accomplished and his genuine love for—his marriage with— —Mrs. Fitzherbert, whom he addressed in his letters as Margaritta, is one of the best-known love affairs in royal history.

Mary Anne Fitzherbert was a Roman Catholic and this greatly confused the issue of their marriage, since the Act Of Settlement stated that if the prince married a Catholic he forfeited the succession to the throne. So they were secretly married by the Rev. R. Burt on 15th December 1785. Nevertheless, though the marriage was denied in Parliament, it was an open secret.

The Prince frequently went into frenzies of despair over his love for Margaritta and rolled, in passion, on the carpet whenever he thought he had lost her. Finally he brutally broke off the marriage of which there were no children, when Lady Jersey began 'exerting her influence' over him in June 1794.

Margaritta retired to Brighton with an annuity of £6,000 and died there in 1837.

[17— ?]

Princes, like woman, find few real friends,
All who approach them their own ends pursue,
Lovers and ministers are seldom true.

So spake a bard—well used to Courts and my sex—to you, my—
[Prince] I ought, agreeable to the style of those who surround you,
to pay an implicit obedience, and meet you as desired on my
quitting the ball-room last night. Meet you!—what you?—
the ****** [Prince] of ***** ⌈Wales]! whose character in the annals
of gallantry is too well known for me to suppose that after
such a meeting—I should have any character at all. This may be
too free—I am unused to address people of excessive rank—my
manners are unaffected—I know not a sentiment that I would wish
to disguise, and I should be happy to know only that behaviour
from your ********* [Royal Highness] that must command silent
respect from—Your father's affectionate subject,

MARGARITTA

112   The Prince of Wales to Margaritta

[17— ?]

I find but too often cause to lament that rank in life—that
perhaps is envied me by all the world—Princes indeed have few
real friends—Even your sex fly me—and does the amiable
Margaritta allow her better judgment to be biassed by public
calumny. It is beneath the heart that reigns in so lovely a bosom!
I do not command—far from it—I only entreat a further knowledge of you, and where is the impropriety of permitting me a
meeting—a condescension that will make me most happy—not

your ***** the son of your ****** [Sovereign] but your admiring, your adoring

*****[Wales]

113 Margaritta to the Prince of Wales

[17—?]

Public calumny I am above—my own reasons and observation are the charms that forbid a private meeting—already has the notice bestowed on me at the ball by your***** ******** [Royal Highness] brought on me, the envy of my own sex, and the impertinence of yours. I like not your associates, particularly that wild man, H*****, he stares me out of countenance, the difference of our rank in life forbids a further knowledge of me, I entreat you to avoid me, I shall be to-night at the ball, not because I like it, but my not having appeared since the last is I find observed, and some of our visitors yesterday told me I was too much engaged by the *****'s [Prince's] notice, to bestow any on those beneath him!—Come to the ball—dance with Lady C******* B*****, and take the slightest notice of me. Why should you wish to take more? there are a hundred much prettier women! Mrs O******* for example—you think her pretty—she is indeed divine! and she has a husband, an officer of spirit, to shield her from the rude attacks of envy. You may enjoy her conversation—she yours—and malice dare not speak—but *me*, an unprotected helpless orphan? It will be cruel to pursue the Humble

MARGARITTA

114 The Prince of Wales to Margaritta

[17—?]

Cold, unkind, Margaritta! Why am I forbid that attention which is your due—which all the world must pay you. Why am I doomed to pass an inspid evening with a woman of fashion *only*, when my heart and my better judgment would lead me to the most elegant, the most accomplished fair that B******* has to boast. Mrs O******** is beauteous, but it is not mere beauty I admire—it is expression, 'a something than beauty dearer.' You know my opinion of Lady C******** B*****; her rank entitles her to my hand, nothing besides could induce me. I respect her Grace for the sake of the best of mothers and S*****'s—and therefore I comply with what politeness and etiquette requires; but why must I give up the enjoyment of your conversation. Be superior to common talk.

Call not yourself unprotected,—all the world must be your friends. I am concerned H***** displeases you. I am certain he never designed it. This wild man has really some good points; that he admires you I wonder not, and perhaps he is not perfectly delicate in that admiration. Does S******** likewise displease you, and little J***** O*****; that you say you do not like my associates? If they do, they shall not trouble you:—I want no company when in yours!

I felt your absence from the ball, and rejoice that you will grace it this evening. It is impossible to see you with indifference! In vain would you exact so hard a task from the tenderest of your friends.—

The obliged

***** [Wales]

115 *The Prince of Wales to Margaritta*

[17—?]

What a disappointment. Ah, cruel Margaritta! I entered the ball-room last night at nine, in the highest spirits. My eyes flew round it with impatience, in search of the only bright object they wished to see—but they sought in vain! I asked H***** and S******** after you, they had seen you airing—not dressed for the ball—I was disconcerted! Is it possible, so gentle a form, a countenance so soft, so tender, can be thus unkind? I danced with Lady C——, B*****, H*****, with a Mrs B*****, pretty and animated, and I was

162

persuaded at about one o'clock to join them in a Scotch reel, with the little C*****, who is far from handsome, but dances well. The small company that remained were diverted—but nothing could re-animate my spirits. Why do you thus fly me?—once more I entreat a meeting; let it be at your own house if you please; where is the impropriety; if you grace not the C**** (which hundreds may rejoice at), why refuse attentions that are most due to you. I wish not to be considered here in my public character—much less by you—than as any other private gentleman, whose eyes and whose heart assure him you are most worthy his regard.

I esteem a character that I would not injure; report says yours is faultless as your form—allow me—permit me—a further knowledge of you; you will not find me, I trust, undeserving of your good opinion—but that I shall always remain—Your devoted and admiring

***** [Wales]

116 *Margaritta to the Prince of Wales*

[17—?]

Surprised that I was not at the ball!—recollect your letter in the morning—*it is impossible to see you with indifference*; what then was I to expect! No one thing that I wish'd.—You imagine I doubt not that my vanity would have been so well gratified, that reason would have been silent. Had I suffered the woman wholly to prevail this must have been the case; but a thousand combining circumstances have almost quell'd the foibles of my sex, and vanity you must suppose dead in me—when I withdraw thus from your notice. And yet I wish your friendship,—am deeply interested in your fame, and desire most ardently that you may be as eminent in goodness as in rank. I cannot receive your visits, the family I am with would leave the place immediately on such an event. They are what the world calls extreme good people—what I should call outrageous. They are not of the number of your friends.

163

Your first unfortunate vote in the house—against our gracious S********* they will never forgive, and it is vain that I urge the impetuosity of youth, that love of independence so natural to all, —that from reason you gave not that vote;—I dare believe you never thought about it. F** desired it, and you was glad to *appear* to have a will of your own.

But why enter I into politics, yet you make me a politician. I was violent for P***,—now dislike him, but like not F** notwithstanding. A man of bad private character,—though of the greatest talents and blest with uncommon genius—can never deserve the love of a worthy heart.

I air'd [journeyed] last night to L****, and paid a very stupid visit, yet was I not dissatisfied. It was a proper sacrifice to prudence. I am now going a sailing. Our party is large, the day is fine, and the gale favourable. If you write again be cautious how your letter is given me. I think it needless to desire you to destroy mine. They have no merit to entitle them to preservation; and as they are not directed or signed with my real name, I think they can never be made public. Yet I am not without fear. Such trash would be a treasure to the printer, and the very initials of your name would sell a book wonderfully.

Adieu.

117   *The Prince of Wales to Margaritta*

[17—?]

Do you indeed wish for my friendship! Ah! Margaritta, I know not how to believe you:— while thus cold thus insensible to all desires. A meeting again refused:—who are these very good people, whom I have so much reason to dislike, they have no paternal authority I understand; why then regard their narrow prejudices? May I entreat your history: yet I almost dread to hear an account of a life in which I am already so much interested, and which may make me still more enamoured of the dear perverse historian. Politics I should never have mentioned to a lady, but as you seem to blame my conduct, I wish to exculpate myself in your

164

opinion, but you must allow me to do it personally, for the subject is too long for a letter. On horseback you might permit me the pleasure of attending you,—I have seen you riding with only a servant;—let me join you without any, I never ride but with one here, and he shall be forbid, because my livery would carry a mark that you would not like. Your servant would not know me, and report would have nothing to say about it. I entreat you to allow me this; and appoint an early day. Your letters I keep as an invaluable treasure, and shall hardly be so careless of them as you expect. So young, so lovely, and yet so coldly prudent. Ah! Margaritta would that you partook of the warmth that burns in the heart of your faithful

***** [Wales]

118 *Margaritta to the Prince of Wales*

[17—?]

I have not been well! that fickle element on which with so much pleasure I embarked greatly disordered me; quiet and gentle exercise has been prescribed and I am at present forbid riding on horseback.

I entreat you attempt not to visit me: you will not be admitted, and *you ought not* to subject yourself to a refusal. Sure there is a haughty inflexibility about me that should make you cease to wish for more acquaintance; why do you pursue me with such unwearied attentions. I saw you on the beach when I was brought on shore; I could not avoid returning your graceful compliments. The sailors who carried me told me it was your H********. Everyone knows you!—My servant I doubt not amongst the rest. I heard S******** pronounce my name with an encomium I did not approve; I perceived that he would have led you towards me. I thank you my friend for retiring: I am above affection, and you may believe me grateful when I say, *I thank you*. To show that gratitude I will comply with your request, and speak of my past life.

Parental authority I never knew; parental love and tenderness once blest me. But now no father, mother or brother can I boast! my adverse fate has snatched each dear relation from me, and left a void no time can ere fill up. Nursed in the lap of tenderness, my infant hours in sweet succession flew; and when, 'dawning reason shed her ray benign,' maternal love watched o'er each growing sense and formed my heart by reason's purest rules. My father who had the honour of a captain's commission in the army, was a man of letters and gave up all the hours he could take from his profession to educate his Frederick; 'so we grew together —like to a double cherry, seeming parted—but yet an union in partition.'

My brother gained with applause his twentieth year; he had a friend who rivall'd him in every grace, and Frederick's virtues shone brighter in the noble Edmund—I loved them both, but something always told me I loved Edmund best. I thought my brother wrong'd by the preference, but it was allow'd by all our charming circle to be just, and hope and fancy painted such a set of bright illusions that happiness seemed all my own. Suddenly the prospect darkened. My parents in one fatal hour were torn from my embrace by death's unrelenting hand!—thus dash'd from joy I thought myself most wretched! but fate soon shew'd me that my woes were not complete. Frederick and Edmund—they are not!—they fell in —— but the hour of anguish insupportable is past!—let me not recall it!—o'er my pensive head calm resignation waves her healing wand and I have learnt to bear disappointment patiently.

The family I am with I have obligations to, but not of a pecuniary kind. The fortunes of our house were not inconsiderable and they, alas! have centred all in me!—Edmund's also— and here I am wooing health for the sake of society, which has some claims on everyone; example not the least. Adieu! recollection overpowers me! I can write no more.

119 *The Prince of Wales to Margaritta*

[17—?]

Your tale of woe has greatly affected me!—how pathetic, how elegant are all your expressions! I apprehended but too justly the effect your history would have over me; for I love, I esteem you more than ever! Start not at the sound, but let me indeed be your friend:—thank you for so kind an appellation, I will deserve it. I rejoice that you was pleased with my self-denial. S******** did indeed want me to welcome you on shore; and I felt that I wish'd it more than him, but I did not know all the party, and was afraid of displeasing you.

I hope you are not indeed indisposed. Though it hurts my vanity to suppose you so unwilling to grant me a meeting; I shou'd be still more pain'd at your illness, and perhaps rashly venture to enter a house where my presence wou'd be unwelcome.

To satisfy your punctilio I never venture to join you on the Steine, and take no other notice of you than what politeness will authorise. To a mind generous as Margaritta's, this wish to oblige cannot pass unnoticed, and I flatter myself the day will come when she will condescend to reward by her presence the respectful distance—the unwearied attention of her.

***** [Wales]

120 *The Prince of Wales to Margaritta*

[17—?]

You reject all my wishes with a haughty disdain that greatly mortifies me. I am open to correction, I avow my errors. I wish you to assume a character which you are most fit to shine in, and which may be of infinite service to me, but I wish and entreat in vain!—unkind Margaritta.

Even the words of an author I passionately admire is quoted against me. Thus you turn me from a book—I might profit from; for when I attempt to read it, it reminds me of the cold, the severe fair one, whose friendship I have most wish'd to cultivate, who attributes to me all the faults of my predecessor Hal, and believes me incapable to finish the character.

Am I to answer all the idle, the unjust things you hear to my disadvantage? Pardon my heat, I am disappointed! Hurt, I acknowledge; but my heart feels now much more so, at the sickly

167

pale of the finest cheek which I beheld this morning! Had I not some merit when I met you on horseback not to join you? I debated it for half a moment; but the reserved air with which you returned my compliments determined me. I was repaid in the look you afterwards gave me, for I thought in that look you approv'd my discretion.

Sickness only, I hope, has chilled that heart formed for more generous sensations. Your restoration to health I earnestly wish, and your return to tender feelings. Judge for yourself if I am not your attentive

TELEMACHUS

121   *Margaritta to the Prince of Wales*

[17—?]

I was beloved by Edmund, I was the sister of Frederick, and can you wonder I have pride. I lov'd Edmund, and are you surprised at my coldness? Perhaps it is not possible for any but a pre-engaged heart to behold you without feeling sentiments of tenderness. My heart is dead to love, but it glows with every other passion with greater ardour. My friendship is warm and constant, nothing but your own prudence can ever deprive you of it.

I feel myself obliged for your attention to my wishes in not joining me when on horseback. I find great benefit by that exercise, and shall pursue it. If my grateful look repaid you I am happy. You think me severe I know, but you know not the just reasons I have to appear so. You are impatient of restraint—above appearances; but, believe me, your rank requires rather more than common attention, for every eye is on you. Adieu, my dear Telemachus.

MARGARITTA

[17—?]

Every eye is, alas, too severely on me—cold Margaritta.—
Yes; you have lov'd, but why mortify me on this subject. I have
(though the world believes it not) some delicacy in my love—here
it aspires to so bright an object, and I could have wish'd you had
never felt this passion so baneful to repose. How happy to have
first awoke in the most gentle breast so sweet a feeling.

The lamented and envied Edmund, why does he engross *all*
of so large, so good a heart! allow me but a share! let the living
supply the place of the valued departed. Convince me of that
flattering sentiment of yours, 'that perhaps none but a pre-
engaged heart'—I cannot have the vanity to finish so great a
compliment: whose only charm is the being wrote by the fair hand
of Margaritta.

HAL

123   *Margaritta to the Prince of Wales*

[17—?]

You will compel me to leave B*******, I am offended at your
behaviour of last night. Why did I seek a walk retired? had we
met on the Steine you would have been more guarded; alas!
you have not the delicacy I wished! When you talk of love you
offer an insult you are insensible of—your friendship confers
honour;—but your love—retain it for some worthy fair, born to
the high honour of becoming your wife, and repine not that fate
has placed my lot—in humble life. I am content with my station:
content has charms that are not to be expressed. I know I am
wrong in continuing this correspondence;—it must—it ought to
cease: write therefore no more to

MARGARITTA

[17—?]

You alarm me with the idea of your leaving ********, you pain me with your coldness. Ah! Margaritta would it were possible to entreat your acceptance of the hand where the heart is all your own. Why is this forbid? cruel situation, forbid that highest pleasure which every subject enjoys. I cannot but repine! temper calm as yours may endure without complaining; you have suffered, you have learned to bear: but I, bred up with high hopes; young, warm and sanguine, disappointment is a dagger that wounds most sorely! Do not then most amiable of women, oh! do not add to my misfortunes your displeasure, forgive a conduct I already see the impropriety of; allow for my unhappy situation.

Painful pre-eminence, would that I could lay it aside; or that I might be permitted to introduce as a daughter to her ******** virtues congenial to her own. To a ***** who greatly wants it— so bright an example. To my subjects so amiable a ********—vain delusion! I know,—I regret the impossiblity; deprive me not of your friendship—of your valued presence; your inestimable letters; but try to give comfort to that heart which is all your own.

***** [Wales]

EMMA HAMILTON

Emma Hamilton is one of those women destined, from humble surroundings, to set the world in gossip, merely by the beauty of her figure and her excess of energy. She was born Amy Lyon, daughter of a blacksmith of Great Neston, Cheshire. She came, after working as a servant, to Up Park, where she met Charles Greville, second son of the Earl of Warwick. Greville lived with her at Paddington, and she changed her name to Emma Hart.

Her great fame did not begin until Romney painted her. He did twenty-three pictures of her and she sat also for Hoppner, Lawrence, and Sir Joshua Reynolds. She was painted as a Bacchante, a Magdalen, St Cecilia and Calypso. She became well known, too, for her 'attitudes' or *poses plastiques* in which she represented classical figures. Such poses were brilliantly dramatic and full of grace.

Greville sent her (after careful education) to Naples under the care of his uncle Sir William Hamilton, the English Ambassador. She became his wife in 1791. She met Nelson in 1793. She was intimate with Queen Maria Carolina and a favourite in Neapolitan society. When Hamilton was recalled to England, she accompanied him and Nelson. In January 1801 she gave birth to Nelson's child, Horatia, and when Hamilton died, she lived with Nelson—now separated from Lady Nelson—at his house at Merton. On his death she was left quite well off but she gambled most of it away and died in obscurity in Calais in 1815.

My dearest Greville,

I arrived at this place the 26th & I should have begun to write sooner but the post does not go out tell to morro & I dreaded setting down to write for I try to apear as chearful before Sr Wm, as I can & I am sure to cry the moment I think of you, for I feil more & more unhappy at being seperatted from you, & if my total ruin depends on seeing you, I will & must in the end of the sumer, for to live without you is impossible. I love you to that degree that at this time their is not a hardship opon hearth, either of poverty, hunger, cold, death, or even to walk barefooted to Scotland to see you, but what I would undergo. Therefore, my dear, dear Greville, if you do love me, for God sake & for my sake, try all you can to come hear as soon as possible. You have a true freind in Sr Wm. and he will be happy to see you & do all he can to make you happy & for me, I will be everything you can wish for. I find it is not either a fine horse or a fine coach or a pack of servants or plays or operas can make me happy, it is you that as it in your power, either to make me very happy, or very miserable. I respect Sr. Wm. I have a great regard for him as the uncle & freind of you & he loves me, Greville, but he can never be anything nearer to me than your Uncle & my sincere freind, he can never be my lover. You do not know how good Sr. Wm. is to me, he is doing everything he can to make me happy, he as never dined out since I came hear & endead to spake the truth he is never out of my sight, he breakfastes, dines, supes & is constantly by me, looking in my face, I cant stir a hand, a legg, or foot but what he is marking as graceful & fine & I am sorry to say it, but he loves me now as much as ever he could Lady Bolingbroke, endead, I am sorry, for I canot make him happy, I can be civil, oblidging, & I do try to make my self as agreable as I can to him, but I belong to you, Greville & to you onely will I belong & nobody shall be your heir apparent. You do not know how glad I was to arrive hear the day I did, as it was my Birthday & I was very low spirited. Oh God, that day that you used to smile on me & stay at home & be kind to me, that that day I should be at such a distance, but my comfort is I rely on your promise & september or october I shall see you, but I am quite unhappy at not hearing from you, no letter for me yet Greville, but I must wait with patience. We have had company most every day since I came, some of Sr. Wm's freinds. They are all very much pleased with me & poor Sr. Wm. is never so happy as when he is pointing out my beauties to them. He thinks I am grown much more ansome than I was, he does nothing all day but look at me & sigh. Yes, last night we had a little concert, but then I was low, for I wanted you to partake of our amusement. Sr Thomas Rumbold is hear with is son who is dying of a decline, it is a son he had by is first wife & poor young man, he canot walk from the bed to the chair & Lady Rumbold, like a tender hearted rretch is gone to Rome to pass her time there with the English & as took the coach & all the English servants with her & left poor Sr. Thomas hear with is heart broken waiting on is sick son.

You cant think what a worthy man he is, he dind with ous & likes me very much & every day as brought is carridge or phaeton, which he as bought hear & carried me & my mother & Sr. W out and shows ous a deal of civelaties, for you are to understand I have a caridge of Sr. Ws, a English one painting & new livereys & new coach man, foot man & the same as Mrs Damer for of her own, for she did not go with us. If I was going about in is carridge they would say I was either is wife or mistress, therefore as I am not or ever can be either, we have made a very good establishment of 4 rooms very pleasant, looking to the sea, our boat comes out to day for the first time & we shall begin to bathe in a day or two & we are going for one day or two to Caserta. I was at Pasilipo yesterday, I think it a very pretty place. Sr. Wm. as given me a camels shawl like my old one. I know you will be pleased to hear that & he as given me a beautiful goun, cost 25 guineas. India painting on wite sattin, & several little things of Lady Hamiltons & is going to by me some muslin dresses loose to tye with a sash for the hot weather, made like the turkey dresses, the sleeves tyed in fowlds with ribban & trimmed with lace, in short he is in all ways contriving what he shall get for me. The people admires my English dresses, but the blue hat, Greville, pleases most. Sr. W. is quite enchanted with it. Oh, how he loves you. He told me he had made is will & left you everything belonging to him; that made me very happy for your sake. Pray, my dear Greville, do write me a word if you want any money. I am affraid I distressd you but I am sure Sr W. will send you some & I told him he must help you a little now & send you some for your jurney hear & he kissd me & the tears came into is eyes & he told me I might command any thing for he loved ous both dearly & oh, how happy shall I be when I can once more see you, my dear, dear Greville. You are every thing that is dear to me on hearth & I hope happier times will soon restore you to me for endead I would rather be with you starving, than from you in the greatest splender in the world. I have onely to say I enclose this I wrote yesterday & I will not venture myself now to wright any more for my mind & heart is so torn by differant passions that I shall go mad, onely Greville, remember your promise, October. Sr. Wm. says you never mentioned to him abbout coming to Naples at all, but you know the consequence of your not coming for me. Endead, my dear Greville, I live but on the hope of seeing you & if you do not come hear, lett what will be the consequence, I will come to England. I have had a conversation this morning with Sr. Wm, that has made me mad. He speaks half I do not know what to make of it, but Greville, my dear Greville, wright some comfort to me, pray do, if you love me, but onely remember you will never be loved by any body like your affectionate & sencere

EMMA

P.S. Pray, for God sake wright to me & come to me, for Sr. W. shall never be any thing to me but your freind.

126 *Emma Hart to Charles Greville*

Naples. 1st of August 1786

I have received your letter, my dearest Greville, at last, and you dont know how happy I am at hearing from you, however I may like some parts of your letter, but I wont complain, it is enough I have paper that Greville as wrote on, he as foldet up, he wet the wafer—happy wafer, how I envy thee to take the place of Emmas lips, that she would give worlds had she them, to kiss those lips, but if I go on in this whay I shall be incapable of writing. I only wish that a wafer was my onely rival, but I

174

submit to what God & Greville pleases. I allways knew, I have ever had a forebodeing, since I first begun to love you, that I was not destined to be happy, for their is not a King or prince on hearth that could make me happy without you: so onely consider when I offer to live with you on a hundred a year Sir Wm. will give me, what can you desire, and this from a girl that a King etc, etc, etc is sighing for. As to what you write to me to oblidge Sr. Wm, I will not answer you for Oh if you knew what pain I feil in reading those lines whare you advise me to W . . . nothing can express my rage, I am all madness, Greville, to advise me, you that used to envy my smiles, now with cooll indifferance to advise me to go to bed to him, Sr. Wm. Oh, thats worst of all, but I will not, no I will not rage for if I was with you, I would murder you & myself boath. I will leave of & try to get more strength for I am now very ill with a cold.

I wont look back to what I wrote. I onely say I have had 2 letters in 6 months nor nothing shall ever do for me but going home to you. If this is not to be, I will except of nothing, I will go to London, their go in to every exess of vice, tell I dye a miserable broken hearted wretch & leave my fate as a warning to young whomin never to be two good, for, now you have made me love you, made me good, you have abbandoned me & some violent end shall finish our connexion if it is to finish, but, Oh Greville, you cannot, you must not give me up, you have not the heart to do it, you love me I am sure & I am willing to do everything in my power that you shall require of me & what will you have more and I onely say this the last time, I will either beg or pray, do as you like.

[She writes much about her 'social' activities, and ends her letter]

I have such a head ake today with my cold I dont know what to do. I shall write next post by Sr. Wm, onely I cant lett a week go without telling you how happy I am at hearing from you. Pray write as often as you can & come as soon as you can & if you come we shall all go home to England in 2 years & go through Spain & you will like that. Pray write to me & dont write in the style of a freind but a lover, for I wont hear a word of a freind, it shall be all love & no freindship. Sr. Wm. is our freind, but we are lovers. I am glad you have sent me a Blue Hat & gloves; my hat is

175

universally admired through Naples. God bless you, my dear Greville prays your ever truly and affectionate.

EMMA HART

P.S. Pray write nothing will make me so angry & it is not to your interest to disoblidge me, for you dont know the power I have hear, onely I will never be his mistress. If you affront me, I will make him marry me. God bless you for ever.

127 *Verses written by Lady Hamilton to Nelson . . . 1805?*

I think, I have not lost my heart;
Since I, with truth, can swear,
At every moment of my life
I feel my Nelson there!

If, from thine Emma's brest, her heart
Were stolen or flown away;
Where! where! should she my Nelson's love
Record each happy day?

If, from thine Emma's brest, her heart
Were stolen or flown away;
Where! Where! should she engrave, my Love!
Each tender word you say!

Where! Where! should Emma treasure up
Her Nelson's smiles and sighs?
Where mark, with joy, each secret look
Of love, from Nelson's eyes?

Then, do not rob me of my heart
Unless you first forsake it;
And, then, so wretched it would be
Despair alone will take it.

176

San Josef, Torbay,
February 1st, 1801

I believe poor dear Mrs. Thomson's friend will go mad with joy. He cries, prays, and performs all tricks, yet dare not show all or any of his feelings, but he has only me to consult with. He swears he will drink your health this day in a bumper, and damn me if I don't join him in spite of all the doctors in Europe, for none regard you with truer affection than myself. You are a dear, good creature, and your kindness and attention to poor Mrs. T. stamps you higher than ever in my mind. I cannot write, I am so agitated by this young man at my elbow. I believe he is foolish; he does nothing but rave about you and her. I own I participate of his joy and cannot write anything.

The *San Josef* left Plymouth yesterday at 1 o'clock, and anchored here at 8 this morning, where I found an order to hoist my flag in the *St. George*, as Lord Spencer says I must go forth as the Champion of England in the North, and my *San Josef* is to be held by Captain Wolseley of the *St. George*, till my return, when I hope to have a knock at the Republicans. In this instance they have behaved handsomely—could not be better. I trust I shall soon be at Portsmouth, and every endeavour of mine shall be used to come to town for three days, and perhaps you and Sir William may like to see Portsmouth. Captain Darby is just come in; he desires me to say everything which is kind, and that he wishes he could see you instead of your picture, which I have handsomely framed and glazed. The post is waiting, and I have been two hours pulling from Lord St. Vincent's house. It is blowing fresh. May the heavens bless you and yours, is the fervent prayer of your unalterable and faithful, &c.

Best regards to Sir William. Instead of under cover, direct as follows: Lord Nelson, &c., &c., to the care of Sir Thomas Troubridge, Bart., Brixham, Devon, which will give them to me four hours sooner.

February 3rd, 1801

Your good and dear friend, does not think it proper at present to write with his own hand (but he hopes the time may not be far distant when he may be united for ever to the object of his wishes, his *only* love. He swears before heaven that he will marry you as soon as it is possible, which he fervently prays may be soon.) He charges me to say how dear you are to him, and that you must, every opportunity, kiss and bless for him his dear little girl, which he wishes to be called Emma, out of gratitude to our dear, good Lady Hamilton; but in either its from Lord N. he says, or Lady H., he leaves to your judgment and choice. I have given Lord N. a hundred pounds this morning, for which he will give Lady Hamilton an order on his agents; and I beg that you will distribute it amongst those who have been useful to you on the late occasion; and your friend, my dear Mrs. Thomson, may be sure of my care of him and his interest, which I consider as dearly as my own, and do you believe me ever, &c.

Lady Hamilton must desire at the back for it to be paid to the person who carries it.

San Josef,
February 4th, 1801

It blows so very hard that I doubt if it will be possible to get a boat on shore, either to receive or send letters, but if it moderates in time for the post of course mine shall go, and I hope from my heart to hear you are better, and it has made my head ache stooping so much, as I have been making memorandums for my will, and, having regularly signed it, if was to die this moment I believe it would hold good. If I am not able to send it, as far as relates to you, this day, I will to-morrow. I have been obliged to be more particular than I would, as a wife can have nothing, and it might be taken from you by will or the heirs of your husband. If you disapprove of any part say so and I will alter it, but I think you must approve; I have done my best that you should. I shall now go to work and save a fortune. Say, shall I bequeath the £2,000 owing me from Sir William for the same purpose? You must keep this letter till you receive a copy of my memo. What a pretty piece of history letting out the French squadron. I was laughed at by some wiseacres in power when I said, if I was a French Admiral I would come out in spite of all the English fleet, as they kept close into Brest, and I would be outside of them before morning.

Your dear, kind letters of Monday are just come on board in a shore boat, and I shall try and get mine ashore, but it is barely possible. (Sir William should say to the Prince that, situated as you are, it would be highly improper for you to admit H.R.H. That the Prince should wish it I am not surprized at, and that he will attempt every means to get into your house and into any place where you may dine. Sir Wm. should speak out, and if the Prince is a man of honour he will quit the pursuit of you. I know his aim is to have you for a mistress. The thought so agitates me that I cannot write. Tell Mrs. T. her friend is grateful for her goodness,) and with my kindest regards to Mrs. Jenkins and Horatia, and ever believe me your sincere, faithful and affectionate, &c.

We drink your health every day. Believe me, your letter cannot be too long or too minute of all particulars. My mind is a little easier having perfect confidence. Make my respects to Sir Wm, the Duke, and Lord Wm Gordon.

131   Lord Nelson to Lady Hamilton

Victory, off Plymouth,
September 17th, 1805

Nine o'clock in the Morning, Blowing fresh at W.S.W., dead foul wind.

I sent, my own dearest Emma, a letter for you, last night, in a Torbay Boat, and gave the man a guinea to put it in the Post

Office. We have had a nasty blowing night, and it looks very dirty. I am now signalling the Ships at Plymouth to join me; but I rather doubt their ability to get to sea. However, I have got clear of Portland, and have Cawsand Bay and Torbay under the lee. I intreat, my dear Emma, that you will cheer up; and we will look forward to many, many happy years, and be surrounded by our children's children. God Almighty can, when he pleases, remove the impediment. My heart and soul is with you and Horatia. I got this line ready in case a Boat should get alongside. For ever, ever, I am yours, most devotedly

NELSON AND BRONTE

132   *Lord Nelson to Lady Hamilton*

Victory, October 19th, 1805

[This letter was written two days before the Battle of Trafalgar. It is Nelson's last letter to Emma which she received after his death.]

My dearest beloved Emma, the dear friend of my bosom. The signal has been made that the Enemy's Combined Fleet are coming out of Port. We have very little wind, so that I have no hopes of seeing them before tomorrow. May the God of Battles crown my endeavours with success; at all events, I will take care that my name shall ever be most dear to you and Horatia, both of whom I love as much as my own life. And as my last writing before the Battle will be to you, so I hope in God that I shall live to finish my letter after the Battle. May Heaven bless you prays your

NELSON AND BRONTE

FREDERICK, DUKE OF YORK

Frederick was the second and favourite son of George III. At the age of six months the King promoted him Bishop of Osnabrück and he remained so until 1803. In 1791 he married Princess Frederica, daughter of Frederick William II of Prussia. The King, after Frederick returned from Flanders with the army, made him Commander-in-Chief. He was not a success as a field commander.

In 1803, Mary Anne Clarke, wife of a stonemason whom she soon deserted, became the mistress of the Duke of York while he was still Commander-in-Chief. Mrs. Clarke, running into debt, sold offices and promotions in the army by her promises to interest the Duke. In May 1809 eight charges of abuse of military patronage were brought against the Duke. A committee of inquiry examined Mrs. Clarke. It was all very obvious what had been going on but the Duke, who knew what his mistress was up to, had not benefited financially by her tricks. However, the result of the hearings was that he resigned as C.-in-C. and, giving his mistress a pension and a sum of money, he had no more to do with her. She died at Boulogne on 21st June 1852.

Standgate, August 24, 1804

How can I sufficiently express to my darling love my thanks for her dear, dear letter or the delight which the assurances of her love give me? Oh my angel! do me justice and be convinced that there never was a woman adored as you are. Every day, every hour convinces me more and more that my whole happiness depends upon you alone. What a time it appears to be since we parted and with what impatience do I look forward to the day after to-morrow. There are, still however, two whole nights before I shall clasp my darling in my arms!

How happy am I to learn that you are better. I still, however, will not give up my hopes of the cause of your feeling uncomfortable. Clavering is mistaken, my angel, in thinking that any new regiments are to be raised; it is not intended, only second Battalions to the existing Corps; you had better, therefore, tell him so, and that you were sure that there would be no use in applying for him.

Ten thousand thanks, my love, for the handkerchiefs, which are delightful; and I need not, I trust, assure you of the pleasure I feel in wearing them, and thinking of the dear hands who made them for me.

Nothing could be more satisfactory than the tour I have made, and the state in which I have found everything. The whole of the day before yesterday was employed in visiting the Works at Dover; reviewing the troops there and examining the coast as far as this place. From Folkstone I had a very good view of those of the French camp.

Yesterday, I first reviewed the camp here, and afterwards the 14th Light Dragoons, who are certainly in very fine order; and from thence proceeded to Brabourne Lees to see four regiments of Militia; which altogether took me up near thirteen hours. I am now setting off immediately to ride along the coast to Hastings, reviewing the different Corps as I pass, which will take me at least as long. Adieu, therefore, my sweetest, dearest love, till the day after to-morrow, and be assured that to my last hour I shall remain yours and yours alone.

134 *Frederick, Duke of York to Mrs. Mary Anne Clarke*

August 4, 1805

How can I sufficiently express to My Sweetest My Darling Love, the delight which her dear, her pretty letter gave me, or how much I feel all the kind things she says to me in it. Millions and millions of thanks for it, My Angel! and be assured that my heart is fully sensible of your affection, and that upon it alone its whole happiness depends.

I am, however, quite hurt that my love did not go to the Lewes Races; how kind of her to think of me upon the occasion; but I trust that she knows me too well not to be convinced that I cannot bear the idea of adding to those sacrifices which I am but too sensible that she has made to me.

News, my Angel cannot expect from me from hence; though the life led here, at least in the family I am in, is very hurrying, there is a sameness in it, which affords little subject for a letter; except Lord Chesterfield's family there is not a single person, except ourselves that I know. Last night we were at the play, which went off better than the first night.

Dr O'Meara called on me yesterday morning and delivered me your letter; he wishes much to preach before Royalty, and if I can put him in the way of it I will.

What a time it appears to me already, my darling, since we parted; how impatiently I look forward to next Wednesday sennight! God bless you, my own dear, dear love! I shall miss the post if I add more, oh! believe me, ever to my last hour,—Yours and yours alone

Addressed— Mrs Clarke
To be left at the Post Office Worthing.
Endorsed— Dr. O'Meara

[1] Fictitious form of address.

PRINCE AUGUSTUS

Prince Augustus Frederick was the sixth son of George III. A man of progressive thought, who favoured the abolition of slavery, the repeal of the Corn Laws, and religious toleration, he was created Duke of Sussex in 1801. When he was only twenty, he went to Italy for health reasons and fell in love, at Rome, with Lady Augusta Murray, daughter of the Countess of Dunmore. She was six years older than he. He was able to persuade an English clergyman, a Mr. Gunn, to marry them in 1793. However, the Court of Arches later declared the marriage illegal under the conditions of the Royal Marriage Act.

On the death of the Duke—Lady Augusta died in 1830—the eldest son of the marriage claimed his father's title but failed, in law, to establish his claim. At the trial these letters between the two lovers were read out and were published in the daily papers.

135 *Lady Augusta Murray to Prince Augustus (afterwards Duke of Sussex)*

March, 1793

Then, my treasure, you say you will talk of honour to him. There is no honour in the case; if there is I will not marry you. I

184

love you, and I have reason to hope and believe you love me; but honour in the sense you take it is out of the question.

I cannot bear to owe my happiness to anything but affection; and all my promises, though sacred in our eyes and in those of heaven, shall not oblige you to do anything towards me that can in the least prejudice your future interests.

As for honour, with the meaning Mr Gunn will annex to it, I am ashamed to fancy it—he will imagine I have been your mistress, and that humanity, commonly termed honour, now induces you to pity me, and so veil my follies by an honourable marriage.

My own beloved Prince, forgive me if I am warm on this subject. I wish you to feel you owe me nothing; and whatever I owe you, I wish to owe to your love, and to your good opinion, but to no other principle.

Tell Mr Gunn, my own Augustus, that you love me—that you are resolved to marry me—that you have pledged your sacred word; tell him, if you please, that upon the Bible you have sworn it—that I have done the same, and nothing shall ever divide us; but don't let him imagine that I have been vile. Do this only, my love; but pray take care of the character of your wife, of your Augusta.

136   *Prince Augustus to Lady Augusta Murray*
26th March 1793

Do, my dearest Augusta, trust me; I will never abuse the confidence you put in me, and more and more will endeavour to deserve it. I only wait for your orders to speak to Mr Gunn. Say only that you wish me to do it, and I will hasten to get a positive answer.

See, my soul, it only depends upon *you* to speak; thy Augustus, *thou* wilt find ready at all times to serve you. He thinks, he dreams of nothing but to make thee happy. Can he not succeed in this, all his hopes are gone; life will be nothing to him; he will pass the days in one constant melancholy, wishing them soon to conclude, and finding every day longer than the other. Indeed, my

Augusta, that cannot be the case; my solemn oath is given, and that can never be recalled. I am, yours, my soul, ever yours.

137 Prince Augustus to Lady Augusta Murray

4th April 1793

Will you allow me to come this evening? It is my only hope. Oh! let me come, and we will send for Mr Gunn. Everything but this is hateful to me. More than forty-eight hours have I passed without the slightest nourishment. Oh, let me not live so. Death is certainly better than this; which, if in forty-eight hours it has not taken place, must follow; for, by all that is holy, till when I am married, I will eat nothing; and if I am not to be married the promise shall die with me! I am resolute. Nothing in the world shall alter my determination. If Gunn will not marry me I will die . . . I will be conducted in everything by you; but I must be married, or die. I would rather see none of my family than be deprived of you.

You alone can make me; you alone shall this evening. I will sooner drop than give you up.

Good God! how I feel! and my love to be doubted sincere and warm. The Lord knows the truth of it, and as I say, if I am not married in forty-eight hours I am no more. Oh! Augusta, my soul, let us try; let me come; I am capable of everything; I fear nothing, and Mr Gunn seeing our resolution, will agree. I am half-dead. Good God! What will become of me? I shall go mad, most undoubtedly.

138 Lady Augusta Murray to Prince Augustus

My treasure, my dearest life and love, how can I refuse you? And yet dare I trust to the happiness your letter promised me?

You shall come if you wish it. You shall do as you like; my whole soul rejoices in the assurance of your love, and to your exertions I will trust

I will send to ——; but I fear the badness of the night will prevent his coming. My mother has ordered her carriage at past seven, and will not, I fear, be out before the half-hour after.

To be yours to-night, seems a dream that I cannot make out; the whole day have I been plunged in misery, and now to awake to joy is a felicity that is beyond my ideas of bliss. I doubt its success; but do as you will; I am what you will; your will must be mine, and no will can ever be dearer to me, more mine, than that of my Augustus, my lover, my all.

1775   1834

CHARLES LAMB

Anyone who loves Lamb loves him this side idolatry. His Letters are some of the finest in the language. He was much loved by all the Romantic poets from Coleridge to Wordsworth. Everyone knows how his sister Mary, in a fit of madness, killed her mother and how Charles looked after her for the rest of his life. The trouble with Lamb is that once one begins writing about him one never stops. Stories, pictures of him as a schoolboy at Christ's Hospital, as a boy wandering round the Great House at Blakesware, 'Nothing fills a child's mind,' he said, 'like an old Mansion'; his walks of twenty miles or more a day; his hissing his own play when the audience hissed it; his friendship with Bernard Barton, the Woodbridge Quaker poet and that wonderful dinner party at the painter's, Haydon's, when Lamb made certain remarks to Wordsworth; his puns, his smoking and his love of pubs. Where does one stop? Not the least delightful are his love letters to the actress Miss Kelly, to whom with the full consent of his sister he proposed marriage in 1819. He bore her refusal with his usual humour and fortitude.

Lamb died from an attack of erysipelas brought on after a fall as he was walking on the London to Edmonton road.

9th July 1819

Dear Miss Kelly,

If your Bones are not engaged on Monday night, will you favour us with the use of them? I know, if you can oblige us, you will make no bones of it; if you cannot, it shall break none betwixt us. We might ask somebody else, but we do not like the bones of any strange animal. We should be welcome to dear Mrs. Liston's, but then she is so plump, there is no getting at them. I should prefer Miss Iver's—they must be ivory I take it for granted—but she is married to Mr. xxx, and become bone of his bone, consequently can have none of her own to dispose of. Well, it all comes to this,—if you can let us have them, you will, I dare say; if you cannot, God rest your bones. I am almost at the end of my bon-mots.

C. LAMB

20 July, 1819

Dear Miss Kelly,

We had the pleasure, *pain* I might better call it, of seeing you last night in the new Play. It was a most consummate piece of Acting, but what a task for you to undergo! at a time when your heart is sore from real sorrow! it has given rise to a train of thinking, which I cannot suppress.

Would to God you were released from this way of life; that you could bring your mind to consent to take your lot with us, and throw off for ever the whole burden of your Profession. I neither expect or wish you to take notice of this which I am writing, in your present over occupied & hurried state.—But do think of it at your leisure. I have quite income enough, if that were all, to justify for me making such a proposal, with what I may call even a handsome provision for my survivor. What you possess of your own would naturally be appropriated to those, for whose sakes chiefly you have made so many hard sacrifices. I am not so foolish as not to know that I am a most unworthy match for such a one as you, but you have for years been a principal object in my mind. In many a sweet assumed character I have learned to love you, but simply as F. M. Kelly I love you better than them all. Can you quit these shadows of existence, & come & be a reality to us? can you leave off harassing yourself to please a thankless multitude, who know nothing of you, & begin at last to live to yourself & your friends?

As plainly & frankly as I have seen you give or refuse assent in some feigned scene, so frankly do me the justice to answer me. It is impossible I should feel injured or aggrieved by your telling me at once, that the proposal does not suit you. It is impossible that I should ever think of molesting you with idle importunity and persecution after your mind [was] once firmly spoken—but happier, far happier, could I have leave to hope a time might come, when our friends might be your friends; our interests yours; our book-knowledge, if in that inconsiderable particular we have any little advantage, might impart something to you, which you would every day have it in your power ten thousand fold to repay by the added cheerfulness and joy which you could not fail to bring as a dowry into whatever family should have the honor and happiness of receiving *you*, the most welcome accession that could be made to it.

In haste, but with entire respect and deepest affection, I subscribe myself,

C. LAMB

141   *Miss Kelly to Charles Lamb*

Henrietta Street, 20th July, 1819

An early & deeply rooted attachment has fixed my heart on one from whom no worldly prospect can well induce me to with-draw it, but while I thus *frankly* and decidedly decline your pro-posal, believe me, I am not insensible to the high honour which the preference of such a mind as yours confers upon me—let me, however, hope that all thought upon this subject will end with this letter, & that you will henceforth encourage no other sentiment towards me than esteem in my private character and a continuance of that approbation of my humble talents which you have already expressed so much & so often to my advantage and gratification.

Believe me I feel proud to acknowledge myself
Your obliged friend
F. M. KELLY

142   *Charles Lamb to Miss Kelly*

July 20th, 1819

Dear Miss Kelly,

Your injunctions shall be obeyed to a tittle. I feel myself in a lackadaisacal no-how-ish kind of a humour. I believe it is the rain, or something. I had thought to have written seriously, but I fancy I succeed best in epistles of mere fun; puns and *that* nonsense. You will be good friends with us, will you not? let what has past 'break no bones' between us. You will not refuse us them next time we send for them?

Yours very truly,
C. L.

Do you observe the delicacy of not signing my full name?
N.B. Do not paste that last letter of mine into your Book.

JOHN CONSTABLE

In 1811 two things happened to John Constable. He exhibited the picture 'Dedham Vale' in which the authentic features of his style appear for the first time and he fell in love with Maria Bicknell. However, Dr. Rhudde, Maria's grandfather, was opposed to their marriage and it was not until five years later, in 1816, that they were married. Maria's letters are full of a deep concern for Constable to look after his health and to 'get on'.

They settled first at No. 1 Keppel Street, Russell Square, where John started to become famous with such paintings as 'Flatford Mill' and 'The White Horse', which was bought by his friend Archdeacon Fisher for £105. In 1828 his financial troubles were over. Maria's father left him £20,000. But it was a bitter freedom for, towards the end of the year Maria, who had been in failing health, died. He never really recovered from the shock, and suffering from rheumatism and depression he himself died on 31st March 1837.

143   John Constable to Maria Bicknell

[November 1811]

... Be assured, we have only to consider our union as an event that must happen, and we shall yet be happy ....

[November 1811]

. . . You grieve and surprise me by continuing so sanguine on a subject altogether hopeless. I cannot endure that you should harbour expectations that must terminate in disappointment. I never can consent to act in opposition to the wishes of my father; how then can I continue a correspondence wholly disapproved of by him? He tells me that I am consulting your happiness as well as my own by putting an end to it. Let me then entreat that you will cease to think of me. Forget that you have ever known me, and I will willingly resign all pretensions to your regard, or even acquaintance, to facilitate the tranquillity and peace of mind which is so essential to your success in a profession, which will ever be in itself a source of continued delight. You must be certain that you cannot write without increasing feelings that must be entirely suppressed. You will, therefore, I am sure, see the impropriety of sending me any more letters. I congratulate you on your change of residence. It is, I think, a very desirable situation. Farewell, my dear sir, and ever believe me your sincere and constant well-wisher

M. E. B.

145 *Maria Bicknell to John Constable*

September 10th, 1812

Continue to write to me, my dear John, without the least reserve; the more I am acquainted with you, the happier I shall be. We are both very unfortunately situated (but really you must think me very silly to tell you what is so evident). We can, however, make writing alleviate many of our troubles, and be to us one of our highest pleasures. I used to dislike it excessively; but now there is no employment I like so well. . . . Have the goodness to remember me kindly to your mother, and tell her how much I am obliged to her for her frequent recollections of me. And you, my dearest John, accept every affectionate wish from

M. E. B.

146 *Maria Bicknell to John Constable*

[December 1812]

. . . By a sedulous attention to your profession, you will very much help to bestow calm on my mind, which I shall look for in vain while I see with sorrow how unsettled you appear, and consequently, unfitted to attend to a study that requires the incessant application of the heart and head. You will allow others, without half your abilities, to outstrip you in the race of fame, and then look back with sorrow on time neglected and opportunities lost, and perhaps blame me as the cause of all this woe. Exert yourself while it is yet in your power; the path of duty is alone the path of happiness. Let us wait with quiet resignation till a merciful Providence shall dispose of us in the way that will be best. Believe me, I shall feel a more lasting pleasure in knowing that you are improving your time, and exerting your talents for the ensuing exhibition, than I should do while you were on a stolen march with me round the Park. Still I am not heroine enough to say, wish, or mean, that we should never meet. I know that to be impossible. But, then, let us resolve it shall be but seldom, not as inclination, but as prudence shall dictate. Farewell, dearest John; may every blessing attend you, and in the interest I feel in your welfare, forgive the advice I have given you, who, I am sure, are better qualified to admonish me. Resolution is, I think, what we now stand most in need of, to refrain for a time, for our mutual good, from the society of each other.

147 *John Constable to Maria Bicknell*

October 25th, 1814

. . . I am happy to hear of some improvement in your mother's health; I hope it may continue to advance. Though any notice or

194

good wishes from me I know will be useless, yet I mention it for your sake. . . . I have had a distressing letter from my friend John Fisher on the death of his uncle, General Fisher. Poor Fisher was acting the part of a comforter when no comfort could be imparted. The distress of the General's daughter, Mrs. Conroy, and of his son-in-law, was beyond all belief. A fine manly soldier weeping like an infant; and Fisher was obliged to tear her from the coffin when they were taking it away. He wishes me to undertake (as it might prove a means of consolation) a portrait of the General from a drawing. He was extremely like the good bishop, mild, sensible, and placid. I could give him little hope of making much of a picture, but shall willingly try. . . . The studies I have made this summer are better liked than any I have done; but I would rather have your opinion of them than that of all others put together. But fate is still savage. I lament every moment the want of your society and feel the loss of it in my mind and heart. *You* deserved a better fate.

148 *Maria Bicknell to John Constable*

Spring Garden Terrace,
February 23rd, 1815

My dearest John,
    I have received, from papa, the sweet permission to see you again under this roof (to use his own words), 'as an occasional visitor'. From being perfectly wretched, I am now comparatively happy. . . .

M. E. BICKNELL

149 *John Constable to Maria Bicknell*

63, Charlotte Street
June 16th, 1815

    I have seen Spilbury again; he still urges me to make him a visit at his cottage, near Tintern Abbey. I ought to see another country, and this is a charming one. I am half inclined to go, but I need not decide for a week or ten days. I pine after dear Suffolk; but is not this indolence? My heart, as you know too well, is not there. At least, not all of it. But you say, you would not give a farthing for a divided heart; however, make yourself easy, you have by far the greatest part; but what vanity is this!

150 *Maria Bicknell to John Constable*

[Although Maria's father had given permission for Constable to visit her occasionally at his house, Dr Rhudde—Maria's grandfather—was unaware of the sanction as he was bitterly opposed to any union between his grand-daughter and Constable. . . .]

February 7th, 1816

. . . The doctor has just sent *such* a letter, that I tremble with having heard only a part of it read. Poor dear papa, to have such a letter written to him! he has a great share of feeling and it has sadly hurt him. . . . I know not how it will end. Perhaps the storm may blow over; God only knows. We must be patient. I am sure your heart is too good not to feel for my father. He would wish to make us all happy if he could. Pray do not come to town just yet. I hope by the end of the month peace will be restored.

151 *John Constable to Maria Bicknell*

February 1816

I am truly sorry anything should have happened to cause us any concern from that quarter. But my sisters trust the calm will not long be disturbed; though I have always feared it was a deceitful one, and that we have been making ourselves happy over a barrel of gunpowder. But, my love, let me hear from you, and tell me whether I may see you when I return to London. All this nonsense has been kept from my father, or it must have vexed him.

196

February 18th, 1816

I trust, my dearest love, you have allowed yourself to be made as little unhappy as possible, by what has been lately passing in your house. You have always been so kind as to believe that my affection for you was never alloyed by worldly motives. I, now, more than ever repeat it: and I assure you, that nothing can be done, by any part of your family, that shall ever make any alteration in me towards you. I shall not concern myself with the justice or injustice of others; that must rest with themselves; it is sufficient for us to know that we have done nothing to deserve the ill opinion of any one. Our business is now more than ever with ourselves. I am entirely free from debt, and, I trust, could I be made happy, to receive a good deal more than I do now by my profession. After this, my dearest Maria, I have nothing more to say, than the sooner we are married the better; and from this time, I shall cease to listen to any arguments the other way, from any quarter. I wish your father to know what I have written if you think with me.

153   *John Constable to Maria Bicknell*

East Bergholt,
July 17th, 1816

My dearest love,

You would certainly have heard from me before, had I left London on the day I mentioned, but I could not get away before Tuesday. I found all my friends here quite well, and we make a large family party, nine with Mrs. Whalley's two children, and your portrait, which gives great pleasure here, as an additional proof of your kindness to me. . . . We are all very happy among ourselves; but so used have I been, on entering these doors, to be received with the affectionate shake of the hand of my father, and the endearing salute of my mother, that I often find myself overcome by a sadness I cannot refrain. . . . I am sitting before your portrait; which when I look off the paper, is so extremely like, that I can hardly help going up to it. I never before knew the real pleasure a portrait can afford.

154 *John Constable to Maria Bicknell*

Wivenhoe Park,
September 7th, 1816

My dearest love,

I hasten to send you the enclosed letter from our friend Fisher. I can only say, that I am ready to adopt any plan that may meet your feelings on this occasion, and I repeat Fisher's words, that, 'I shall be happy and ready to marry you,' at the time he mentions. I am advised by my good friends here, to try one more effort with the doctor; but I shall do entirely in this as you direct.

[The following is the letter enclosed.]

Osmington, near Dorchester,
August 27th, 1816

My dear Constable,

I am not a great letter writer, and when I take pen in hand, I generally come to the point at once. I, therefore, write to tell you, that I intend to be in London on Tuesday evening, the 24th, and on Wednesday, shall hold myself ready and happy to marry you. There, you see, I have used no roundabout phrases, but said the thing at once, in good plain English. So, do you follow my example, and get to your lady, and instead of blundering out long sentences about 'the Hymeneal altar', &c., say that on Wednesday, September 25th, you are ready to marry her. If she replies, like a sensible woman, as I suspect she is, 'Well, John, here is my hand, I am ready,'—all well and good. If she says, 'Yes, but another day will be more convenient,' let her name it, and I am at her service.[1]

[1] They were married on 2nd October, 1816, at St. Martin's Church, by Mr. Fisher. Maria's father and Constable became excellent friends, and eventually Dr. Rhudde, her grandfather, became reconciled to the marriage.

CHARLOTTE CARPENTER

Charlotte Carpenter was the ward of Lord Downshire at the time Sir Walter Scott met her. Writing to his mother he described her: 'Without flying into raptures, for I must assure you that my judgement as well as my affections are consulted upon this occasion—without flying into raptures, then, I may safely assure you, that her temper is sweet and cheerful, her understanding good, and what I know will give you pleasure, her principles of religion very serious.'

They became engaged in the autumn of 1797.

155   *Charlotte Carpenter to Sir Walter Scott*

Carlisle, Nov. 27 1797

You have made me very *triste* all day. Pray never more complain of being poor. Are you not ten times richer than I am? Depend on yourself and your profession. I have no doubt you will rise very high, and be a *great rich man*, but we should look down to be contented with our lot, and banish all disagreeable thoughts. We shall do very well. I am sorry to hear you have such a *bad head*.

I hope I shall nurse away all your aches. I think you write too much. When I am *mistress* I shall not allow it. How very angry I should be if you were to part with *Lenore*. Do you really believe I should think it an *unnecessary expense* where your health and pleasure can be concerned? I have a better opinion of you, and I am very glad you don't give up the cavalry, as I love anything that is *stylish*.

Don't forget to find a stand for the old carriage, as I shall like to keep it, in case we should have to go any journey; it is so much more convenient than the post-chaises, and will do very well till we can keep *our carriage*.

What an idea of yours was that to mention where you wish to have your *bones laid*! If you were married, I should think you were tired of me. A very pretty compliment *before marriage*. I hope sincerely that I shall not live to see that day. If you always have those cheerful thoughts, how very pleasant and gay you must be.

Adieu, my dearest friend. Take care of yourself, if you love me, as I have *no wish* that you should visit that *beautiful* and *romantic* scene, the burying-place. Adieu, once more, and believe that you are loved very sincerely by

C. C.

156   *Charlotte Carpenter to Sir Walter Scott*

Dec. 10, [1797]

If I could but really believe that my letter only gave you half the pleasure you express, I should almost think, my dearest Scott, that I should get very fond of writing them for the pleasure to *indulge* you—that is saying a great deal.

I hope you are sensible of the compliment I pay you, and don't expect I shall *always* be so pretty behaved. You may depend on me, my dearest friend, for fixing as early a day as I possibly can; and if it happens to be not quite so soon as you wish, you must not be angry with me.

It is very unlucky you are such a bad housekeeper, as I am no better. I shall try. I hope to have very soon the pleasure of seeing

you, and to tell you how much I love you; but I wish the first
fortnight was over. With all my love, and those sort of pretty
things—adieu.

CHARLOTTE

P.S.—Etudiez votre Français? Remember you are to teach me
Italian in return, but I shall be but a stupid scholar. *Aimez Charlotte.*

PATRICK BRONTË

The father of the famous novelists, Charlotte, Emily and Anne, was born at Emsdale, Co. Down on 17th March 1777. He changed his name from Brunty as soon as he came to England. Shortly after taking his degree at Cambridge he became curate at Wethersfield, Essex. From there he went to Hartshead-cum-Clifton, in Yorkshire, and was appointed examiner at the Wesleyan Academy, at Woodhouse Grove, Apperley Bridge. It was here that he first met Maria Branwell who had come up from Penzance to help her aunt, Mrs. Fennell, run the school.

Maria was, then, 29 years old, having been born on 15th April 1783. She was the fifth daughter of Thomas Branwell. In their book *Man of Sorrow*, John Lock and Canon W. T. Dixon give a most moving description of the courtship of Patrick and Maria. All his letters to her have been lost but nine of hers have been preserved. On Saturday, 15th September 1821, Maria died. Her last words were, 'Oh my poor children, my poor children.'

At the end of 1821 Patrick proposed marriage to Elizabeth Firth but she rejected him. He then turned to his first love, Mary Burder. He wrote first to her mother and received a brief reply. He then wrote direct to Mary but the result was, as might have been expected, rejection again.

To Rev. Patrick Bronte, A.B., Hartshead.

Wood House Grove, August 26th 1812

My dear Friend, This address is sufficient to convince you
that I not only permit, but approve of yours to me—I do indeed
consider you as my *friend;* yet when I consider how short a time I
have had the pleasure of knowing you, I start at my own rashness,
my heart fails, and did I not think that you would be disappointed
and grieved, I believe I should be ready to spare myself the task of
writing. Do not think I am so wavering as to repent of what I have
already said. No, believe me, this will never be the case, unless
you give me cause for it.

You need not fear that you have been mistaken in my character. If I know anything of myself, I am incapable of making an
ungenerous return to the smallest degree of kindness, much less to
you whose attentions and conduct have been so particularly obliging. I will frankly confess that your behaviour and what I have
seen and heard of your character has excited my warmest esteem
and regard, and be assured you shall never have cause to repent of
any confidence you may think proper to place in me, and that it
will always be my endeavour to deserve the good opinion which
you have formed, although human weakness may in some instances
cause me to fall short. In giving you these assurances I do not
depend upon my own strength, but I look to Him who has been
my unerring guide through life, and in whose continued protection
and assistance I confidently trust.

I thought on you much on Sunday, and feared you would not
escape the rain. I hope you do not feel any bad effects from it? My
cousin wrote you on Monday and expects this afternoon to be
favoured with an answer. Your letter has caused me some foolish
embarrassment, tho' in pity to my feelings they have been very
sparing of their raillery.

I will now candidly answer your questions. The *politeness of
others* can never make me forget your kind attentions, neither can *I
walk our accustomed rounds* without thinking on you, and, why should
I be ashamed to add, wishing for your presence. If you knew what
were my feelings whilst writing this you would pity me. I wish to
write the truth and give you satisfaction, yet fear to go too far, and

exceed the bounds of propriety. But whatever I may say or write I will *never deceive* you, or *exceed the truth*. If you think I have not placed the *utmost confidence* in you, consider my situation, and ask yourself if I have not confided in you sufficiently, perhaps too much. I am very sorry that you will not have this till after to-morrow, but it was out of my power to write sooner. I rely on your goodness to pardon everything in this which may appear either too free or too stiff, and beg that you will consider me as a warm and faithful friend.

My uncle, aunt, and cousin unite in kind regards.

I must now conclude with again declaring myself to be

Yours sincerely, MARIA BRANWELL

158   Maria Branwell to Patrick Brontë

To Rev. Patrick Bronte, A.B., Hartshead.

Wood House Grove, September 5th, 1812

My Dearest Friend, I have just received your affectionate and very welcome letter, and although I shall not be able to send this until Monday, yet I cannot deny myself the pleasure of writing a few lines this evening, no longer considering it a task, but a pleasure, next to that of reading yours. I had the pleasure of hear-ing from Mr. Fennell, who was at Bradford on Thursday after-noon, that you had rested there all night. Had you proceeded, I am sure the walk would have been too much for you; such exces-sive fatigue, often repeated, must injure the strongest constitution. I am rejoiced to find that our forebodings were without cause. I had yesterday a letter from a very dear friend of mine, and had the satisfaction to learn by it that all at home are well. I feel with you the unspeakable obligations I am under to a merciful Providence —my heart swells with gratitude, and I feel an earnest desire that I may be enabled to make some suitable return to the Author of all my blessings. In general, I think I am enabled to cast my care upon Him, and then I experience a calm and peaceful serenity of mind which few things can destroy. In all my addresses to the throne of grace I never ask a blessing for myself but I beg the same for you, and considering the important station which you are called to fill, my prayers are proportionately fervent that you may be favoured with all the gifts and graces requisite for such a calling. O my dear friend, let us pray much that we may live lives holy and useful to each other and all around us!

Monday morn. My cousin and I were yesterday at Calverley Church, where we heard Mr. Watman preach a very excellent sermon from 'learn of Me, for I am meek and lowly of heart'. He displayed the character of our Saviour in a most affecting and amiable light. I scarcely ever felt more charmed with his excellences, more grateful for his condescension, or more abased at my own unworthiness; but I lament that my heart is so little retentive of those pleasing and profitable impressions.

I pitied you in your solitude, and felt sorry that it was not in my power to enliven it. Have you not been too hasty in informing your friends of a certain event? Why did you not leave them to guess a little longer? I shrink from the idea of its being known to everybody. I do, indeed, *sometimes* think of you, but I will not say how often, lest I raise your vanity; and we sometimes talk of you and the doctor. But I believe I should seldom mention your name myself were it not now and then introduced by my cousin. I have never mentioned a word of what is past to anybody. Had I thought this necessary I should have requested you to do it. But I think there is no need, as by some means or other they seem to have a pretty correct notion how matters stand betwixt us; and as their hints, etc., meet with no contradiction from me, my silence passes for confirmation. Mr. Fennell has not neglected to give me some serious and encouraging advice, and my aunt takes frequent opportunities of dropping little sentences which I may turn to some advantage. I have long had reason to know that the present state of things would give pleasure to all parties. Your ludicrous account of the scene at the Hermitage was highly diverting, we laughed heartily at it; but I fear it will not produce all that compassion in Miss Fennell's breast which you seem to wish. I will now tell you what I was thinking about and doing at the time you mention. I was then toiling up the hill with Jane and Mrs Clapham to take our tea at Mr. Tatham's, thinking on the evening when I first took the same walk with you, and on the change which had taken place in my circumstances and views since then—not wholly without a wish that I had your arm to assist me, and your conversation to shorten the walk. Indeed, all our walks have now an insipidity in them which I never thought they would have possessed. When I work, if I wish to get *forward* I may be glad that you are at a distance. Jane begs me to assure you of her kind regards. Mr. Morgan is expected to be here this evening. I must assume a bold and steady countenance to meet his attacks!

I have now written a pretty long letter without reserve or caution, and if all the sentiments of my heart are not laid open to you believe me it is not because I wish them to be concealed, for, I hope there is nothing there that would give you pain or displeasure. My most sincere and earnest wishes are for your happiness and welfare, for this includes my own. Pray much for me that I may be made a blessing and not a hindrance to you. Let me not interrupt your studies nor intrude on that time which ought to be dedicated to better purposes. Forgive my freedom, my dearest friend, and rest assured that you are and ever will be dear to

MARIA BRANWELL

Write very soon.

159   Maria Branwell to Patrick Brontë

To Rev. Patrick Bronte, A.B., Hartshead.
Wood House Grove, September 11th, 1812

My dearest Friend, Having spent the day yesterday at Miry Shay, a place near Bradford, I had not got your letter till my return in the evening, and consequently have only a short time this morning to write if I send it by this post. You surely do not think you *trouble* me by writing? No, I think I may venture to say if such were your opinion you would *trouble* me no more. Be assured, your letters are and I hope always will be received with extreme pleasure and read with delight. May our Gracious Father mercifully grant the fulfillment of your prayers! Whilst we depend entirely on Him for happiness, and receive each other and all our blessings as from His

206

hands, what can harm us or make us miserable? Nothing temporal or spiritual.

Jane had a note from Mr. Morgan last evening, and she desires me to tell you that the Methodists' service in church hours is to commence next Sunday week. You may expect frowns and hard words from her when you make your appearance here again, for, if you recollect, she gave you a note to carry to the Doctor, and he has never received it. What have you done with it? If you can give a good account of it you may come to see us as soon as you please and be sure of a hearty welcome from all parties. Next Wednesday we have some thoughts, if the weather be fine, of going to Kirkstall Abbey once more, and I suppose your presence will not make the walk less agreeable to any of us.

The old man is come and waits for my letter. In expectation of seeing you on Monday or Tuesday next,—I remain, Yours faithfully and affectionately,

M. B.

160   Maria Branwell to Patrick Brontë

To Rev. Patrick Bronte, A.B., Hartshead.
Wood House Grove, September 23rd, 1812

My Dearest Friend, Accept of my warmest thanks for your kind affectionate letter, in which you have rated mine so highly that I really blush to read my own praises. Pray that God would enable me to deserve all the kindness you manifest towards me, and to act consistently with the good opinion you entertain of me —then I shall indeed be a helpmeet for you, and to be this shall at all times be the care and study of my future life. We have had to-day a large party of the Bradford folks—the Rands, Fawcetts, Dobsons, etc. My thoughts often strayed from the company, and I would have gladly left them to follow my present employment. To write to and receive letters from my friends were always among my chief enjoyments, but none ever gave me so much pleasure as those which I receive from and write to my newly adopted friend. I am by no means sorry you have given up all thought of the house you mentioned. With my cousin's help I have made known your plans to my uncle and aunt. Mr. Fennell immediately coincided with that which respects your present abode, and observed that it had occurred to him before, but that he had not had an opportunity of mentioning it to you. My aunt did not fall in with it so readily, but her objections did not appear to me to be very weighty. For my own part, I feel all the force of your arguments in favour of it, and the objections are so trifling that they can scarcely be called objections. My cousin is of the same opinion. Indeed, you have such a method of considering and digesting a plan before you make it known to your friends, that you run very little risk of incurring their disapprobations, or of having your schemes frustrated. I greatly admire your talents this way—may they never be perverted by being used in a bad cause! And whilst they are exerted for good purposes, may they prove irresistible! If I may judge from your letter, this middle scheme is what would please you best, so that if there should arise no new objection to it, perhaps it will prove the best you can adopt. However, there is yet sufficient time to consider it further. I trust in this and every other circumstance you will be guided by the wisdom that cometh from above—a portion of which I doubt not has guided you hitherto. A belief of this, added to the complete satisfaction with which I read your reasonings on the subject, made me a ready convert to your opinions. I hope nothing will occur to induce you to change your intention of spending the next week at Bradford. Depend on it you shall have letter for letter; but may we not hope to see you here during that time, surely you will not think the way more tedious than usual? I have not heard any particulars respecting the church since you were at Bradford. Mr. Rawson is now there, but Mr. Hardy and his brother are absent, and I understand nothing decisive can be accomplished without them. Jane expects to hear something more to-morrow. Perhaps ere this reaches you, you will have received some intelligence respecting it from Mr. Morgan. If you have no other apology to make for your blunders than that which you have given me, you must not expect to be excused, for I have not mentioned it to any one, so that, however it may clear your character in my opinion it is not likely to influence any other person. Little, very little, will induce me to cover your faults with a veil of charity. I already feel a kind of participation in all that concerns you. All praises and censures

208

bestowed on you must equally affect me. Your joys and sorrows must be mine. Thus shall the one be increased and the other diminished. While this is the case we shall, I hope, always find 'life's cares' to be 'comforts'. And may we feel every trial and distress, for such must be our lot at times, bind us nearer to God and to each other! My heart earnestly joins in your comprehensive prayers. I trust they will unitedly ascend to a throne of grace, and through the Redeemer's merits procure for us peace and happiness here and a life of eternal felicity hereafter. Oh, what sacred pleasure there is in the idea of spending an eternity together in perfect and uninterrupted bliss! This should encourage us to the utmost exertion and fortitude. But whilst I write, my own words condemn me—I am ashamed of my own indolence and backwardness to duty. May I be more careful, watchful, and active than I have ever yet been!

My uncle, aunt, and Jane request me to send their kind regards, and they will be happy to see you at any time next week whenever you can conveniently come down from Bradford. Let me hear from you soon—I shall expect a letter on Monday. Farewell, my dearest friend. That you may be happy in yourself and very useful to all around you is the daily earnest prayer of yours truly,

MARIA BRANWELL

160a *Maria Branwell to Patrick Brontë*

To Rev. Patrick Bronte, A.B., Hartshead.
Wood House Grove, October 3rd, 1812

How could my dear friend so cruelly disappoint me? Had he known how much I had set my heart on having a letter this afternoon, and how greatly I felt the disappointment when the bag arrived and I found there was nothing for me, I am sure he would not have permitted a little matter to hinder him. But whatever was the reason of your not writing, I cannot believe it to have been neglect or unkindness, therefore I do not in the least blame you, I only beg that in future you will judge of my feelings by your own, and if possible never let me expect a letter without receiving one . . . May I hope that there is now some intelligence on the way to me? or must my patience be tried till I see you on Wednesday? But what nonsense am I writing! Surely after this you can have no doubt that you possess all my heart. Two months ago I could not possibly have believed that you would ever engross so much of my thoughts and affections, and far less could I have thought that I should be so forward as to tell you so. I believe I must forbid you to come here again unless you can assure me that you will not steal any more of my regard . . .

I must now take my leave. I believe I need scarcely assure you that I am yours truly and very affectionately,

MARIA BRANWELL

161 Maria Branwell to Patrick Brontë

To Rev. Patrick Bronte, A.B., Hartshead.
Wood House Grove, October 21st, 1812

With the sincerest pleasure do I retire from company to converse with him whom I love beyond all others. Could my beloved friend see my heart he would then be convinced that the affection I bear him is not at all inferior to that which he feels for me—indeed I sometimes think that in truth and constancy it excels. But do not think from this that I entertain any suspicions of your sincerity— no, I firmly believe you to be sincere and generous, and doubt not in the least that you feel all you express. In return, I entreat that you will do me the justice to believe that you have not only a *very large portion* of my *affection* and *esteem*, but *all* that I am capable of feeling, and from henceforth measure my feelings by your own. Unless my love for you were very great how could I so contentedly give up my home and all my friends—a home I loved so much that I have often thought nothing could bribe me to renounce it for any great length of time together, and friends with whom I have been so long accustomed to share all the vicissitudes of joy and sorrow? Yet these have lost their weight, and though I cannot always think of them without a sigh, yet the anticipation of sharing with you all the pleasures and pains, the cares and anxieties of life, of contributing to your comfort and becoming the companion of your pilgrimage, is more delightful to me than any other prospect which this world can possibly present. I expected to have heard from you on Saturday last, and can scarcely refrain from thinking you unkind to keep me in suspense two whole days longer than was necessary, but it is well that my patience should be sometimes tried, or I might entirely lose it, and this would be a loss indeed! Lately I have experienced a considerable increase of hopes and fears, which tend to destroy the calm uniformity of my life. These are not unwelcome, as they enable me to discover more of the evils and errors of my heart, and discovering them I hope through grace to be enabled to correct and amend them. I am sorry to say that my cousin has had a very serious cold, but to-day I think she is better; her cough seems less, and I hope we shall be able to come to Bradford on Saturday afternoon, where we intend to stop till Tuesday. You may be sure we shall not soon think of taking such another journey as the last. I look forward with pleasure to Monday, when I hope to meet with you, for as we are no *longer twain* separation is painful, and to meet must ever be attended with joy.

Thursday morning.—I intended to have finished this before breakfast, but unfortunately slept an hour too long. I am every moment in expectation of the old man's arrival. I hope my cousin is still better to-day; she requests me to say that she is much obliged to you for your kind enquiries and the concern you express for her recovery. I take all possible care of her, but yesterday she was naughty enough to venture into the yard without her bonnet!

As you do not say anything of going to Leeds I conclude you have not been. We shall most probably hear from the Dr. this afternoon. I am much pleased to hear of his success at Bierley! O that you may both be zealous and successful in your efforts for the salvation of souls, and may your own lives be holy, and your hearts greatly blessed while you are engaged in administering to the good of others! I should have been very glad to have had it in my power to lessen your fatigue and cheer your spirits by my exertions on Monday last. I will hope that this pleasure is still reserved for me. In general, I feel a calm confidence in the providential care and continued mercy of God, and when I consider His past deliverances and past favours I am led to wonder and adore. A sense of my small returns of love and gratitude to Him often abases me and makes me think I am little better than those who profess no religion. Pray for me, my dear friend, and rest assured that you possess a very, very large portion of the prayers, thoughts, and heart of yours truly,

M. BRANWELL

162 *Maria Branwell to Patrick Brontë*

To Rev. Patrick Bronte, A.B., Hartshead.
Wood House Grove, November 18th, 1812

My Dear Saucy Pat, Now don't you think you deserve this epithet far more than I do that which you have given me? I really know not what to make of the beginning of your last; the winds, waves, and rocks almost stunned me. I thought you were giving me the account of some terrible dream, or that you had a presentiment of the fate of my poor box, having no idea that your lively imagination could make so much of the slight reproof conveyed in my last. What will you say when you get a *real, downright scolding*? Since you show such a readiness to atone for your offences after receiving a mild rebuke, I am inclined to hope you will seldom deserve a severe one. I accept with pleasure your atonement, and send you a free and full forgiveness. But I cannot allow that your affection is more deeply rooted than mine. However, we will dispute no more about this, but rather embrace every opportunity to prove its sincerity and strength by acting in every respect as friends and fellow-pilgrims travelling the same road, actuated by the same motives, and having in view the same end. I think if our lives are spared twenty years hence I shall then pray for you with the same, if not greater, fervour and delight that I do now. I am pleased that you are so fully convinced of my candour, for to know that you suspected me of a deficiency in this virtue would grieve and mortify me beyond expression. I do not derive any merit from the possession of it, for in me it is constitutional. Yet I think where it is possessed it will rarely exist alone, and where it is wanted there is reason to doubt the existence of almost every other virtue. As to the other qualities which your partiality attributes to me, although I rejoice to know that I stand so high in your good opinion, yet I blush to think in how small a degree I possess them. But it shall be the pleasing study of my future life to gain such an increase of grace and wisdom as shall enable me to act up to your highest expectations and prove to you a helpmeet. I firmly believe the Almighty has set us apart for each other; may we, by earnest, frequent prayer, and every possible exertion, endeavour to fulfil His will in all things! I do not, cannot, doubt your love, and here I freely declare I love you above all the world besides. I feel very, very grateful to the great Author of all our mercies for His unspeakable love and condescension towards us, and desire 'to show forth my gratitude not only with my lips, but by my life and conversation'. I indulge a hope that our mutual prayers will be answered, and that our intimacy will tend much to promote our temporal and eternal interest.

I suppose you never expected to be much the richer for me, but I am sorry to inform you that I am still poorer than I thought myself. I mentioned having sent for my books, clothes, etc. On Saturday evening about the time you were writing the description of your imaginary shipwreck, I was reading and feeling the effects of a real one, having then received a letter from my sister giving me an account of the vessel in which she had sent my box being stranded on the coast of Devonshire, in consequence of which the box was dashed to pieces with the violence of the sea, and all my little property, with the exception of a very few articles, swallowed up in the mighty deep. If this should not prove the prelude to something worse, I shall think little of it, as it is the first disastrous circumstance which has occurred since I left my home, and having been so highly favoured it would be highly ungrateful in me were I to suffer this to dwell much on my mind.

Mr. Morgan was here yesterday, indeed he only left this morning. He mentioned having written to invite you to Bierley on Sunday next, and if you complied with his request it is likely that we shall see you both here on Sunday evening. As we intend going to Leeds next week, we should be happy if you would accompany us on Monday or Tuesday. I mention this by desire of Miss Fennell, who begs to be remembered affectionately to you. Notwithstanding Mr. Fennell's complaints and threats, I doubt not but he will give you a cordial reception whenever you think fit to make your appearance at the Grove. Which you may likewise be assured of receiving from your ever truly affectionate

MARIA

Both the doctor and his lady very much wish to know what kind of address we make use of in our letters to each other. I think they would scarcely hit on *this!!*

163   *Maria Branwell to Patrick Brontë*

To Rev. Patrick Bronte, A.B., Hartshead.

Wood House Grove, December 5th, 1812

My Dearest Friend, So you *thought* that *perhaps I might* expect to hear from you. As the case was so doubtful, and you were in such great haste, you might as well have deferred writing a few days longer, for you seem to suppose it is a matter of perfect indifference to me whether I hear from you or not. I believe I once requested you to judge of my feelings by your own—am I to think that *you* are thus indifferent? I feel very unwilling to entertain such an opinion, and am grieved that you should suspect me of such a cold, heartless, attachment. But I am too serious on the subject; I only meant to rally you a little on the beginning of your last, and to tell you that I fancied there was a coolness in it which none of your former letters had contained. If this fancy was groundless, forgive me for having indulged it, and let it serve to convince you of the sincerity and warmth of my affection. Real love is ever apt to suspect that it meets not with an equal return; you must not wonder then that my fears are sometimes excited. My pride cannot bear the idea of a diminution of your attachment, or to think that it is stronger on my side than on yours. But I must not permit my pen so fully to disclose the feelings of my heart, nor will I tell you whether I am pleased or not at the thought of seeing you on the appointed day.

Miss Fennell desires her kind regards, and, with her father, is extremely obliged to you for the trouble you have taken about

214

the carpet, and has no doubt but it will give full satisfaction. They think there will be no occasion for the green cloth.

We intend to set about making the cakes here next week, but as the fifteen or twenty persons whom you mention live probably somewhere in your neighbourhood, I think it will be most convenient for Mrs. B. [Bedford] to make a small one for the purpose of distributing there, which will save us the difficulty of sending so far.

You may depend on my learning my lessons as rapidly as they are given me. I am already tolerably perfect in the A B C, etc. I am much obliged for you for the pretty little hymn which I have already got by heart, but cannot promise to sing it scientifically, though I will endeavour to gain a little more assurance.

Since I began this Jane put into my hand Lord Lyttleton's 'Advice to a Lady'. When I read those lines, 'Be never cool reserve with passion joined, with caution choose, but then be fondly kind, etc.,' my heart smote me for having in some cases used too much reserve towards you. Do you think you have any cause to complain of me? If you do, let me know it. For were it in my power to prevent it, I would in no instance occasion you the least pain or uneasiness. I am certain no one ever loved you with an affection more pure, constant, tender, and ardent than that which I feel. Surely this is not saying too much; it is the truth, and I trust you are worthy to know it. I long to improve in every religious and moral quality, that I may be a help, and if possible an ornament to you. Oh let us pray much for wisdom and grace to fill our appointed stations with propriety, that we may enjoy satisfaction in our own souls, edify others, and bring glory to the name of Him who has so wonderfully preserved, blessed, and brought us together.

If there is anything in the commencement of this which looks like pettishness, forgive it; my mind is now completely divested of every feeling of the kind, although I owe I am sometimes too apt to be overcome by this disposition.

Let me have the pleasure of hearing from you again as soon as convenient. This writing is uncommonly bad, but I too am in haste.

Adieu, my dearest, I am your affectionate and sincere

MARIA

215

Haworth, near Keighley, Yorkshire
[28th July 1823]

Dear Madam,

The circumstance of Mrs. Burder not answering my letter for so long a time gave me considerable uneasiness; however, I am much obliged to her for answering it at last. Owing to a letter which I received from Miss Sarah, and to my not receiving any answer to two letters which I wrote subsequently to that, I have thought for *years* past that it was highly probable you were married, or at all events, you wished to hear nothing of me, or from me, and determined that I should learn nothing of you. This not unfrequently gave me pain, but there was no remedy, and I endeavoured to resign, to what appeared to me to be the will of God.

I experienced a very agreeable sensation in my heart, at this moment, on reflecting that you are *still* single, and am so selfish as to wish you to remain so, even if you would never allow me to see you. *You* were the *first* whose hand I solicited, and no doubt I was the *first* to whom *you promised to give that hand.*

However much you may dislike me now, I am sure you once loved me with an unaffected innocent love, and I feel confident that after all which you have seen and heard you cannot doubt my love for you. This is a long interval of time and may have effected many changes. It has made me look something older. But I trust, I have gained more than I have lost, I hope I may venture to say I am wiser and better. I have found this world to be but vanity, and I trust I may aver that my heart's desire is to be found in the ways of divine Wisdom, and in her paths, which are pleasantness and peace. My dear Madam, I earnestly desire to know how it is in these respects with you. I wish, I ardently wish your *best* interests in *both* the worlds. Perhaps you have not had much trouble since I saw you, nor such experience as would unfold to your view in well-defined shapes the unsatisfactory nature of all earthly considerations. However, I trust you possess in your soul a sweet peace and serenity arising from communion with the Holy Spirit, and a well-grounded hope of eternal felicity. Though I have had much bitter sorrow in consequence of the sickness and death of my dear Wife, yet I have ample cause to praise God for his numberless mercies. I have a *small* but *sweet* little family that often soothe my heart and afford me pleasure by their endearing little ways, and I have what I consider a competency of the good things of this life. I am *now settled* in a part of the country *for life* where I have many friends, and it has pleased God in many respects to give me favour in the eyes of the people, and to prosper me in my ministerial labours. I want but *one* addition to my comforts, and then I think I should wish for no more on this side eternity. I want to see a dearly Beloved Friend, kind as I *once* saw her, and as *much* disposed to promote my happiness. If I have ever given her any pain I only wish for an opportunity to make her ample amends, by every attention and kindness. Should that very dear Friend doubt respecting the veracity of any of my statements, I would beg leave to give her the most satisfactory reference, I would beg leave to refer her to the Rev. John Buckworth, Vicar of Dewsbury, near Leeds, who is an excellent and respectable man, well known both as an *Author* and an able Minister of the Gospel to the religious world.

My dear Madam, all that I have to request at present is that you will be so good as to answer this letter as soon as convenient, and tell me candidly whether you and Mrs. Burder would have any objection to seeing me at Finchingfield Park as an *Old Friend*. If you would allow me to call there in a friendly manner, as soon as I could get a supply for my church and could leave home I would set off for the South. Should you object to my stopping at Finchingfield Park overnight I would stop at one of the Inns in Braintree—as most likely my old friends in that town are either dead or gone. Should you and Mrs. Burder kindly consent to see me as an old friend, it might be necessary for me before I left home to write *another* letter in order that I might know when you would be at home. I cannot tell how *you* may feel on reading this, but I must say *my* ancient love is rekindled, and I have a *longing* desire to see you. Be so kind to give my best respects to Mrs. Burder, to Miss Sarah, your brothers, and the *Little Baby*. And *whatever* you resolve upon, believe me to be yours *Most Sincerely*,

P. BRONTË

Finchingfield Park,
August 8th, 1823

Reverend Sir,

As you must reasonably suppose, a letter from you presented
to me on the 4th inst. naturally produced sensations of surprise
and agitation. You have thought proper after a lapse of fifteen
years and after various changes in circumstances again to address
me, with what motives I cannot well define. The subject you have
introduced, so long buried in silence and until now almost forgotten, cannot, I should think, produce in your mind anything
like satisfactory reflection. From a recent persual of many letters
of yours bearing date eighteen hundred and eight, nine and ten
addressed to myself and my dear departed Aunt, many circumstances are brought with peculiar force afresh to my recollection.
With my present feelings I cannot forbear in justice to myself
making some observations which may possibly appear severe—of
their justice I am convinced. This review, Sir, excites in my bosom
increased gratitude and thankfulness to that wise, that indulgent,
Providence which then watched over me for good and withheld
me from forming in very early life an indissoluble engagement
with one whom I cannot think was altogether clear of duplicity. A
union with you under then existing circumstances must have
embittered my future days and would, I have no doubt, been pro-
ductive of reflections upon me as unkind and distressing as events
have proved they would have been unfounded and unjust. Happily
for me I have not been the ascribed cause of hindering your
promotion, of preventing any brilliant alliance, nor have those
great and affluent friends that you used to write and speak of
withheld their patronage on my account, young, inexperienced,
unsuspecting, and ignorant as I was of what I had a right to look
forward to.

Many communications were received from you in humble
silence which ought rather have met with contempt and indigna-
tion ever considering the sacredness of a promise. Your confidence
I have never betrayed, strange as was the disclosure you once made
unto me; whether those ardent professions of devoted lasting
attachment were sincere is now to me a matter of little con-

sequence. 'What I have seen and heard' certainly leads me to conclude very differently. With these my present views of past occurrences is it possible, think you, that I or my dear Parent could give you a cordial welcome to the Park as an *old friend*? Indeed, I must give a *decided* negative to the desired visit. I know of no ties of friendship *ever* existing between us which the last eleven or twelve years have not severed or at least placed an insuperable bar to any revival. My present condition, upon which you are pleased to remark, has hitherto been the state of my choice and to me a state of much happiness and comfort, tho' I have not been exempted from some severe trials. Blessed with the kindest and most indulgent of friends in a beloved Parent, Sister, and Brother, with a handsome competency which affords me the capability of gratifying the best feelings of my heart, teased with no domestic cares and anxieties and without anyone to control or oppose me, I have felt no willingness to risk in a change so many enjoyments in my possession. Truly I may say, 'My Cup over-floweth', yet it is ever my desire to bear in mind that mutability is inscribed on all earthly possession. 'This is not my rest', and I humbly trust that I have been led to place all my hopes of present and future happiness upon a surer foundation, upon that tried foundation stone which God has laid in Zion. Within these last twelve months I have suffered a severe and protracted affliction from typhus fever. For twenty-eight weeks I was unable to leave my bedroom, and in that time was brought to the confines of an eternal world. I have indeed been brought low, but the Lord has helped me. He has been better to me than my fears, has delivered my soul from death, my eyes from tears, and my feet from falling, and I trust the grateful language of my heart is, 'What shall I render unto the Lord for all his benefits?' The life so manifestly redeemed from the grave I desire to devote more unreservedly than I have ever yet done to His service.

With the tear of unavailing sorrow still ready to start at the recollection of the loss of that beloved relative whom we have been call'd to mourn since you and I last saw each other, I can truly sympathize with you and the poor little innocents in your bereavement. The Lord can supply all your and their need. It gives me pleasure always to hear the work of the Lord prospering. May He enable you to be as faithful, as zealous, and as successful a labourer in His vineyard as was one of your predecessors, the good old Mr. Grimshaw, who occupied the pulpit at Haworth more than half a century ago, then will your consolations be neither few nor small. Cherishing no feeling of resentment or animosity, I remain, Revd. Sir, sincerely your Well Wisher,

MARY D. BURDER

WILLIAM HAZLITT

William Hazlitt was born at Maidstone on 10th April 1778, where his father was a Unitarian minister. At first he had ambitions as a portrait painter and went, in 1802, to Paris to copy in the Louvre. His last portrait—Charles Lamb as a Venetian Senator—proved to him that he would not succeed and, in 1805, he published his first book, *An Essay on the Principles of Human Action.* . . . In 1808 he married Sarah Stoddart. But his marriage, too, was not to be a success. Although they were not divorced for fourteen years, Hazlitt went, in 1819, to live alone in Southampton Buildings where he became infatuated with Sarah Walker, his landlord's daughter. Of this infatuation he wrote an account in *Liber Amoris,* or the *New Pygmalion* (1823). He died on 18th September 1830 and Charles Lamb sat with him to the end.

Of his letters to Sarah Walker, his grandson says, 'They are the unconnected and inconsequent outpourings of an imagination always superlatively vivid, and now morbidly so.' Reading them today, however, they seem genuine love letters, truthful, modest and sincere. The sadness and tenderness is evident when Hazlitt writes, 'She came (I know not how) and sat by my side, and was folded in my arms, a vision of love and joy—as if she had dropped from the heavens to bless me by some special dispensation of a favouring providence—to make me amends for all. And, now, without any fault of mine but too much love, she has vanished from me and I am left to wither.' It was in vain for Sarah to say, 'Sir, I told you I could feel no more for you than friendship,' in

vain for Hazlitt to discover her in the arms of some other man; he
loved her to the end of his life.

166 *William Hazlitt to Sarah Walker*

Feb. 1822

You will scold me for this, and ask me if this is keeping my
promise to mind my work. One half of it was to think of Sarah;
and besides I do not neglect my work either, I assure you. I
regularly do ten pages a day, which mounts up to thirty guineas'
worth a week, so that you see I should grow rich at this rate, if I
could keep on so; *and I could keep on so*, if I had you with me to
encourage me with your sweet smiles, and share my lot. The
Berwick smacks sail twice a week, and the wind sets fair. When I
think of the thousand endearing caresses that have passed between
us, I do not wonder at the strong attachment that draws me to
you, but I am sorry for my own want of power to please. I hear the
wind sigh through the lattice, and keep repeating over and over to
myself two lines of Lord Byron's tragedy—

> So shalt thou find me ever at thy side,
> Here and hereafter, if the last may be.

applying them to thee, my love, and thinking whether I shall ever
see thee again. Perhaps not—for some years at least—till both
thou and I are old—and then when all else have forsaken thee, I
will creep to thee, and die in thine arms.

You once made me believe I was not hated by her I loved:
and for that sensation—so delicious was it, though but a mockery
and a dream—I owe you more than I can ever pay. I thought to
have dried up my tears for ever the day I left you: but as I write
this they stream again. If they did not, I think my heart would
burst.

I walk out here of an afternoon and hear the notes of the
thrush that comes up from a sheltered valley below, welcome in

the spring; but they do not melt my heart as they used; it is grown cold and dead. As you say it will one day be colder.

God forgive what I have written above; I did not intend it; but you were once my little all, and I cannot bear the thought of having lost you for ever, I fear through my own fault.

Has anyone called? Do not send any letters that come. I should like you and your mother (if agreeable) to go and see Mr Kean in 'Othello', and Miss Stephens in 'Love in a Village,' if you will, I will write to Mr T—— to send you tickets. Has Mr P—— called? I think I must send to him for the picture to kiss and talk to. Kiss me, my best beloved. Ah! if you can never be mine, still let me be your proud and happy slave.

H.

167 William Hazlitt to Sarah Walker

[no date]

My dear Miss L.—*Evil to them that evil think* is an old saying; and I have found it a true one. I have ruined myself by my unjust suspicions of you. Your sweet friendship was the balm of my life, and I have lost it I fear for ever, by one fault and folly after another.

What would I give to be restored to the place in your esteem which you assured me I held only a few months ago! Yet I was not contented, but did all I could to torment myself and harass you by endless doubts and jealousy. Can you not forget and forgive the past, and judge of me by my conduct in future? Can you not take all my follies in the lump, and say, like a good, generous girl, 'Well, I'll think no more of them.' In a word, may I come back and try to behave better. A line to say so would be an additional favour to so many already received by,—Your obliged friend, and sincere well-wisher.

1784   1859

JAMES HENRY LEIGH HUNT

Leigh Hunt and his brother John were sent to prison for attacking the Prince Regent in their journal, *The Examiner*. They called him 'a fat Adonis of 50'. Here came all the famous liberals of the day to visit them—Byron, Moore, Brougham, and others.

James Henry Leigh Hunt was born at Southgate. His father was a lawyer in Philadelphia until his loyalist sympathies caused him to leave the States. His son was sent to Christ's Hospital. Anyone reading the *Essays of Elia* or Lamb's *Letters* will come to know Leigh Hunt very well. He was something of an opportunist but dearly loved by Lamb and Byron (who was exasperated by him, but still provided for him and his family during his stay in Italy which his wife had arranged with Mrs. Shelley), Haydon, the painter, C. W. Dilke, and William Hazlitt. His wife, Marianne, is spoken of as being 'rather unattractive' but from this selection of his letters he seems to have loved her well enough. He met her when she was a little girl of thirteen and he a young man of seventeen. Once when he tried to thrust his superior 'learning' down her throat, she replied 'that she resented dictations which tended to put a bent upon her own personal feelings and turn of thought'. They were married on 3rd July 1809.

[Date 1803 or 1804]

My dearest Marian,—I am very uncomfortable; I get up at five in the morning, say a word to nobody, curse my stars till eleven at night, and then creep into bed to curse my stars for to-morrow; and all this because I love a little, black-eyed girl of fifteen, whom nobody knows, with my heart and soul.

You must not suppose I love you a bit the better for being fifty miles out of my reach in the day time; for you must know that I travel at a pretty tolerable pace every night, and have held many a happy chat with you about twelve or one o'clock at midnight, though you may have forgotten it by this time.

> Oft by yon sad and solitary stream
> Sweet visions gild the youthful poet's dream;
> Calm as *the* [he] slumbers in the roseate shade,
> Unvarying Fancy clasps his absent maid,
> Hangs on each charm that captivates the heart,
> The smile, the glance, too eloquent for art,
> The whispers trembling as of love they tell,
> And the smooth bosom's undulating swell;
> Paints the bright prospect of approaching years,
> And all Elysium opens to his prayers.

You see lovers can no more help being poets than poets can help being lovers. . .

I shall see you again and I'll pay you prettily for running away from me, for you shall not stir from *my* side the whole evening when you return; tell Betsy too that she is a very malicious prophetess, and that if she comes to me again with such ill news as she gave me in her last epistle, I shall pray heaven to cut at least two inches of plumpness from her round face, and at nineteen to give her a husband of ninety. If you are well and *have* been so at Brighton, you are everything I could wish you. God bless you and yours! You see I can still pray for myself. Heaven knows that every blessing it bestows on you is a tenfold one bestowed on your

H.

Gainsborough, Thursday, Feb. 1806

Dearest Girl,— . . . I worshipped the magnificence and the love of the God of Nature, and I thought of you; these two sensations always arise in my heart in the quiet of a rural landscape, and I have often considered it a proof of the purity and the reality of my affection for you, that it always feels most powerful in my religious moments—and it is very natural. Are you not the greatest blessing Heaven has bestowed upon me? Your image attends me, not only in my rural rambles, not only in those healthful walks, when escaped from the clamour of streets and the glare of theatres, I am ready to exclaim with Cowper,

'God made the country, and man made the town;' it is present with me even in the bustle of life; it gives me a dislike to frivolous and riotous society; it excites me to improve myself in order to preserve your affection, and it quenches the little flashes of caprice and impatience which disturb the repose of existence.

If I feel my anger rising at trifles, it checks me instantaneously; it seems to say to me, 'Why do you disturb yourself? Marian loves you; you deserve her love, and you ought to be above these little marks of a little mind.' Such is the power of virtuous love.

I am naturally a man of violent passions, but your affection has taught me to subdue them. Whenever you feel any little disquietudes or impatiences arising in your bosom, think of the happiness you bestow upon me and real love will produce the same effects on you as it has produced on me. No reasoning person ought to marry who cannot say, 'My love has made me better and more desirous of improvement than I have been!'

. . . I do not write I acknowledge either the best or the straightest hand in the world, but I endeavour to avoid blots and interpolations. I suppose you guess by this preamble that I am going to find fault with your letters. I would not dare, however, to find fault were I not sure that you would receive my lectures cheerfully; you have no false shame to induce you to conceal or to deny your faults, quite the contrary; you think sometimes too much of them, for I know of none which you cannot easily remedy. Besides, my faithful and attentive affection would induce me to ask with confidence any little sacrifice of your time and your care; and as you have done so much for me in correcting the errors of my *head*, you will not feel very unpleasant when I venture to correct the errors of your *hand*.

Now, cannot you sit down on Sunday, my sweet girl, and write me a fair, even-minded honest hand, unvexed with desperate blots or skulking interlineations. Mind, I do not quarrel with the contents or with the subject; what you tell of others amuses me and what you tell me of myself delights me; it is merely the fashion of your lines; in short, as St. Paul saith—'The spirit giveth life, but the *letter* killeth.' I know you can do this easily and I know also you will do it cheerfully, because it will give me pleasure . . .[1]

It is astonishing to me that I could ever be melancholy when I possess friends like these; and when above all, I am able to tell my dearest Marian how infinitely she is beloved by her

HENRY

170 *James Henry Leigh Hunt to Marianne Kent*
[Extract]
Margate, 30th July 1807

. . . Margate is still the same mere fashionable lump of chalk, but it serves for a sort of looking-glass of Brighton, and when I look upon the sea, I think we are both regarding the same object, or that the same waves are destined to bathe both you and me. . . . Tell me when you write what time you go into the sea, or rather into the woolsack, for I do not see the vast benefit that can be derived from bathing in huge gowns of thick cloth. . . .[2] You see I hardly know when to leave off when once I am in your company. God bless you again and again. Your most affectionate

HENRY

[1] Passage omitted concerning friends.
[2] Recommends her to read good novels only.

In the Garden, Hermitage, Nottingham
Saturday Noon, 25th June 1808

My dearest Love,—The Hermitage ink is very bad, but perhaps it will get brighter as it comes nearer you . . .

Hermits might have been very comfortable for aught I know, but I am persuaded there is no such thing after all as a perfect enjoyment of solitude, for the more delicious the solitude the more one wants a companion. You know what sort of a companion, and you know whom too for me. I know that if you were with me just now, I could forget London entirely, but I cannot manage to forget it while I am alone.

LORD BYRON

When he was 10 years old Byron succeeded to the title and when 15 he fell in love with Mary Anne Chaworth, ten years his senior. She refused him and married John Musters. She was, said Byron, 'all that his youthful fancy could paint of beautiful'. Byron settled in the family seat, Newstead Abbey, in 1808, but soon after he went abroad with John Carn Hobhouse.

Lady Caroline Lamb, daughter of the Earl of Bessborough, who was a little mad, fell in love with Byron and 'absolutely beseiged him'. The story went that, at a party in July 1813, she quarrelled with Byron and tried to stab herself with a knife and some fragments of glass. Byron, later, wrote the cruel letter which Caroline Lamb printed in her novel *Glenarvon*.

On 2nd January 1815 Byron was married to Miss Millbanke, a marriage which was unhappy. A separation eventually took place and Byron left England for ever. In April 1819 he met Teresa, daughter of Count Gamba of Ravenna who, at 16, had recently married Count Guiccioli. Byron fell in love with her and they lived together. In 1823 he offered to join the Greeks in their rebellion against Turkey. He died of marsh fever at Missolonghi in 1824. Lady Caroline Lamb lived in retirement after Byron's exile and is said to have died from the shock of meeting his funeral procession.

[August 1812?]

My dearest Caroline,

If tears which you saw and know I am not apt to shed,—if the agitation in which I parted from you,—agitation which you must have perceived through the *whole* of this most *nervous* affair, did not commence until the moment of leaving you approached,—if all I have said and done, and am still but too ready to say and do, have not sufficiently proved what my real feelings are, and must ever be towards you, my love, I have no other proof to offer. God knows, I wish you happy, and when I quit you, or rather you, from a sense of duty to your husband and mother, quit me, you shall acknowledge the truth of what I again promise and vow, that no other in word or deed, shall ever hold the place in my affections, which is, and shall be, most sacred to you, till I am nothing. I never knew till *that moment* the *madness* of my dearest and most beloved friend; I cannot express myself; this is no time for words, but I shall have a pride, a melancholy pleasure, in suffering what you yourself can scarcely conceive, for you do not know me. I am about to go out with a heavy heart, because my appearing this evening will stop any absurd story which the event of the day might give rise to. Do you think *now* I am *cold* and *stern* and *artful*? Will even *others* think so? Will your *mother* ever—that mother to whom we must indeed sacrifice much, more, much more on my part than she shall ever know or can imagine? 'Promise not to love you!' ah, Caroline, it is past promising. But I shall attribute all concessions to the proper motive, and never cease to feel all that you have already witnessed, and more than can ever be known but to my own heart,—perhaps to yours. May God protect, forgive, and bless you. Ever, and even more than ever,

Your most attached,

BYRON

P.S.—These taunts which have driven you to this, my dearest Caroline, were it not for your mother and the kindness of your connections, is there anything on earth or heaven that would have made me so happy as to have made you mine long ago? and not less *now* than *then*, but *more* than ever at this time. You know I would with pleasure give up all here and all beyond the grave for you, and in refraining from this, must my motives be misunderstood? I care not who knows this, what use is made of it,—it is to *you* and to *you* only that they are *yourself* [*sic*]. I was and am yours freely and most entirely, to obey, to honour, love,—and fly with you when, where, and how you yourself *might* and *may* determine.

173   Lord Byron to the Countess Guiccioli

Bologna, August 25, 1819

My Dear Teresa,

I have read this book[1] in your garden;—my love, you were absent, or else I could not have read it. It is a favourite book of yours, and the writer was a friend of mine. You will not understand these English words, and *others* will not understand them— which is the reason I have not scrawled them in Italian. But you will recognize the handwriting of him who passionately loved you, and you will divine that, over a book which was yours, he could only think of love. In that word, beautiful in all languages, but most so in yours—Amor mio—is comprised my existence here and hereafter. I feel I exist here, and I fear that I shall exist hereafter,—to *what* purpose you will decide; my destiny rests with you, and you are a woman, eighteen years of age, and two out of a convent. I wish that you had stayed there, with all my heart,—or, at least, that I had never met you in your married state.

But all this is too late. I love you, and you love me,—at least you *say so*, and *act* as if you *did* so, which last is a great consolation in all events. But *I* more than love you, and cannot cease to love you.

Think of me, sometimes, when the Alps and the ocean divide us,—but they never will, unless you *wish* it.

BYRON

[1] The book to which Byron referred was the Countess's copy of *Corinne* by Madame de Staël, and it was on the last page that Byron penned his love letter to the Countess.

PERCY BYSSHE SHELLEY

Shelley is the prototype revolutionary, the undergraduate who revolts against authority and whose whole life is influenced by the way authority reacts to him.

He was born at Field Place, near Horsham, Sussex, and educated at Eton and University College, Oxford, from which he was expelled for writing and publishing *The Necessity of Atheism*. He went out of his way to draw attention to his ideas by sending a copy of the pamphlet to all Heads of Colleges.

'Love is free,' he declared. It was a philosophy which hurt only those with whom he was in love—and discarded. Before he died he wrote to a friend, 'I think one is always in love with something or other; the error, and I confess it is not easy for spirits cased in flesh and blood to avoid it, consists in seeking in a mortal image the likeness of what is perhaps eternal.'

For a year, after he left Oxford, he had a mild love affair with Elizabeth Hitchener, a school teacher at Hurstpierpoint, to whom he wrote many letters. In 1811, however, he eloped with Harriet Westbrook. They were married in Edinburgh in August. The marriage was a disaster and they separated in 1814. Beautiful and educated as she was, Shelley said of her that she could not 'feel poetry and understand philosophy'. Perhaps the truth was that he had met and fallen in love with Mary Godwin, daughter of Mary Wollstonecraft, authoress of *A Vindication of the Rights of Women*. Shelley and Mary eloped to Italy in 1814. Harriet committed suicide by drowning herself in the Serpentine. Shelley and Mary were married in 1816.

York, [15th] October 1811

I write to-day, because *not* to answer such a letter as yours instantly, eagerly—I will add, gratefully—were impossible, but I shall be at Cuckfield on Friday night. My dearest friend (for I will call you so), *you* who understand my motives to action which, I flatter myself, unisonize with your own, *you*, who can contemn the world's prejudices, whose views are mine, I will dare to say I *love*: nor do I risk the possibility of that degrading and contemptible interpretation of this sacred word, nor do I risk the supposition that the lump of organized matter which enshrines *thy* soul excites the love which that soul alone *dare* claim. . . . Henceforth will I be yours—yours with truth, sincerity, and unreserve. Not a thought shall arise which shall not seek its responsion in your bosom, not a motive of action shall be unenwafted by your cooler reason: and, (by) so doing, do I not choose a criterion more infallible than my own consciousness of right and wrong (tho' this may not be required) for what conflict of a frank mind is more terrible than the balance between two opposing importances of morality . . . this is surely the only wretchedness to which a mind who only acknowledges virtue its master can feel. I leave York to-night for Cuckfield where I shall arrive on Friday. That mistaken man, my father, has refused us money, and commanded that our names should never be mentioned. . . . Sophisticated by falsehood as society is I had thought that this blind resentment had long been banished to the regions of dullness, comedies, and farces, or was used merely to augment the difficulties, and consequently the attachment of the hero and heroine of a modern novel. I have written frequently to this thoughtless man, and am now determined to visit him, in order to try the force of truth, tho' I must confess I consider it nearly as hyperbolical as 'music rending the knotted oak.' Some philosophers have ascribed indefiniteness to the power of intellect; but I question whether it ever would make an ink-stand capable of free-agency. Is this too severe? But you know *I*, like the god of the Jews, set myself up as no respecter of persons, and relationship is considered by me as bearing that relation to reason which a band of straw does to fire. I love you more

233

than any relation; I profess you are the sister of my soul, its dearest sister, and I think the component parts of that soul must undergo complete dissolution before its sympathies can perish.

Some Philosophers have taken a world of pains to persuade us that congeniality is but romance . . . certainly *reason* can never either account for, or prove the truth of, *feeling*. . . . I have considered it in every possible light; and reason tells me that death is the boundary of the life of man, yet I feel, I believe the direct contrary. . . . The senses are the only inlets of knowledge, and there is an inward sense that has persuaded me of this. How I digress, how does one reasoning lead to another, involving a chain of endless considerations! Certainly, everything is connected, both in the moral and physical world there is a train of events, and tho' not likely, it is impossible to deny, but that the turn which my mind has taken, originated from the conquest of England by William of Normandy. By the bye, I have something to talk to you of— Money. . . . I covet it.—'What you? you a miser, you desire gold, you a slave to the most contemptible of ambitions!' No, I am not; but I still desire money, and I desire it because I think I know the use of it. It commands labor, it gives leisure, and to give leisure to those who will employ it in the forwarding of truth is the noblest present an individual can make to the whole. . . . I will open to you my views . . . on my *coming* to the estate which, worldly considered is mine, but which actually I have not more, perhaps not so great, a right to as you; Justice demands that it should be shared between my sisters? Does it, or does it not? Mankind are as much my brethren and sisters as they: *all* ought to share. This cannot be; it must be confined. But thou art a sister of *my soul, he* is its brother: surely these have a right. . . . Consider this subject, write to me on it. Divest yourself of individuality, dare to place *self* at a distance which I know you can, spurn those bugbears *gratitude, obligation*, and *modesty* . . . the world calls these virtues, they are well enough for the world. It wants a chain, it hath forged one for itself, but with the sister of my soul I have no obligation, to her I feel no gratitude, I stand not on etiquette, alias insincerity. . . . The ideas excited by these words are varying, frequently unjust, always *selfish*. . . . *Love* in the sense in which we understand it, needs not these succedanea. Consider the questions which I have proposed to you. I know you are above that pretended confession of your own imbecility which the world has nicknamed modesty, and you must be conscious of your own high worth. To underrate your powers is an evil of greater magnitude than the contrary, the former benumbs, whilst the latter excites to action. My friend Hogg and myself consider our property as common, that the day will arrive when *we* shall do the same, is the wish of my soul, whose consummation I most eagerly anticipate.

My uncle is a most generous fellow, had he not assisted us, we should still [have] been chained to the filth and *commerce* of Edinburgh. Vile as aristocracy is, commerce—purse-proud ignorance and illiterateness—is more contemptible. . . . I still see Religion to be immoral. When I contemplate these gigantic piles of superstition—when I consider too the leisure for the exercise of mind, which the labor which erected them annihilated—I set them down as so many retardations of the period when truth becomes omnipotent. . . . Every useless ornament, the pillars, the iron railings, the juttings of wainscot, and as Southey says, the cleaning of grates are all exertions of bodily labor which tho' trivial, separately considered, when united, destroy a vast proportion of this invaluable leisure. . . . How many things could we do without! How unnecessary are *mahogany* tables, silver vases, myriads of viands and liquor, expensive printing, that, worst of all. Look even [around some] little habitation,—the dirtiest cottage, which [exhibits] myriads of instances where ornament is sacrificed to cleanliness or leisure. Whither do I wander? Certainly I wish to prove by my own proper prowess that the chain which I spoke of is real. The letter at Field Place has been opened and read, exposed to all the remarks of impertinence, not that they understood it. Henceforth I shall have no secrets for [? from] you; and indeed I have much then to tell you—wonderful changes! Direct to me at the Capt.'s until you hear again, but I only stay two days in Sussex, but I shall see you.

Sister of my soul, adieu.—With, I hope, *eternal* love, Your

PERCY SHELLEY

Padua, Mezzogiorno,
[? 22nd September 1818]

My Best Mary,

I found at Mount Selice a favourable opportunity for going to Venice, where I shall try to make some arrangement for you and little Ca to come for some days, and shall meet you, if I do not write anything in the meantime, at Padua, on Thursday morning. Clare says she is obliged to come to see the Medico, whom we missed this morning, and who has appointed as the only hour at which he can be at leisure—$\frac{1}{2}$ past 8 in the morning. You must, therefore, arrange matters so that you should come to the Stella d'Oro a little before that hour—a thing to be accomplished only by setting out at $\frac{1}{2}$ past 3 in the morning. You will by this means arrive at Venice very early in the day, and avoid the heat, which might be bad for the babe, and take time, when she would at least sleep great part of the time. Clare will return with the return carriage, and I shall meet you, or send you to Padua.

Meanwhile remember Charles the 1st—and do you be prepared to bring at least *some* of Myrrha translated; bring the book also with you, and the sheets of 'Prometheus Unbound,' which you will find numbered from one to twenty-six on the table of the pavilion. My poor little Clara, how is she to-day? Indeed I am somewhat uneasy about her, and though I feel secure that there is no danger, it would be very comfortable to have some reasonable person's opinion about her. The Medico at Padua is certainly a man in great practice, but I confess he does not satisfy me.

Am I not like a wild swan to be gone so suddenly? But, in fact, to set off alone to Venice required an exertion. I felt myself capable of making it, and I knew that you desired it. What will not be—if so it is destined—the lonely journey through that wide, cold France? But we shall see. As yet I do not direct to you *Lady* Shelley.

Adieu, my dearest love—remember, remember Charles the I and Myrrha. I have been already imagining how you will conduct some scenes. The second volume of St. Leon begins with this proud and true sentiment—'There is nothing which the human mind can conceive, which it may not execute.' Shakespeare was only a human being. Adieu till Thursday. Your ever affectionate

P. B. S.

JOHN KEATS

Keats's letters to Fanny Brawne tear the heart with an almost unbearable agony, for he was in the first months of the illness which was to kill him and she was a healthy girl. In the middle of December 1818 he wrote of her, shortly after meeting her, in a letter to his brother George:

'She is about my height—with a fine style of countenance of the lengthen'd sort—she wants sentiment in every feature—she manages to make her hair look well—her nostrils are fine—though a little painful—her mouth is bad and good—her profile is better than her full-face which indeed is not full but pale and thin without showing any bone—Her shape is very graceful and so are her movements—her Arms are good her hands badish—her feet tolerable—she is not seventeen—but she is ignorant—monstrous in her behaviour flying out in all directions, calling people such names—that I was forced lately to make use of the term *Minx*—this is I think not from any innate vice but for a penchant she has for acting stylishly. I am however tired of such style and shall decline any more of it.'

On 3rd February 1820 Keats had his real first attack of consumption. His friend Brown has left an account of how the poet knew it to be his death warrant. In July the last great volume of poems was published, and on 18th September Keats and his friend Severn sailed for Italy. From Naples they went to Rome where, on 10th December, Keats had his final relapse. He died on 23rd February 1821.

1 July 1819
Shanklin,
Isle of Wight, Thursday

My dearest Lady,

I am glad I had not an opportunity of sending off a Letter which I wrote to you on Tuesday night—'twas too much like one out of Ro[u]sseau's Heloise. I am more reasonable this morning. The morning is the only proper time for me to write to a beautiful Girl whom I love so much: for at night, when the lonely day has closed, and the lonely, silent, unmusical Chamber is waiting to receive me as into a Sepulchre, then believe me my passion gets entirely the sway, then I would not have you see those R[h]apsodies which I once thought it impossible I should ever give way to, and which I have often laughed at in another, for fear you should think me either too unhappy or perhaps a little mad. I am now at a very pleasant Cottage window, looking onto a beautiful hilly country, with a glimpse of the sea; the morning is very fine. I do not know how elastic my spirit might be, what pleasure I might have in living here and breathing and wandering as free as a stag about this beautiful Coast if the remembrance of you did not weigh so upon me. I have never known any unalloy'd Happiness for many days together: the death or sickness of some one has always spoilt my hours—and now when none such troubles oppress me, it is you must confess very hard that another sort of pain should haunt me. Ask yourself my love whether you are not very cruel to have so entrammelled me, so destroyed my freedom. Will you confess this in the Letter you must write immediately and do all you can to console me in it—make it rich as a draught of poppies to intoxicate me—write the softest words and kiss them that I may at least touch my lips where yours have been. For myself I know not how to express my devotion to so fair a form: I want a brighter word than bright, a fairer word than fair. I almost wish we were butterflies and liv'd but three summer days—three such days with you I could fill with more delight than fifty common years could ever contain. But however selfish I may feel, I am sure I could never act selfishly: as I told you a day or two before I left Hampstead, I will never return to London if my Fate does not turn up Pam[1] or at least a Court-card. Though I could centre my Happiness in you, I cannot expect to engross your heart so entirely —indeed if I thought you felt as much for me as I do for you at this moment I do not think I could restrain myself from seeing you again tomorrow for the delight of one embrace. But no—I must live upon hope and Chance. In case of the worst that can happen, I shall still love you—but what hatred I shall have for another! Some lines I read the other day are continually ringing a peal in my ears:

> To see those eyes I prize above mine own
> Dart favors on another—
> And those sweet lips (yielding immortal nectar)
> Be gently press'd by any but myself—
> Think, think Francesca, what a cursed thing
> It were beyond expression!

J.

Do write immediately. There is no Post from this Place, so you must address Post Office, Newport, Isle of Wight. I know before night I shall curse myself for having sent you so cold a Letter; yet it is better to do it as much in my senses as possible. Be as kind as the distance will permit to your

J. KEATS

Present my Compliments to your mother, my love, to Margaret and best remembrances to your Brother—if you please so.

177   *John Keats to Fanny Brawne*

[Thursday 8th July 1819]
[Newport I.O.W.]

My sweet Girl,

Your letter gave me more delight, than any thing in the world but yourself could do; indeed I am almost astonished that any absent one should have that luxurious power over my senses which I feel. Even when I am not thinking of you I receive your influence and a tenderer nature stealing upon me. All my thoughts,

[1] In the game of loo, Pam is the knave of clubs.

my unhappiest days and nights have I find not at all cured me of my love of Beauty, but made it so intense that I am miserable that you are not with me: or rather breathe in that dull sort of patience that cannot be called Life. I never knew before, what such a love as you have made me feel, was; I did not believe in it; my Fancy was affraid of it, lest it should burn me up. But if you will fully love me, though there may be some fire, 'twill not be more than we can bear when moistened and bedewed with Pleasures. You mention 'horrid people' and ask me whether it depend upon them, whether I see you again. Do understand me, my love, in this. I have so much of you in my heart that I must turn Mentor when I see a chance of harm beffaling you. I would never see anything but Pleasure in your eyes, love on your lips, and Happiness in your steps. I would wish to see you among those amusements suitable to your inclinations and spirits; so that our loves might be a delight in the midst of Pleasures agreeable enough, rather than a resource from vexations and cares. But I doubt much, in case of the worst, whether I shall be philosopher enough to follow my own Lessons: if I saw my resolution give you a pain I could not. Why may I not speak of your Beauty, since without that I could never have lov'd you. I cannot conceive any beginning of such love as I have for you but Beauty. There may be a sort of love for which, without the least sneer at it, I have the highest respect and can admire it in others: but it has not the richness, the bloom, the full form, the enchantment of love after my own heart. So let me speak of you[r] Beauty, though to my own endangering; if you could be so cruel to me as to try elsewhere its Power. You say you are affraid I shall think you do not love me—in saying this you make me ache the more to be near you. I am at the diligent use of my faculties here, I do not pass a day without sprawling some blank verse or tagging some rhymes; and here I must confess, that, (since I am on that subject,) I love you the more in that I believe you have liked me for my own sake and for nothing else. I have met with women whom I really think would like to be married to a Poem and to be given away by a Novel. I have seen your Comet,[1] and only wish it was a sign that poor Rice would get well whose illness makes him rather a melancholy companion: and the more so as so to conquer his feelings and hide them from me,

[1] The head of a comet passed across the face of the sun 26th June 1819, and became visible generally at the beginning of July.

with a forc'd Pun. I kiss'd your writing over in the hope you had indulg'd me by leaving a trace of honey—What was your dream? Tell it me and I will tell you the interpretation thereof.

Ever yours, my love!

JOHN KEATS

Do not accuse me of delay—we have not here an opportunity of sending letters every day. Write speedily.

178 *John Keats to Fanny Brawne*

[Monday 13th September 1819]
Fleet Street, Monday Morn

My dear Girl,

I have been hurried to Town by a Letter from my brother George; it is not of the brightest intelligence. Am I mad or not? I came by the Friday night coach and have not yet been to Ham[p]stead. Upon my soul it is not my fault. I cannot resolve to mix any pleasure with my days: they go one like another undistinguishable. If I were to see you today it would destroy the half comfortable sullenness I enjoy at present into dow[n]right perplexities. I love you too much to venture to Hampstead, I feel it is not paying a visit, but venturing into a fire. Que ferai je? as the french novel writers say in fun, and I in earnest: really what can I do? Knowing well that my life must be passed in fatigue and trouble, I have been endeavouring to wean myself from you: for to myself alone what can be much of a misery? As far as they regard myself I can despise all events: but I cannot cease to love you. This morning I scarcely know what I am doing. I am going to Walthamstow. I shall return to Winchester to-morrow; whence you shall hear from me in a few days. I am a Coward, I cannot bear the pain of being happy; 'tis out of the question; I must admit no thought of it.

Yours ever affectionately

JOHN KEATS

[Monday 11th October 1819]
College Street

My sweet Girl,

I am living to day in yesterday: I was in a complete fa[s]cination all day. I feel myself at your mercy. Write me ever so few lines and tell you (*for* me) you will never for ever be less kind to me than yesterday—. You dazzled me. There is nothing in the world so bright and delicate. When Brown came out with that seemingly true story again[s]t me last night, I felt it would be death to me if you had ever believed it—though against any one else I could muster up my obstinacy. Before I knew Brown could disprove it I was for the moment miserable. When shall we pass a day alone? I have had a thousand kisses, for which with my whole soul I thank love—but if you should deny me the thousand and first—'twould put me to the proof how great a misery I could live through. If you should ever carry your threat yesterday into execution— believe me 'tis not my pride, my vanity or any petty passion would torment me—really 'twould hurt my heart—I could not bear it. I have seen Mrs Dilke this morning; she says she will come with me any fine day.

Ever yours

JOHN KEATS

Ah hertè mine!

[Wednesday 13th October 1819]
25 College Street

My dearest Girl,

This moment I have set myself to copy some verses out fair. I cannot proceed with any degree of content. I must write you a line or two and see if that will assist in dismissing you from my Mind for ever so short a time. Upon my Soul I can think of nothing else. The time is passed when I had power to advise and warn you against the unpromising morning of my Life. My love has made me selfish. I cannot exist without you. I am forgetful of every thing but seeing you again—my Life seems to stop there—I see no further. You have absorb'd me. I have a sensation at the present moment as though I was dissolving—I should be exquisitely miserable without the hope of soon seeing you. I should be affraid to separate myself far from you. My sweet Fanny, will your heart never change? My love, will it? I have no limit now to my love—You[r] note came in just here—I cannot be happier away from you. 'Tis richer than an Argosy of Pearles. Do not threat me even in jest. I have been astonished that Men could die Martyrs for religion—I have shudder'd at it. I shudder no more—I could be martyr'd for my Religion—Love is my religion—I could die for that. I could die for you. My Creed is Love and you are its only tenet. You have ravish'd me away by a Power I cannot resist; and yet I could resist till I saw you; and even since I have seen you I have endeavoured often 'to reason against the reasons of my Love'.[1] I can do that no more—the pain would be too great. My love is selfish. I cannot breathe without you.

Yours for ever

JOHN KEATS

181   *John Keats to Fanny Brawne*

[19th October 1819]
Great Smith Street
Tuesday Morn

My sweet Fanny,

On awakening from my three days dream ('I cry to dream again')[2] I find one and another astonish'd at my idleness and thoughtlessness. I was miserable last night—the morning is always restorative. I must be busy, or try to be so. I have several things to speak to you of tomorrow morning. Mrs Dilke I should think will tell you that I purpose living at Hampstead. I must impose chains upon myself. I shall be able to do nothing. I sho[u]ld like to cast the die for Love or death. I have no Patience with any thing else—if you ever intend to be cruel to me as you

---

[1] John Ford, '*Tis Pity She's a Whore*, I.iii.   [2] *The Tempest*, III.ii, 152–5.

say in jest now but perhaps may sometimes be in earnest be so now
—and I will—my mind is in a tremble, I cannot tell what I am
writing.

Ever my love yours

JOHN KEATS

182   *John Keats to Fanny Brawne*

[Thursday 10th February 1820?]

My dearest Girl,

If illness makes such an agreeable variety in the manner of
you[r] eyes I should wish you sometimes to be ill. I wish I had
read your note before you went last night that I might have
assured you how far I was from suspecting any coldness. You had a
just right to be a little silent to one who speaks so plainly to you.
You must believe you shall, you will that I can do nothing say
nothing think nothing of you but what has its spring in the Love
which has so long been my pleasure and torment. On the night I
was taken ill when so violent a rush of blood came to my Lungs
that I felt nearly suffocated—I assure you I felt it possibly I
might not survive and at that moment though[t] of nothing but
you. When I said to Brown 'this is unfortunate'[1] I thought of you.
'Tis true that since the first two or three days other subjects have
entered my head. I shall be looking forward to Health and the
Spring and a regular routine of our old Walks.

Your affectionate

J. K.

813   *John Keats to Fanny Brawne*

[February 1820?]

My dear Fanny,

Do not let your mother suppose that you hurt me by writing
at night. For some reason or other your last night's note was not so

[1] Cf. *A Midsummer-Night's Dream*, IV.i.33.

244

treasureable as former ones. I would fain that you call me *Love* still. To see you happy and in high spirits is a great consolation to me—still let me believe that you are not half so happy as my restoration would make you. I am nervous, I own, and may think myself worse than I really am; if so you must indulge me, and pamper with that sort of tenderness you have manifested towards me in different Letters. My sweet creature when I look back upon the pains and torments I have suffer'd for you from the day I left you to go to the isle of Wight; the extasies in which I have pass'd some days and the miseries in their turn, I wonder the more at the Beauty which has kept up the spell so fervently. When I send this round I shall be in the front parlour watching to see you show yourself for a minute in the garden. How illness stands as a barrier betwixt me and you! Even if I was well—I must make myself as good a Philosopher as possible. Now I have had opportunities of passing nights anxious and awake I have found other thoughts intrude upon me. 'If I should die,' said I to myself, 'I have left no immortal work behind me—nothing to make my friends proud of my memory—but I have lov'd the principle of beauty in all things, and if I had had time I would have made myself remember'd.' Thoughts like these came very feebly while I was in health and every pulse beat for you—now you divide with this (may *I* say it?) 'last infirmity of noble minds'[1] all my reflection.

God bless you, Love.

J. KEATS

184   *John Keats to Fanny Brawne*

[February 1820?]

My dearest Fanny,

The power of your benediction is of not so weak a nature as to pass from the ring in four and twenty hours—it is like a sacred Chalice once consecrated and ever consecrate. I shall kiss your name and mine where your Lips have been—Lips! why should a poor prisoner as I am talk about such things. Thank God, though

[1] *Lycidas*, I.71.

I hold them the dearest pleasures in the universe, I have a consolation independent of them in the certainty of your affection. I could write a song in the style of Tom Moore's Pathetic about Memory if that would be any relief to me. No 'twould not. I will be as obdurate as a Robin. I will not sing in a cage. Health is my expected heaven and you are my Houri—this word I believe is both singular and plural—if only plural, never mind—you are a thousand of them.

Ever yours affectionately
my dearest—

J. K.

You had better not come to-day.

185 *John Keats to Fanny Brawne*

[March 1820?]

Sweetest Fanny,

You fear, sometimes, I do not love you so much as you wish? My dear Girl I love you ever and ever and without reserve. The more I have known you the more have I lov'd. In every way—even my jealousies have been agonies of Love, in the hottest fit I ever had I would have died for you. I have vex'd you too much. But for Love! Can I help it? You are always new. The last of your kisses was ever the sweetest; the last smile the brightest; the last movement the gracefullest. When you pass'd my window home yesterday, I was fill'd with as much admiration as if I had then seen you for the first time. You uttered a half complaint once that I only lov'd your Beauty. Have I nothing else then to love in you but that? Do not I see a heart naturally furnish'd with wings imprison itself with me? No ill prospect has been able to turn your thoughts a moment from me. This perhaps should be as much a subject of sorrow as joy—but I will not talk of that. Even if you did not love me I could not help an entire devotion to you: how much more deeply then must I feel for you knowing you love me. My Mind has been the most discontented and restless one that ever was put into a body too small for it. I never felt my Mind repose upon

246

anything with complete and undistracted enjoyment—upon no person but you. When you are in the room my thoughts never fly out of window: you always concentrate my whole senses. The anxiety shown about our Loves in your last note is an immense pleasure to me: however you must not suffer such speculations to molest you any more: nor will I any more believe you can have the least pique against me. Brown is gone out—but here is Mrs Wylie—when she is gone I shall be awake for you.—Remembrances to your Mother.

Your affectionate

J. KEATS

[May 1820]
Tuesday Morn—

My dearest Girl,

I wrote a Letter for you yesterday expecting to have seen your mother. I shall be selfish enough to send it though I know it may give you a little pain, because I wish you to see how unhappy I am for love of you, and endeavour as much as I can to entice you to give up your whole heart to me whose whole existence hangs upon you. You could not step or move an eyelid but it would shoot to my heart—I am greedy of you. Do not think of any thing but me. Do not live as if I was not existing—Do not forget me—But have I any right to say you forget me? Perhaps you think of me all day. Have I any right to wish you to be unhappy for me? You would forgive me for wishing it, if you knew the extreme passion I have that you should love me—and for you to love me as I do you, you must think of no one but me, much less write that sentence. Yesterday and this morning I have been haunted with a sweet vision—I have seen you the whole time in your shepherdess dress. How my senses have ached at it![1] How my heart has been devoted to it! How my eyes have been full of Tears at it! I[n]deed I think a real Love is enough to occupy the widest heart—Your going to town alone, when I heard of it was a shock to me—yet I

---

[1] Cf. *Othello*, IV.ii.68.

247

expected it—*promise me you will not for some time, till I get better.* Promise me this and fill the paper full of the most endearing names. If you cannot do so with good will, do my Love tell me— say what you think—confess if your heart is too much fasten'd on the world. Perhaps then I may see you at a greater distance, I may not be able to appropriate you so closely to myself. Were you to loose a favorite bird from the cage, how would your eyes ache after it as long as it was in sight; when out of sight you would recover a little. Perhaps if you would, if so it is, confess to me how many things are necessary to you besides me, I might be happier, by being less tantaliz'd. Well may you exclaim, how selfish, how cruel, not to let me enjoy my youth! to wish me to be unhappy! You must be so if you love me—upon my Soul I can be contented with nothing else. If you could really what is call'd enjoy yourself at a Party—if you can smile in peoples faces, and wish them to admire you *now*, you never have nor ever will love me. I see *life* in nothing but the certainty of your Love—convince me of it my sweetest. If I am not somehow convinc'd I shall die of agony. If we love we must not live as other men and women do—I cannot brook the wolfsbane[1] of fashion and foppery and tattle. You must be mine to die upon the rack if I want you. I do not pretend to say I have more feeling than my fellows—but I wish you seriously to look over my letters kind and unkind and consider whether the Person who wrote them can be able to endure much longer the agonies and uncertainties which you are so peculiarly made to create—My recovery of bodily hea[l]th will be of no benefit to me if you are not all mine when I am well. For God's sake save me— or tell me my passion is of too awful a nature for you. Again God bless you

J. K.

No—my sweet Fanny—I am wrong. I do not want you to be unhappy—and yet I do, I must while there is so sweet a Beauty— my loveliest my darling! Good bye! I kiss you—O the torments!

[1] Cf. 'Ode on Melancholy', 1.2.

[5th July? 1820]
Wednesday Morng.

My dearest Girl,

I have been a walk this morning with a book in my hand, but
as usual I have been occupied with nothing but you I wish I could
say in an agreeable manner. I am tormented day and night. They
talk of my going to Italy. 'Tis certain I shall never recover if I am
to be so long separate from you yet with all this devotion to you I
cannot persuade myself into any confidence of you. Past experience
connected with the fact of my long separation from you gives me
agonies which are scarcely to be talked of. When your mother
comes I shall be very sudden and expert in asking her whether you
have been to Mrs Dilke's, for she might say no to make me easy. I
am literally worn to death, which seems my only recourse. I cannot
forget what has pass'd. What? nothing with a man of the world,
but to me deathful. I will get rid of this as much as possible. When
you were in the habit of flirting with Brown you would have left
off, could your own heart have felt one half of one pang mine did.
Brown is a good sort of Man—he did not know he was doing me to
death by inches. I feel the effect of every one of those hours in my
side now; and for that cause, though he has done me many services,
though I know his love and friendship for me, though at this
moment I should be without pence were it not for his assistance, I
will never see or speak to him until we are both old men, if we
are to be. I *will* resent my heart having been made a football. You
will call this madness. I have heard you say that it was not unpleasant to wait a few years—you have amusements—your mind
is away—you have not brooded over one idea as I have, and how
should you? You are to me an object intensely desireable—the air
I breathe in a room empty of you is unhealthy. I am not the same
to you—no—you can wait—you have a thousand activities—you
can be happy without me. Any part, any thing to fill up the day
has been enough. How have you pass'd this month? Who have
you smil'd with? All this may seem savage in me. You do not feel
as I do—you do not know what it is to love—one day you may—
your time is not come. Ask yourself how many unhappy hours
Keats has caused you in Loneliness. For myself I have been a
Martyr the whole time, and for this reason I speak; the confession

is forc'd from me by the torture. I appeal to you by the blood of that Christ you believe in: Do not write to me if you have done anything this month which it would have pained me to have seen. You may have altered—if you have not—if you still behave in dancing rooms and other societies as I have seen you—I do not want to live—if you have done so I wish this coming night may be my last. I cannot live without you, and not only you but *chaste you; virtuous you.* The Sun rises and sets, the day passes, and you follow the bent of your inclination to a certain extent—you have no conception of the quantity of miserable feeling that passes through me in a day.—Be serious! Love is not a plaything—and again do not write unless you can do it with a crystal conscience. I would sooner die for want of you than—

Yours for ever

J. KEATS

188 *John Keats to Fanny Brawne*

[July 1820]

My dearest Fanny,

My head is puzzled this morning, and I scarce know what I shall say though I am full of a hundred things. 'Tis certain I would rather be writing to you this morning, notwithstanding the alloy of grief in such an occupation, than enjoy any other pleasure, with health to boot, unconnected with you. Upon my soul I have loved you to the extreme. I wish you could know the Tenderness with which I continually brood over your different aspects of countenance, action and dress. I see you come down in the morning: I see you meet me at the Window—I see every thing over again eternally that I ever have seen. If I get on the pleasant clue I live in a sort of happy misery, if on the unpleasant 'tis miserable misery. You complain of my illtreating you in word thought and deed—I am sorry,—at times I feel bitterly sorry that I ever made you unhappy —my excuse is that those words have been wrung from me by the sha[r]pness of my feelings. At all events and in any case I have been wrong; could I believe that I did it without any cause, I should be the most sincere of Penitents. I could give way to my repentant feelings now, I could recant all my suspicions, I could mingle with your heart and Soul though absent, were it not for some parts of your Letters. Do you suppose it possible I could ever leave you? You know what I think of myself and what of you. You know that I should feel how much it was my loss and how little yours. My friends laugh at you! I know some of them—when I know them all I shall never think of them again as friends or even acquaintances. My friends have behaved well to me in every instance but one, and there they have become tattlers, and inquisitors into my conduct: spying upon a secret I would rather die than share it with any body's confidence. For this I cannot wish them well, I care not to see any of them again. If I am the Theme, I will not be the Friend of idle Gossips. Good gods what a shame it is our Loves should be so put into the microscope of a Coterie. Their laughs should not affect you (I may perhaps give you reasons some day for these laughs, for I suspect a few people to hate me well enough, *for reasons I know of,* who have pretended a great friendship for me) when in competition with one, who if he never should see you again would make you the Saint of his memory. These Laughers, who do not like you, who envy you for your Beauty, who would have God-bless'd me from you for ever: who were plying me with discouragements with respect to you eternally. People are revengeful —do not mind them—do nothing but love me—if I knew that for certain life and health will in such event be a heaven, and death itself will be less painful. I long to believe in immortality. I shall never be able to bid you an entire farewell. If I am destined to be happy with you here—how short is the longest Life. I wish to believe in immortality—I wish to live with you for ever. Do not let my name ever pass between you and those laughers, if I have no other merit than the great Love for you, that were sufficient to keep me sacred and unmentioned in such Society. If I have been cruel and unjust I swear my love has ever been greater than my cruelty which last[s] but a minute whereas my Love come what will shall last for ever. If concession to me has hurt your Pride, god knows I have had little pride in my heart when thinking of you. Your name never passes my Lips—do not let mine pass yours —Those people do not like me. After reading my Letter you even then wish to see me. I am strong enough to walk over—but I dare not. I shall feel so much pain in parting with you again. My dearest love, I am affraid to see you, I am strong but not strong enough to

251

see you. Will my arm be ever round you again. And if so shall I be obliged to leave you again. My sweet Love! I am happy whilst I believe your first Letter. Let me be but certain that you are mine heart and soul, and I could die more happily than I could otherwise live. If you think me cruel—if you think I have sleighted you—do muse it over again and see into my heart. My Love to you is 'true as truth's simplicity and simpler than the infancy of truth' as I think I once said before How could I slight you? How threaten to leave you? not in the spirit of a Threat to you—no—but in the spirit of Wretchedness in myself. My fairest, my delicious, my angel Fanny! do not believe me such a vulgar fellow. I will be as patient in illness and as believing in Love as I am able.

Yours for ever my dearest

JOHN KEATS

189 *John Keats to Fanny Brawne*

[August 1820?]

My dearest Girl,

I wish you could invent some means to make me at all happy without you. Every hour I am more and more concentrated in you; every thing else tastes like chaff in my Mouth. I feel it almost impossible to go to Italy—the fact is I cannot leave you, and shall never taste one minute's content until it pleases chance to let me live with you for good. But I will not go on at this rate. A person in health as you are can have no conception of the horror that nerves and a temper like mine go through. What Island do your friends propose retiring to? I should be happy to go with you there alone, but in company I should object to it; the backbitings and jealousies of new colonists who have nothing else to amuse themselves, is unbearable. M*r* Dilke came to see me yesterday. and gave me a very great deal more pain than pleasure. I shall never be able any more to endure to [*for* the] society of any of those who used to meet at Elm Cottage and Wentworth Place. The last two years taste like brass upon my Palate. If I cannot live with you I will live alone. I do not think my health will improve much while I am separated from you. For all this I am averse to seeing you—I cannot bear flashes of light and return into my glooms again. I am not so unhappy now as I should be if I had seen you yesterday. To be happy with you seems such an impossibility! it requires a luckier Star than mine! it will never be. I enclose a passage from one of your Letters which I want you to alter a little—I want (if you will have it so) the matter express'd less coldly to me. If my health would bear it, I could write a Poem which I have in my head, which would be a consolation for people in such a situation as mine. I would show some one in Love as I am, with a person living in such Liberty as you do. Shakspeare always sums up matters in the most sovereign manner. Hamlet's heart was full of such Misery as mine is when he said to Ophelia 'Go to a Nunnery, go, go!'[1] Indeed I should like to give up the matter at once—I should like to die. I am sickened at the brute world which you are smiling with. I hate men and women more. I see nothing but thorns for the future—wherever I may be next winter in Italy or nowhere Brown will be living near you with his indecencies—I see no prospect of any rest. Suppose me in Rome—well, I should there see you as in a magic glass going to and from town at all hours, —— I wish you could infuse a little confidence in human nature into my heart. I cannot muster any—the world is too brutal for me—I am glad there is such a thing as the grave—I am sure I shall never have any rest till I get there. At any rate I will indulge myself by never seeing any more Dilke or Brown or any of their Friends. I wish I was either in your arms full of faith or that a Thunder bolt would strike me.

God bless you.

J. K.

[1] *Hamlet*, III.i, 124–58.

1799   1845

THOMAS HOOD

Thomas Hood was a great comic writer who came to fame for his editing of the *Comic Annual*. Given, like Charles Lamb, to punning he defended himself in a couplet;

> However critics may take offense
> A double meaning has a double sense.

What schoolboy does not know his poem 'Eugene Aram' which first appeared in another annual called *The Gem*.

His wife, sister of John Hamilton Reynolds, was said to have had one of the sweetest tempers in the world, loved a joke even if it went against herself, and was a woman of excellent sense. They were married on 5th May 1824.

190   *Thomas Hood to his wife*

Coblenz, March 13th [1835]

At last, my own dearest and best, I sit down to write to you, and I fear you have been looking anxiously for news from me. . . . I am writing but a business letter, and you must give me credit, my own dearest, for everything else, as I wish to devote all the space I can to describing what will be for your comfort. . . . I have been like the wandering Jew. How my thoughts and wishes fly over the vine-covered hills to meet yours; my love set towards you like the mighty current of the great Rhine itself, and will brook no impediments.

I grudge the Common-place I have been obliged to write; every sentence should claim you, as my own dear wife, the pride of my youth, the joy of my manhood, the hope of all my after days. Twice has the shadow of death come between us, but our hearts are preserved to throb against each other. I am content for your sake to wait the good time when you may safely undertake the voyage, and do not let your heart run away with your head. . . . I forgot to say at Coblenz the men frequent the Casinos, and the women make evening parties of their own, but I do not mean to give up my old domestic habits. We shall set an example of fire-side felicity, if that can be said of a stove, for we have no grates here—the more's the pity. God bless you. Ever—your own

T. H.

191   *Thomas Hood to his wife*

[Coblenz—1835?]

My own dearest and best Love, . . . I do hope you will soon be able to come, and in the meantime I will do everything I can think of to facilitate your progress . . .

I saw a vision of you, dearest, to-day, and felt you leaning on me, and looking over the Moselle at the blue mountains and vine-yards. I long but to get to work with you and the pigeon pair by my side, and then I shall not sigh for the past. . . . Get yourselves strong, there is still a happy future; fix your eyes forward on our meeting, my best and dearest.

Our little home, though homely, will be happy for us, and we do not bid England a very long good-night. Good-night, too, my dearest wife, my pride and comfort.

255

And from these mountains where I now respire,
Fain would I waft much blessing unto thee,
As with a sigh I deem thou now might'st be to me—

192   *Thomas Hood to his wife*

[no date]

My own dearest and best,—We parted manfully and
womanfully as we ought. I drank only half a bottle of the Rhine
wine, and only the half of that, ere I fell asleep on the sofa, which
lasted two hours. It was the reaction, for your going tired me
more than I cared to show. Then I drank the other half, and as that
did not do, I went and retraced our walk in the park, and sat down
in *the same seat*, and felt happier and better. Have you not a
romantic old husband?

JANE CARLYLE

Jane Baillie Welsh was the only child of Dr Welsh of Haddington. She was married to Thomas Carlyle (after a love affair with Edward Irving, a schoolmaster at Haddington) on 17th October 1826. They were miserably poor and Carlyle at first thought of living, as a farmer, at Craigenputtock, a remote and depressing farmhouse belonging to his wife's mother. Jane poured scorn on his idea of farming about which he knew nothing. And, indeed, it is amusing to think of Carlyle, the man who fled from Edward FitzGerald's house near Woodbridge, because the cock's crowing disturbed him at night, running a farm at all. However, they lived for a short time in a cottage on the estate with only one servant.

But it was London which attracted Carlyle, apart from being nearer sources for his material on his book *The French Revolution* and, in 1834, they took No. 5 Cheyne Row, Chelsea, and here Carlyle lived until his death. In her letters to her mother, to her friends, even to Thomas when he was away from home, Jane tells how she battled with fleas, dull, if not actually stupid maids, and redecorating the house, in order that Thomas should have a noise-free room in which to work.

At the end of 1865 Carlyle was elected to the Rectorship of Edinburgh University and went to deliver an address there on 2nd April 1866. He was still in Scotland when Jane, thought to have recovered from a hopeless illness, died suddenly as she was getting out of her carriage. Her death is supposed to be due to shock caused by an accident to her dog.

That night, as she lay dead in her bedroom, the candles were lighted about her. Years ago she had upset her mother by refusing to use some wax candles. These she had kept until they were used in this way.

The letters she wrote to Carlyle are always full of affection and concern for a man who was difficult at the best of times. The real truth of their marriage, their love, is that it flourished only when they were apart from each other. One cannot imagine either of them married to anyone else, yet, together in London, they worked upon each other until one or the other was driven away from home. After her death Carlyle lived on, overcome by remorse and very lonely. He died in 1881.

193   Jane Carlyle to Thomas Carlyle, Craigenputtock

Templand,
December 30th, 1828

Goody, Goody, dear Goody,—you said you would weary and I do hope in my heart you are wearying. It will be so sweet to make it all up to you in kisses when I return. You will *take me* and hear all my bits of experiences, and your heart will beat when you find how I have longed to return to you. Darling, Dearest, Loveliest, 'The Lord bless you.' I think of you every hour, every moment. I love you and admire you like,—like anything. My own Good Good! But to get away on Sunday was not in my power, my mother argued, entreated, and finally *grat*. I held out on the ground of having appointed Alick to meet me at Church; but he was untenable, John Kerr could be sent off at break of day to tell that I could not come. I urged that the household would find themselves destitute of every Christian *comfoart*, unless I were home before Wednesday. That could be taken care of by sending anything that was wanted from here. Tea, sugar, butcher's meat, everything was at my service. Well, but I wanted, I said, to be your *first foot* on New Year's Day. I might be gratified in this also. She would *hire a post-chaise and take me over for that day* on condition

258

that I returned at night! In short, she had a remedy for everything but death, and I could not without seeming unkind and ungracious, refuse to stay longer than I proposed. So I write this letter 'with my own hand' that you may not be *disappointed* from day to day but prepare to welcome me in 'your choicest mood' on Sunday. If the day is at all tolerable, perhaps Alick or you will meet me at Church. Mrs. Crichton, of Dabton, was very pressing that you and I should spend some days with them just now, 'when their house was full of company'. But I assured her it would be losing labour to ask you. However, by way of consolation, I have agreed to 'refresh' a party for her with my presence on Friday, and held out some hope that you would visit them at your leisure. 'I am sure the kindness of those people . . .' 'The Lord bless them'!

Dearest, I wonder if you are getting any victual. There must be cocks at least, and the chickens will surely have laid their eggs. I have many an anxious thought about you; and I wonder if you sleep at nights, or if you are wandering about—on, on—smoking and killing mice. Oh, if I was there I could put my arms so close about your neck, hush you into the softest sleep you have had since I went away. Goodnight—you will get a parcel by Macnight and Andrew Watsons in which there is a little tea in case it be needed, for I do not expect the things from Ednr. this week as I understand Eliza is gone out of town for a few days to some great house-heating.

Good night, my beloved. Dream of me.

I am ever,

Your own GOODY

194 *Jane Carlyle to Thomas Carlyle, Chelsea*

Liverpool,
July 2nd, 1844

Indeed, dear, you look to be almost unhappy enough already! I do not want you to suffer physically, only morally, you understand,

and to hear of your having to take coffee at night and all that gives me *no wicked satisfaction*, but makes me quite unhappy. It is curious how much more uncomfortable I feel without you, when it is I who am going away from you, and not, as it used to be, you gone away from me. I am always wondering since I came here how I can, even in my angriest mood, talk about leaving you for good and all; for to be sure, if I were to leave you today *on that principle*, I should need absolutely to go back tomorrow *to see how you were taking it*.

195 *Jane Carlyle to Thomas Carlyle, Chelsea*

Seaforth House
Friday, July 12th, 1844

Dearest Good,

You are really a jewel of a Husband in the article of writing! It is *such* a comfort to me when the nice looking little letter drops surely in! . . .

My cold is pretty well gone. I dare not take all the liberty I should like with myself in this beautiful place; but I can go now in *moderation*, and can enjoy what joy is going. It is really curious, however, how the Devil is always busy! No sooner have I got rid of my headache and sore-throat, than a new botheration arises for me in what Geraldine *rightly* termed her 'Tiger-jealousy.' You will hardly be able to conceive how *this* could be anything but *laughable*; but I assure you it has entirely spoiled my comfort for the last twenty-four hours; and not mine only, but Mrs. Paulet's and everybody else's in the house. We were fancying her [Geraldine] bilious, and it turned out to have been all rage at *me* for 'giving such a *stab* to her feelings as she had never suffered the like of from man or woman!' She came here on the understanding that I was to go back with her to Manchester and stay there a few days on the road to London. But the day before yesterday, when she was alone with me, in my room, I, wearied out with my cold, and feeling that I had to go back to Maryland Street in the first instance, it very naturally fell from me, 'but since we are together *here*, Geraldine, the going to Manchester does not seem to be any longer

260

necessary?' she answered me pettishly that 'if I *wished* to *sacrifice* her to Mrs. Paulet and the Welshes, in God's name to do it!' and went off in a nice little tiff. But I never thought of her being seriously offended. And she had thrown the whole company into consternation by her rudeness to Mrs. Paulet and myself, before we fancied that she was anything else than 'out of sorts'. All yesterday, however, her vagaries exceeded my reminiscences of Mrs. Jordan in the 'Jealous Wife'! Nothing but outbursts of impertinence and hysterics from morning till night, which finished off with a grand *scene* in my room after I had gone up to bed—a full and faithful account of which I shall entertain you with at meeting. It was a *revelation* to me not only of Geraldine but of human nature. Such mad, *lover-like* jealousy on the part of one woman towards another, it has never entered into my heart to conceive. By a wonderful effort of *patience* on my part,—made more on Mrs. Paulet's account, who was quite vexed, than from the *flattering* consideration that *I* was the object of this incomprehensible passion,—the affair was brought to a happy conclusion. I got her to laugh over her own absurdity, promised to go by Manchester, if she would behave herself like a reasonable creature; and with her hair all dishevelled, and her face all bewept, she thereupon sat down at my feet and—smoked a cigarette!! with all the placidity in life! She keeps a regular supply of these little things, and smokes them before all the world. In fact, I am not at all sure that she is not *going mad*! and Mrs. Paulet, too, declares she often feels quite anxious about her.

I like this Mrs. Darbyshire very much; and another lady who was here yesterday enchanted me with her music. I never heard such singing in my life. So send the *trio*, for God's sake. I keep to my purpose of going back to Maryland Street on Monday.

Ever your own JANE CARLYLE

CHARLES JAMES MATHEWS

In his *Autobiography*, 1879, Charles James Mathews relates how he first saw Madame Vestris. He had been ill and, at a visit to 'the Olympic' theatre, he was carried downstairs in the arms of his Italian servant, in order to avoid the crowds at the doors. 'After our departure', he says, 'a lady remarked to the stage-manager, looking at me as I was lifted into the carriage, "Ah, poor young man, it's all over with him—he's not long for this world!" How astonished would that lady have been had she been told that she would be my wife of eighteen years which, however, turned out to be the case.'

The lady was, of course, Madame Vestris, some six years older than Charles and whom he married in 1838. In 1856 Charles was confined in Lancaster Castle gaol for debt. It was then he wrote her these tender letters.

196　*Charles James Mathews to Madame Vestris (his wife)*

Lancaster, July 5, 1856

My own dearest Love,—In spite of all my hard struggles, I have the sad task to announce to you that I have been arrested and brought here. For God's sake, do not let the news overwhelm you! I know no other mode of acquainting you with it, and think that a long beginning is almost worse than the truth at once. . . .

I leave you to conceive the agony of my despair. But one thought rushed upon me—the thought of you, my poor, suffering, beloved wife. How were you to be informed of it, and what would be the effect it would have on you? I shall never forget that moment. All I have gone through for the last twenty years saw nothing to the supreme anguish of that moment. . . . I had never before been within a real *bona fide* prison in all its horrors. I will not describe them, my beloved one; I do not wish to add to your misery. . . .

I have telegraphed to Knowles and to Smith, also to Manchester to Knowles's lawyer, and am writing in every direction and to everybody I can think of. I am totally helpless, and in the depths of despair till I know what my fate is to be. Oh what a day I shall pass to-morrow, instead of passing it in my own beloved home. When I think of your state of mind and body, I dread to hear of the consequences. I will not attempt to preach quiet and calmness —the position is beyond all that; and I cannot expect from you, in your sad state, that which I cannot command myself. . . .

God bless and protect you, my own beloved, adored wife. . . . Forgive me the misery I cause you; I am sufficiently punished.

Your ever affectionate, miserable husband

C. J. MATHEWS

God help me! a thousand, thousand kisses!

197 *Charles James Mathews to Madame Vestris*

Lancaster, July 9, 1856

My own dearest Love,—As to the coming here, I can only say it is *madness*. If we could meet, or be together in private even for an hour, it would be different; though to bring you away from your room in your state, and without the power to have the slightest comfort in this beastly town, and away from your doctor, would be to urge you to your complete prostration, and to bring you to your grave at once. But to see you in a stone room, in the presence of a horrid turnkey, without the means of even giving you a seat after a walk of many hundred yards through paved courts and stone staircases, in the midst of prisoners and convicts, would be actually *making* misery of so dreadful a nature as not to be borne for a moment, even in contemplation. You would never arrive to the frightful reality—you would sink in the attempt.

For mercy's sake, let me implore—let me intreat and conjure you to dismiss such an idea from your mind! Think what it would be! . . .

Do, pray do, dearest beloved Lizzy, listen to me, and try to bear up. Think what agony it is for me to know you are in such an awful state as that Mrs Morrisson describes. It is truly heart-rending, and my feelings are not to be described. I am positively annihilated. God bless you.

Your affectionate husband,

C. J. MATHEWS

198   *Charles James Mathews to Madame Vestris*

July 19, 1856

My own dearest beloved Wife,—Your reminder of our wedding-day brought the tears into my eyes; for though I may be inattentive to such anniversaries generally, my heart must be made of stone not to care to mind and contrast the happiness experienced on that blessed day and the misery endured yesterday.

Believe me, my darling Lizzie, when I swear that my love for you is as true at this moment as it was eighteen years ago, and that sufferings and your fortitude under all the ills of this world endear you more to me every hour. All this I hoped to have been able to say to you instead of write, but after spending a day of expectation and hope, I have been cruelly disappointed . . .

You will get this on Monday morning, for though there is no delivery in London to-morrow, the post goes to-night, consequently I avoid the annoyance of not being able to write to-morrow. On Monday, I will send you a telegram to announce the judge's decision, and if favourable, shall follow it myself by the first train that starts. It is an age to look forward to, and I cannot look it in the face at all. I am quite broken down and broken-hearted.

This long separation has already unmanned me, and if I have still to remain here, I am sure my spirits and fortitude must give way.

God bless and protect you, my own beloved, adored wife, and give you strength and courage to support our dreadful calamities, better than I am able to do, and grant that we may soon meet to part no more, but to live to comfort each other for the future in peace and tranquillity.

Believe ever, my beloved wife, in weal and in woe,
Your truly affectionate husband,

C. J. MATHEWS

ELIZABETH BARRETT

The love affair between Robert Browning and Elizabeth Barrett is too well known to comment on. Perhaps not so well known are the noble love letters they wrote each other. Elizabeth, herself, is enshrined for us in the words of Miss Mitford who described her as a young woman: 'A slight, delicate figure with a shower of dark curls falling on each side of a most expressive face: large, tender eyes, richly fringed by dark eyelashes and a smile like a sunbeam.'

Elizabeth Barrett is the prisoner figure of Romance, held captive in the cage of her father's house in Wimpole Street, London. From this prison she, a fine poet, languishing with love and ill-health, is rescued by another poet, Robert Browning, who by the force of his character and energy restores her to health and happiness. The wicked father is left to long years of regret after his beloved daughter has eloped.

Whatever truth there is in such a picture, it is a fact that Elizabeth suffered from fragile health, that she fell ideally in love with Robert Browning and he with her and that, in 1846, they eloped to Italy. The marriage was wonderfully happy. Elizabeth died in Florence in 1861, leaving one son. Robert Browning lived until 1889 and is buried in Westminster Abbey.

Tuesday
(Postmark, February 24, 1846)

Ah, sweetest, in spite of our agreement, here is the note that sought not to go, but must—because, if there is no speaking of Mrs Jamesons and such like without bringing in your dear name (not *dearest* name, my Ba!) what is the good of not writing it down, now, when I, though possessed with the love of it no more than usual, yet *may* speak, and to a hearer? And I have to thank you with all my heart for the good news of the increasing strength and less need for the opium—how I do thank you, my dearest—and desire to thank God through whose goodness it all is! This I could not but say now, tomorrow I will write at length, having been working a little this morning, with whatever effect. So now I will go out and see your elm-trees and gate, and think the thoughts over again, and coming home I shall perhaps find a letter.

Dearest, dearest—my perfect blessing you are!

May God continue his care for us.   R

[September 1846]

Dearest take this word, as if it were many. I am so tired—and then it shall be the right word.

Sunday and Friday are impossible. On Saturday I will go to you, if you like—with half done,—nothing done—scarcely. Will you come for me to Hodgson's? or shall I meet you at the station? At what o'clock should I set out, to be there at the hour you mention?

Also, for the boxes—we cannot carry them out of the house, you know, Wilson and I. They must be sent on Friday evening to the Vauxhall station, 'to be taken care of.' Will the people keep them carefully? Ought someone to be spoken to beforehand? If we sent them to New Cross, they would not reach you in time.

Hold me my beloved—with your love. It is very hard—But Saturday seems the only day for us. Tell me if you think so indeed.

Your very own B A

1 p.m. Saturday[1] [Post-mark, September 12, 1846]

You will only expect a few words—what will those be? When the heart is full it may run over, but the real fulness stays within.

You asked me yesterday 'if I should repent?' Yes—my own Ba,—I could wish all the past were to do over again, that in it I might somewhat more,—never so little more, conform in the outward homage to the inward feeling. What I have professed . . . (for I have performed nothing) seems to fall short of what my first love required even—and when I think of *this* moment's love . . . I could repent, as I say.

Words can never tell you, however,—form them, transform them anyway,—how perfectly dear you are to me—perfectly dear to my heart and soul.

I look back, and in every one point, every word and gesture, *every* letter, every silence—you have been entirely perfect to me—I would not change one word, one look.

My hope and aim are to preserve this love, not to fall from it —for which I trust to God who procured it for me, and doubtlessly can preserve it.

Enough now, my dearest, dearest, own Ba! You have given me the highest, completest proof of love that ever one human being gave another. I am all gratitude—and all pride (under the proper feeling which ascribes pride to the right source) all pride that my life has been so crowned by you.

God bless you prays your very own R.

I will write to-morrow of course. Take every care of *my life* which is in that dearest little hand; try and be composed, my beloved.

Remember to thank Wilson for me.

[1] They were married on 12th September 1846 in St. Marylebone Parish Church.

Sunday [Post-mark, September 14, 1846]

My Own Beloved, if ever you should have reason to complain of me in things voluntary and possible, all other women would have a right to tread me underfoot, I should be so vile and utterly unworthy. There is my answer to what you wrote yesterday of wishing to be better to me . . . you! What could be better than lifting me from the ground and carrying me into life and the sunshine? I was yours rather by right than by gift (yet by gift also, my beloved!); for what you have saved and renewed is surely yours. All that I am, I owe you—if I enjoy anything now and henceforth, it is through you. You know this well. Even as *I*, from the beginning, knew that I had no power against you . . . or that, if I *had* it was for your sake.

Dearest, in the emotion and confusion of yesterday morning, there was yet room in me for one thought which was not a feeling —for I thought that, of the many, many women who have stood where I stood, and to the same end, not one of them all perhaps, not one perhaps, since that building was a church, has had reasons strong as mine, for an absolute trust and devotion towards the man she married,—not one! And then I both thought and felt, that it was only just, for them . . . those women who were less happy, . . . to have that affectionate sympathy and support and presence of their nearest relations, parent or sister . . . which failed to *me*, . . . needing it less through being happier!

All my brothers have been here this morning, laughing and talking, and discussing this matter of the leaving town,—and in the room, at the same time, were two or three female friends of ours, from Herefordshire—and I did not dare to cry out against the noise, though my head seemed splitting in two (one-half for each shoulder), I had such a morbid fear of exciting a suspicion. Treppy too being one of them, I promised to go to see her to-morrow and dine in her drawing-room if she would give me, for dinner, some bread and butter. It was like having a sort of fever. And all in the midst, the bells began to ring. 'What bells are those?' asked one of the provincials. 'Marylebone Church bells,' said Henrietta, standing behind my chair.

And now . . . while I write, having escaped from the great din, and sit here quietly,—comes . . . who do you think?—Mr. Kenyon.

269

He came with his spectacles, looking as if his eyes reached to their rim all the way round; and one of the first words was, *'When did you see Browning?'* And I think I shall make a pretension to presence of mind henceforward; for, though *certainly* I changed colour and he saw it, I yet answered with a tolerably quick evasion, . . . 'He was here on Friday'—and leapt straight into another subject, and left him gazing fixedly on my face. Dearest, he saw something, but not all. So we talked, talked. He told me that the 'Fawn of Sertorius' (which I refused to cut open the other day) was ascribed to Landor and he told me that he meant to leave town again on Wednesday, and would see me once more before then. On rising to go away, he mentioned your name a second time . . . 'When do you see Browning again?' To which I answered that I did not know.

Is not *that* pleasant? The worst is that all these combinations of things make me feel so bewildered that I cannot make the necessary arrangements, as far as the letters go. But I must break from the dream-stupor which falls on me when left to myself a little, and set about what remains to be done.

A house near Watford is thought of now—but, as none is concluded on, the removal is not likely to take place in the middle of the week even, perhaps.

I sit in a dream, when left to myself. I cannot believe, or understand. Oh! but in all this difficult, embarrassing and painful situation, I look over the palms to Troy—I feel happy and exulting to belong to you, past every opposition, out of sight of every will of man—none can put us asunder, now, at least. I have a right now openly to love you, and to hear other people call it a *duty*, when I do, . . . knowing that if it were a sin, it would be done equally. Ah—*I* shall not be the first to leave off *that*—see if I shall! May God bless you, ever and ever dearest! Beseech for me the indulgence of your father and mother, and ask your sister to love me. I feel so as if I had slipped down over the wall into some-body's garden—I feel ashamed. To be grateful and affectionate to them all, while I live; is all that I can do, and it is too much a matter of course to need to be promised. Promise it however for your very own Ba whom you made so happy with the dear letter last night. But say in the next how you are—and how your mother is.

I did hate so, to have to take off the ring. You will have to take the trouble of putting it on again, some day.

1809   1882

CHARLES ROBERT DARWIN

In *Emma Darwin, a Century of Family Letters* by H. E. Litchfield there is a delightful picture of Charles Darwin as a young man before he was internationally famous.

Darwin was born at Shrewsbury on 12th February 1809. He was the grandson of Dr Erasmus Darwin (who believed that plants could feel) and of Josiah Wedgwood, the famous potter. In 1838 he proposed to his cousin Emma and the job of house-hunting began. They eventually settled at Downe in Kent.

On 24th November 1859, Darwin published his great work *On the Origin of Species*, the first edition of which was sold out on the day of publication.

He died on 19th April 1882 and is buried in Westminster Abbey.

203   *Charles Darwin to Emma Wedgwood*
                    [30th November 1838], Friday Evening

[After many details on house hunting and domestic affairs . . .]

Powers of sentimentality forgive me for sending such a letter; it surely ought to have been written on foolscap paper, and closed with a wafer. I told you I should write to you as if you really were

271

my own dear, dear wife, and have not I kept my word most stoutly? My excuse must be, I have seen no one for these two days: and what can a man have to say, who works all morning in describing hawks and owls, and then rushes out and walks in a bewildered manner up one street and down another, looking out for the words 'To let'. I called, however, to-day on the Lyells. I cannot tell you how particularly pleasant and cordial Lyell's manner has been to me: I am sure he will be a steady and sure friend to both of us. He told me he heard from his sister (whom I know) in Scotland this morning, and she says, 'So Mr. Darwin is going to be married: I suppose he will be buried in the country, and lost to geology.' She little knows what a good, strict wife I am going to be married to, who will send me to my lessons and make me better, I trust, in every respect, as I am sure she will infinitely happier and happier the longer I live to enjoy my good fortune. Lyell and Madame gave me a very long and *solemn* lecture on the *extreme* importance, for our future comfort during our whole London lives, of choosing slowly and deliberately our visiting acquaintance: every disagreeable or commonplace acquaintance must separate us from our relations and real friends (that is without we give up our whole lives to visiting), for the evenings we sacrifice might have been spent with them *or at the theatre*. Lyell said we shall find the truth of his words before we have lived a year in London. How provokingly small the paper is, my own very dear Emma.

Good-night, C. D.

204   *Charles Darwin to Emma Wedgwood*

Shrewsbury, Wednesday Morning
[14th November 1838]

My dear Emma,

Marianne and Susan will have told you what joy and happiness the news gave all here. We have had innumerable cogitations; and the one conclusion I exult in is that there was never anyone so lucky as I have been, or so good as you. Indeed I can assure you, many times since leaving Maer, I have thought how little I expressed how much I owe to you; and as often as I think this, I vow to try to make myself good enough somewhat to deserve you. I hope you have taken deep thought about the sundry knotty points you will have to decide on. We must have a great deal of talk together when I come back on Saturday. Do have a fire in the Library—it is such a good place to have some quiet talk together. The question of houses, suburbs versus central London—rages violently around each fireplace in this house. Suburbs have rather the advantage at present; and this, of course, rather inclines one to seek out the arguments on the other side. The Governor gives much good advice to live, wherever it may be, the first year prudently and quietly. My chief fear is, that you will find, after living all your life with such large and agreeable parties as Maer only can boast of, our quiet evenings dull. You must bear in mind, as some young lady said, 'all men are brutes,' and that I take the line of being a solitary brute, so you must listen with much suspicion to all arguments in favour of retired places. I am so selfish, that I feel to have you to myself is having you so much more completely that I am not to be trusted. Like a child that has something it loves beyond measure, I long to dwell on the words *my own* dear Emma. As I am writing just as things come uppermost in my mind, I beg of you not to read my letters to anyone, for then I can fancy I am sitting by the side of my own dear future wife, and to her own self I do not care what nonsense I talk—so let me have my way, and scribble, without caring whether it be sense or nonsense. . . .

My father echoes and re-echoes uncle Jos's words, 'You have drawn a prize!' Certainly no man could by possibility receive a more cordial welcome than I did from every one at Maer on Monday morning. My life has been very happy and very fortunate, and many of my pleasantest remembrances are mingled up with scenes at Maer, and now it is crowned. My own dear Emma, I kiss the hands with all humbleness and gratitude, which have so filled up for me the cup of happiness—It is my most earnest wish I may make myself worthy of you. Good-bye.

Most affectionately yours,

CHAS. DARWIN

I would tear this letter up, and write it again, for it is a very silly one, but I can't write a better one.

Since writing the former part the post has brought in your own dear note to Katty. You tell me to be a good boy, and so I must be, but let me earnestly beg of you not to make up your mind in a hurry: you say *truly* Elizabeth never thinks of herself, but there is another person who never thinks of herself, but now she has to think of two people, and I am, thank Heaven for it, that other person. You must be absolute arbitress, but do, dear Emma, remember life is short, and two months is the sixth part of the year, and that year, the first, from which for my part, things shall hereafter date. Whatever you do will be right, but it will be *too* good to be unselfish for me until I am part of you—Dearest Emma, good-bye.

205   *Charles Darwin to Emma Wedgwood*

Saturday Afternoon [29th December 1838]

My dear Emma,

I am tired with having been all day at business work, but I cannot let a post go by without writing to tell you Gower Street is ours, yellow curtains and all. I have to-day paid some advance money, signed an agreement, and had the key given over to me, and the old woman informed me I was her master henceforth. . . . I long for the day when we shall enter the house together; how glorious it will be to see you seated by the fire of our own house. Oh, that it were the 14th instead of the 24th. Good-bye my own dear Emma.

I find I must wait in town till the latter end of next week, on account of the lease and paying the money, and I suspect I must attend the Geolog. Soc. on the 9th, so my plans are hampered. But what does anything signify to the possessor of Macaw Cottage?

JOHN RUSKIN

I was brought up in a house that was dominated by Ruskin's works. They were stiff, green-bound volumes on one shelf; on another the same works appeared in limp, green leather-bound volumes. Their titles were formidable to a small boy, *Modern Painters, The Stones of Venice, The Elements of Drawing*, and so on. It is very possible that most homes of this period had similar collections of Ruskin's works which, at least with me, were never opened. When later I did happen to open one of the books it was full of long words and high-flown ideas about architecture, beauty, truth and so on, which I did not understand. Ruskin seemed to me a hard, ruthless man, an exquisite draughtsman to be sure, but unreadable. It was not until I came to read *Praeterita* that I realised that this man I had taken to be strong and unbreakable like the 'Stones' he was so fond of writing about, was, in fact, one of the most tragic figures of the Victorian Age. For *Praeterita* is graceful, naïve, pathetic, one of the great books of 'Confessions', and deals with Ruskin's early memories.

The real trouble was the strong Calvinist faith of his mother, Margaret, who brought the child up under a rigid system of discipline and corporal punishment which coloured his whole life. John was born on 8th February 1819, in London. His father founded, in 1809, the sherry business of Ruskin, Telford and Domecq. He was a cultured man with a taste for literature and the arts which was to be of enormous benefit to his son, who accompanied him on travels to Cumberland, Scotland, the Black

Forest and to Switzerland where John first saw the Alps, a dominating passion in his life.

John Ruskin married—or was married by his parents to—Euphemia (Effie) Chalmers Gray. It was an unhappy time for both of them for John was completely incapable of satisfying Effie sexually and socially. She was a brilliant woman who enjoyed society, and after six years of a Calvinist hell, she left Ruskin, their marriage nullified under Scots law, and married the painter John Everett Millais. A great deal of mystery surrounded this Victorian 'scandal', and it was not fully resolved until Sir William James published his book *The Order of Release* (from which the following letters are extracted) in 1948. John Ruskin died on 20th January 1900 at Brantwood and is buried in Coniston churchyard.

206   *John Ruskin to Effie Gray*

Denmark Hill
9 November 1847

My own Effie—my kind Effie—my mistress—my friend—my queen—my darling—my only love—how good of you—and I can't answer you a word today. I am going into town with my mother in half an hour—and have all manner of things to do, first —but I am so glad that you have my letter speaking about this very thing—Indeed I *never* will be jealous of you—and I will keep that purer form of jealousy—that longing for more love—within proper limits—and you will soon find out how to manage this weakness—and perhaps to conquer it altogether; I can't enter into details today—but indeed it was anxiety and weakness of nerve which made me so fretful when you were here—natural enough I think—and even then, I was only jealous of *some people*—and that because I was hurt by your *condescension*—it was, I think—at the root—more pride than jealousy—I was speaking of large parties to my mother yesterday for you—she said 'You would'nt like to see her surrounded by a circle of gentlemen like Mrs Loddell?' 'Indeed I should,' I said.

207 *John Ruskin to Effie Gray*
[Extract]

Denmark Hill
11 November 1847

When we are *alone*—You and I—together—Mais—c'est inconceivable—I was just trying—this evening after dinner—to imagine our sitting after dinner at Keswick—vous et moi.—I couldn't do it—it seemed so impossible that I should ever get you all to myself—and then I said to myself 'If she should be dull—if she should not be able to think but of her sweet sisters—her deserted home—her parents—giving up their chief joy—if she should be sad—what *shall* I do—And—if she should *not*—what shall I do—either—how shall I ever tell her my gladness—Oh—my own Love—what shall I do indeed—I shall not be able to speak a word—I shall be running round you—and kneeling to you —and holding up my hands to you as Dinah does her paws—speechless—I shan't do it so well as Dinah though—I shall be clumsy and mute—at once perfectly oppressed with delight—if you speak to me I shall not know what you say—you will have to pat me—and point to something for me to fetch and carry for you —or make me lie down on the rug and be quiet—or send me out of the room until I promise to be a good dog; and when you let me in again—I shall be worse—What *shall* I do?

208 *John Ruskin to Effie Gray*
[Extract]

Folkestone
21 November 1847

I have been thinking how long it will be before I know all your letters by heart. Not long—Yet I should *so* like to have them printed, in a little pocket volume—to carry about with me always. And so—love—you did not know how to tell me how heartsick you were! Do not you think that for once you might have told me to judge you by *myself*. Think—my Effie—what a difference between you—with brother and sisters—and many many—countless, friends about you—not to speak of Papa and Mama; —and me—alone here on the sea beach—. May not you—when you are heartsick another time tell me that you feel a little—as I do?

I really must not go on. I never intended to write at night at all—and yet I cannot be happy till I have said a word or two. You say—you wish you could make me more happy—Have you ever felt yourself *unable* to make me so—when you chose?—Very little will do it—Effie—*So* little!—a kind word—a touch of the hand—a little commission to fetch or do something—so it be for you—a single look—a smile—nay the mere sight of you—(Except when you are sitting in a corner—reading history—or with that peculiar expression about the Lips). Oh—Effie—that's what I have been going to ask you this month—Do tell me what that expression means! Do! It used to come on so suddenly, sometimes —Qu'est-ce que ça veut dire! Goodbye. Only pray tell me what it means—or I shall be so frightened when I see it lest it should mean that I have been naughty.

209   *John Ruskin to Effie Gray*
       [Extract]

                                                    Folkestone
                                              30 November 1847

My Beloved Effie
       I never thought to have felt time pass slowly any more—but —foolish that I am, I cannot help congratulating myself on this being the last day of November—Foolish, I say—for what pleasure soever may be in store for us, we ought not to wish to lose the treasure of time—nor to squander away the heap of gold even though its height should keep us from seeing each other for a little while. But your letter of last night shook all the philosopher out of me. That little undress bit! Ah—my sweet Lady—What naughty thoughts had I. Dare I say?—I was thinking—thinking, naughty —happy thought, that you would soon have— some one's arms to

278

keep you from being cold! Pray don't be angry with me. How *could* I help it?—how can I? I'm thinking so just now, even. Oh—my dearest—I am not so 'scornful' neither, of all that I hope for—Alas—I know not what I would not give for one glance of your fair eyes.—your fair—saucy eyes. You cruel, cruel girl—now that was *just* like you—to poor William at the Ball. I can see you at this moment—*hear* you. '*If* you wanted to dance with *me*, William! *If!*' You saucy—wicked—witching—malicious—merciless—mischief loving—torturing—martyrizing—unspeakably to be feared and fled—mountain nymph that you are—'If!' When you knew that he would have given a year of his life for a touch of your hand. Ah's me—what a world this is, when its best creatures and kindest —will do such things. What a sad world. Poor fellow,—How the lights of the ballroom would darken and its floor sink beneath him—Earthquake and eclipse at once, and to be 'if'd' at by you, too; Now—I'll take up his injured cause—I'll punish you for that—Effie—some time—see if I don't—*If* I don't. It deserves—oh—I don't know what it doesn't deserve—nor what I can do.

P.S. Ah—my mysterious girl—I forgot one little bit of the letter—but I can't forget *all*, though 'a great many things.'

My heart is yours—my thoughts—myself—all but my memory, but that's mine. Now it is cool—as you say—to give me all that pain—and then tell me—'Never mind, I won't do it again.' Heaven forbid! How could you—puss? You are not thinking of saying that you have 'been thinking about it—' or 'writing to a friend'—and that you won't have me now! Are you?

210   *John Ruskin to Effie Gray*
[Extract]

Denmark Hill
15 December 1847

I don't know anything dreadful enough to liken you to—You are like a sweet forest of pleasant glades and whispering branches—where people wander on and on in its playing shadows they know not how far—and when they come near the centre of it, it is all cold and impenetrable—and when they would fain turn, lo —they are hedged with briers and thorns and cannot escape, but all torn and bleeding—You are like a wrecker on a rocky coast— luring vessels to their fate—Every flower that you set in your hair —every smile that you bestow—nay—every gentle frown even— is a false light lighted on the misty coast of a merciless gulph— Once let the ships get fairly *embayed* and they are all to pieces in no time—You are like a fair mirage in the desert—which people follow with weary feet and longing eyes—until they faint on the burning sands—or come to some dark salt lake of tears—You are like the bright—soft—swelling—lovely fields of a high glacier covered with fresh morning snow—which is heavenly to the eye— and soft and winning on the foot—but beneath, there are winding clefts and dark places in its cold—cold ice—where men fall, and rise not again—And then you say you 'don't know how it is—'— No—there's the dreadfulness of it,—there's the danger—Ah, Effie—you have such sad, wicked ways without knowing it— Such sweet silver under-tones of innocent voice—that when one hears, one is lost—such slight—short—inevitable—arrowy glances from under the bent eyelashes—such gentle changes of sunny and shadowy expression about the lovely lips—such *desperate* ways of doing the most innocent things—Mercy on us—to hear you ask anybody 'whether they take sugar with their peaches'?—don't you recollect my being 'temporarily insane' for all the day afterwards— after hearing you ask such a thing—and then all *that* is the least of it—but you are such a good girl, too—and so sorry for all the harm you do—and so ready to like everybody, in reason,—and so surprised when you find they don't understand reason—and so ready to promise after you've half-killed them or driven them mad, that if they won't mind that *once*, you 'won't do it again', and so everything that you ought to be, and can be—, that I think you ought to be shut up in an iron cage—or in one of those things which you have got in the Perth Tolbooth—and not allowed to speak to or see anybody—until you are married. A strict convent might do—bye-the-bye—if there are any near Perth.

[Extract]

Denmark Hill
19 January 1848

I have been thinking a good deal over that hard question of yours—whether I shall always love you as I do now—and I still have but the same answer—it will depend upon yourself—a wife has it in her power to make her husband love her more and more daily, and so he, with her, and I do so thoroughly intend to do everything that I *can* do, for your good and happiness, that I do faithfully believe I shall gain your love more and more as we live on—and I hope deserve it more and more, and if you love *me* I am certain to continue to find all my happiness in you. But I suppose it to be a melancholy and undeniable fact that something of the romance of love must pass away—something of its outer flush and bloom—I can think of you or conceive you as old—50 or sixty—and fancy myself a lover still—at 70—But to tell you the very truth—I *cannot* look fairly in the face of the Great Fact that you must one day—(God willing)—be *Forty*. It sounds very unpleasant indeed—to be sure—I shall be 50—if I see that day,—and I don't know what my views of things in general—and of you in particular, may be by that time. And that's all the philosophy I have—upon this great and interesting question—for indeed, I am not in possession of sufficient data to reason from.

I don't regret our little quarrels, now; I think even at the time there was a kind of luxury in them—I don't know what it was—but I cannot help suspecting myself—now and then—of having in some slight degree, made matters worse for the sake of the delight of making friends again. Do you think we shall be able to quarrel in that sort of amateur fashion at Bowers Well. I'm afraid not—I don't think I could even *play* a quarrel—now. I am quite passive—in your power—you may do what you will with me—if you were to put me into Bowers *Well* and put the top on, I should think it was all right, and the kindest thing in the world. You said I was cross the other day—peutetre—but in the first place I was more anxious than cross—and in the second place—I don't profess to be in a good humour when I am away from you—A little thing puts me out now—but when I once get near you—Ah, what will become of me. I shall have no more independent existence than your shadow has—I feel as if I should faint away for love of you—and become a mist or a smoke, like the Genie in the Arabian nights—and as if the best you could do with me would be to get me all folded and gathered into a little box—and put on your toilet-table—and let me out a little now and then—when I wouldn't be troublesome—

212 *Effie Gray to John Ruskin*

Bowerswell
8 February 1848

I told Papa the other day that you said you never would be really jealous without cause and he says unfortunately jealous people always *find cause* which I think quite true but I hope at heart you are really not a jealous being, and the absurdity of your giving as a reason that my manner to you and other people was quite the same is really the most preposterous thing I ever heard. You must have been thinking of something else when you wrote that! but really John I love you so much that I don't think much about *the* jealous part of you for I do not believe you will be at all so after we are married and I daresay you will allow me to ask anybody I like to take some pudding without behaving afterwards as madly as Mr. Munn.

213 *Effie Gray to John Ruskin*

Bowerswell
10 February 1848

I do not know how I can sufficiently thank you for your inestimable letter this morning so full of tenderness and affection almost too kind and good. You will quite spoil me, my love, it almost

282

made me weep with joy to think myself so beloved not but that I was fully impressed with that before, but this morning's letter almost made me rejoice too much in thinking that so much happiness was permitted to me who am so unworthy of it. I am indeed happy beyond telling in thinking you love me so much and truly glad am I if by expressing my earnest desires for continued happiness on your part I added one moment of pleasure on your birthday to you I wish I could have added my thoughts more fully to my wishes for you and was much dissatisfied that my letter was so unexpressive of my feelings for had you been here much much more should I have said to what I wrote. You will indeed be a kind husband to me. Many trials we shall probably have but not from want of love on either part—that must be the greatest trial I think in married life finding that the only being perhaps in the world whose affection is necessary to you as a part of your being not loving and assisting you in all your joys and cares, leaving you with the utmost indifference when you are in trouble to get out of it the best way you can, and in Joy not partaking the feeling but perhaps trying to subdue it if not in a similar mood, this would be I think the summit of wretchedness and misery. You who are so kind as a son will be a perfect lover as a husband. What I meant by saying that we had much to find out in each other was not that I expected to find great faults in you, I think I know all that I have to expect, and I shall see your coat brushed and mend your gloves and especially keep you from wearing white hats and in order to compromise the matter with you I shall promise never to wear an *excessively* Pink Bonnet which can be seen all over the Exhibition although I suppose you have not particular objection to one of a paler hue. Pink is a very favourite colour of mine but I will subdue the shade out of respect to your superior discernment in these matters.

283

COVENTRY PATMORE

Coventry Patmore was born on 23rd July 1823, at Woodford, Essex. He numbered among his friends Browning, Tennyson, Thackeray and Lord Houghton.

At the age of 24 he met and married Emily Augusta Andrews—an outstanding beauty and extremely accomplished. They adored each other and the marriage was gloriously happy. Emily was the inspiration for his famous poem 'The Angel in the House' which achieved world-wide fame and was a sensational success in the United States.

Her death at the early age of 37 proved a shattering blow and for some considerable time Patmore became almost a recluse.

His finest work—'The Unknown Eros' was unhappily overshadowed by the popularity of 'The Angel in the House' and did not receive the acclaim it merited.

214 *Coventry Patmore to Emily Augusta Andrews*

1847

. . . I have been meditating a poem for you; but I am determined not to give you anything I write unless it is the best thing I have written. O, how much the best it ought to be if it would do justice to its subject. . . .

From THE REVULSION

'Twas when the spousal time of May
   Hangs all the hedge with bridal wreaths,
And air's so sweet the bosom gay
   Gives thanks for every breath it breathes;
When like to like is gladly moved,
   And each thing joins in Spring's refrain,
'Let those love now who never loved;
   Let those who have loved love again;'
That I, in whom the sweet time wrought,
   Lay stretch'd within a lonely glade,
Abandon'd to delicious thought,
   Beneath the softly twinkling shade.
The leaves, all stirring, mimick'd well
   A neighbouring rush of rivers cold
And, as the sun or shadow fell,
   So these were green and those were gold;
In dim recesses hyacinths droop'd,
   And breadths of primrose lit the air,
Which, wandering through the woodland, stoop'd
   And gather'd perfumes here and there;
Upon the spray the squirrel swung,
   And careless songsters, six or seven,
Sang lofty songs the leaves among,
   Fit for their only listener, Heaven.
I sigh'd, 'Immeasurable bliss
   Gains nothing by becoming more!
Millions have meaning; after this
   Cyphers forget the integer.'

[From 'The Angel in the House', Bk. II, Canto VII]

THE LOVER

He meets, by heavenly chance express,
　　The destined maid; some hidden hand
Unveils to him that loveliness
　　Which others cannot understand.
His merits in her presence grow,
　　To match the promise in her eyes,
And round her happy footsteps blow
　　The authentic air of Paradise.
For joy of her he cannot sleep;
　　Her beauty haunts him all the night;
It melts his heart, it makes him weep
　　For wonder, worship, and delight.
O, paradox of love, he longs,
　　Most humble when he most aspires,
To suffer scorn and cruel wrongs
　　From her he honours and desires.
Her graces make him rich, and ask
　　No guerdon; this imperial style
Affronts him; he disdains to bask,
　　The pensioner of her priceless smile.
He prays for some hard thing to do,
　　Some work of fame and labour immense,
To stretch the languid bulk and thew
　　Of love's fresh-born magnipotence.
No smallest boon were bought too dear
　　Though barter'd for his love-sick life;
Yet trusts he, with undaunted cheer,
　　To vanquish heaven, and call her Wife.
He notes how queens of sweetness still
　　Neglect their crowns, and stoop to mate;
How, self-consign'd with lavish will,
　　They ask but love proportionate;
How swift pursuit by small degrees,
　　Love's tactic, works like miracle;
How valour, clothed in courtesies,
　　Brings down the haughtiest citadel;

And therefore, though he merits not
To kiss the braid upon her skirt,
His hope, discouraged ne'er a jot,
Out-soars all possible desert.

[From 'The Angel in the House', Bk. I, Canto III]

217 *Coventry Patmore*

SPONSA DEI

What is this Maiden fair,
The laughing of whose eye
Is in man's heart renew'd virginity;
Who yet sick longing breeds
For marriage which exceeds
The inventive guess of Love to satisfy
With hope of utter binding, and of loosing endless
    dear despair?
What gleams about her shine,
More transient than delight and more divine!
If she does something but a little sweet,
As gaze towards the glass to set her hair,
See how his soul falls humbled at her feet!
Her gentle step, to go or come,
Gains her more merit than a martyrdom;
And, if she dance, it doth such grace confer
As opes the heaven of heavens to more than her,
And makes a rival of her worshipper.
To die unknown for her were little cost!
So is she without guile,
Her mere refused smile
Makes up the sum of that which may be lost!
Who is this Fair
Whom each hath seen,
The darkest once in this bewailed dell,
Be he not destin'd for the glooms of hell?

Whom each hath seen
And known, with sharp remorse and sweet, as Queen
And tear-glad Mistress of his hopes of bliss,
Too fair for man to kiss?
Who is this only happy She,
Whom, by a frantic flight of courtesy,
Born of despair
Of better lodging for his Spirit fair,
He adores as Margaret, Maude, or Cecily?
And what this sigh,
That each one heaves for Earth's last lowlihead
And the Heaven high
Ineffably lock'd in dateless bridal-bed?
Are all, then, mad, or is it prophecy?
'Sons now we are of God,' as we have heard,
'But what shall we be hath not yet appear'd.'
O, Heart, remember thee,
That Man is none,
Save One.
What if this Lady be thy Soul, and He
Who claims to enjoy her sacred beauty be,
Not thou, but God; and thy sick fire
A female vanity,
Such as a Bride, viewing her mirror'd charms,
Feels when she sighs, 'All these are for his arms!'
A reflex heat
Flash'd on thy cheek from His immense desire,
Which waits to crown, beyond thy brain's conceit,
Thy nameless, secret, hopeless longing sweet,
Not by-and-by, but now,
Unless deny Him thou!

[From 'The Unknown Eros']

ISABELLA MARY MAYSON
(MRS. BEETON)

Bella, as she was known to her sisters and relations, accomplished a vast amount in her short life. Before she married Sam Beeton she was helping him with his publishing firm, writing editorials for his magazines and suggesting fashion plates for his *Englishwoman's Domestic Magazine*. After their marriage on 10th July 1856 Sam came to depend upon her much more and there were exhausting trips to Paris to arrange for colour plates for the magazine. It was then that she decided on writing her famous book *Household Management* and Sam, in his magazines, enquired for recipes from 'high and low'. Thousands flowed in. All of them had to be worked out in Bella's kitchen in the house they bought and lived in, in Pinner. They lived in mid-Victorian times, yet they were anything but Victorian in their outlook on life. Bella wanted the crinoline abolished; Sam used to walk up from Pinner to his office in Bouverie Street and back again at night. Sam mourned her death. He died, a young man himself, on 6th June 1877, and was buried in her grave. He was 46.

Nancy Spain, a great-niece of Isabella Beeton, wrote Mrs. Beeton's biography. The following letters are taken from her highly entertaining and witty book *The Beeton Story*.

Epsom, May 26 1856

My own darling Sam,

As I have two or three little matters in your note of yesterday that rather puzzled me, I thought I must write and ask an explanation; very stupid of me you will say, as I am going to see you on Wednesday morning. No doubt you will think that I could just as well have [asked you] myself then, as trouble you with one of my unintelligible epistles. . . .

Secondly, what right has he to conjure up in his fertile brain such nasty things as rough corners to smooth down when there is one who loves him better and more fondly than ever one being did another, on this earth at least.

Oh Sam, I think it is so wrong of you to fancy such dreadful things. You say also you don't think I shall be able to guide myself when I am left to my own exertions. I must say, I have always looked up to, and respected, both parents and perhaps been mindful of what they say (I mean respecting certain matters) but in a very short time you will have the entire management of me and I can assure you that you will find in me a most docile and yielding pupil.

Pray don't imagine when I am yours—that things will continue as they are now. God forbid. Better would it be to put an end to this matter altogether if we thought there was the slightest possibility of *that*. So pray don't tremble for our future happiness.

Look at things in a more rosy point of view and I have no doubt with the love *I am sure* there is existing between us, we shall get on as merrily as crickets with only an occasionally sharp point to soften down and not as many as you fancy . . .

I could not sleep without writing to you, so you must excuse this nonsense. Good-night my precious pet, may angels guide and watch over you and give you pleasant dreams, not drab colours, and accept the fondest and most sincere love of your

BELLA

Burn this as soon as read.

[Sam, of course, did not burn the letter but wrote back]

. . . A dear little brick and blessed must have been the earth on which you were baked. I could not find the slightest spec. of a fault in any one of your remarks for there exists no one more mindful of the respect and love due to a parent than your cavaliero, who is now writing to you . . .

You have made me so much happier and more comfortable to-day, as I see you write so firmly, yet so prettily, upon that dread subject of interference, that I now do quite hope that matters will not remain as they *now* are . . .

I don't desire, I assure you, to *manage* you—*you* can do that quite well yourself—my only desire, my sweetest darling, is that *no one else* should manage you. You, as you know, can do anything with me—any one else, in your account, nothing!

219   Bella Mayson to Sam Beeton

Epsom, July 7th 1856

My dearest Sam,

Father thinks he will be in town to-morrow and we will call at Bouverie between 1 and 2 o'clock if you will be visible about that time.

We had a very tedious ride down; if you had been with me it would have been a very different case.

Trusting you are perfectly serene, and happy as your humble servant and that I shall see you jolly on Thursday morning,

Believe me, my loved one, yours eternally,

BELLA   MAYSON

P.S. If you see Mrs Beeton please tell her father is going to Gunter's, where he will order an extra cake for her, God bless you.

Pinner, Sunday Evening 1856

My beloved Bella,

I have been wandering through the fields, full of newly cut hay, for the last hour or so, and have returned home perfectly envious and full of bile—for I assure you I was the only unhappy mortal who was alone.

I met many happy maidens with many happy men, sometimes one male with two females, at other times the animal and panniers were reversed, but there was always somebody with somebody else, so to this fact do you owe, my dearest, this letter, as I have made up my mind to be even with the people I have seen, in some way or other. And if they are *with* those they love, they cannot, at any rate, be experiencing this pleasure now felt by me of writing to her 'in whose hands are all the corners of my heart'.

You must have had a lovely day at Brighton, for here it has been charmingly sunshiny—the moon is electro-typing at this moment with its beautiful silvery light all around and I instinctively am walking with you on Brighton pier, and almost hear you ejaculate 'Oh, Sam, if you only knew'. I don't know why it is, Bella Mia, but you never get any further than that. . . .

1850   1894

ROBERT LOUIS STEVENSON

Robert Louis Stevenson is the greatest romantic of all English literature. Who was not, in his youth, swayed by *Treasure Island* and *Kidnapped*? What better place for a romantic to live but in the South Seas? Besides, Louis was dying from a lung disease. Yet he continued to work.

He was born in Edinburgh on 13th November 1850. His father and grandfather were romantics too. They built lighthouses. Robert, unable to become an engineer because of his weak lungs, studied law and was called to the Scottish bar in 1875.

To add to the picture of a romantic, Robert travelled in France with nobody but a donkey for companion. It was on such a journey that he met and fell in love with Fanny Osbourne, *née* Vandergrift, an American lady, ten years his senior, who was in Europe 'to study art'. They met in a pub in Grez-sur-Loing and Robert was swept off his feet. Fanny returned to the States and he followed her on an emigrant boat. It was, once again, a romantic, almost penniless journey but, in 1879, after the divorce from Osbourne which caused a minor scandal, they were married. They travelled together a good deal and eventually found their permanent home in Samoa, at the house Robert built called 'Vailima'. The islanders adored them both and nicknamed Robert Tusitala, the Teller of Tales.

Fanny Stevenson, though often in ill health herself, looked after Robert with extreme care. He owed his life to her. She was a brilliant gardener, creating gardens everywhere she went, collecting rare plants and sending them to Kew and other places. In her Diary, for 23rd October 1890, she wrote, 'Louis says that I have the soul of a peasant, not so much that I love working in the earth and with the earth, but because I like to know that it is my own earth that I am delving in. Had I the soul of an artist, the stupidity of possessions would have no power over me. He may be right. I would as soon think of renting a child of love as a piece of land. When I plant a seed or a root, I plant a bit of my heart with it and do not feel that I have finished when I have had my exercise and amusement. But I do not feel so far removed from God when the tender leaves put forth and I know that in a manner I am a creator. My heart melts over a bed of young peas, and a blossom on my rose tree is like a poem written by my son.'

Robert died of a brain haemorrhage at the age of 44 and is buried in Samoa. *On Falling in Love* is really a love letter to Fanny and is the longest such letter in the language.

221   *Robert Louis Stevenson*

ON FALLING IN LOVE

Lord, what fools these mortals be!

There is only one event in life which really astonishes a man and startles him out of his prepared opinions. Everything else befalls him very much as he expected. Event succeeds to event, with an agreeable variety indeed, but with little that is either startling or intense; they form together no more than a sort of background, or running accompaniment to the man's own reflections; and he falls naturally into a cool, curious, and smiling habit of mind, and builds himself up in a conception of life which expects to-morrow to be after the pattern of to-day and yesterday. He may be accustomed to the vagaries of his friends and acquaintances under the influence of love. He may sometimes look forward to it for himself with an incomprehensible expectation. But it is a subject in which neither intuition nor the behaviour of others will help the philosopher to the truth. There is probably nothing rightly thought or rightly written on this matter of love that is not a piece of the person's experience. I remember an anecdote of a well-known French theorist, who was debating a point eagerly in his cénacle. It was objected against him that he had never experienced love. Whereupon he arose, left the society, and made it a point not to return to it until he considered that he had supplied the defect. 'Now,' he remarked, on entering, 'now I am in a position to continue the discussion.' Perhaps he had not penetrated very deeply into the subject after all; but the story indicates right thinking, and may serve as an apologue to readers of this essay.

When at last the scales fall from his eyes, it is not without something of the nature of dismay that the man finds himself in such changed conditions. He has to deal with commanding emotions instead of the easy dislikes and preferences in which he has hitherto passed his days; and he recognises capabilities for pain and pleasure of which he had not yet suspected the existence. Falling in love is the one illogical adventure, the one thing of which we are tempted to think as supernatural, in our trite and reasonable world. The effect is out of all proportion with the cause. Two persons, neither of them, it may be, very amiable or very beautiful, meet, speak a little, and look a little into each other's eyes. That has been done a dozen or so of times in the experience of either with no great result. But on this occasion all is different. They fall at once into that state in which another person becomes to us the very gist and centre-point of God's creation, and demolishes our laborious theories with a smile; in which our ideas are so bound up with the one master-thought that even the trivial cares of our own person become so many acts of devotion, and the love of life itself is translated into a wish to remain in the same world with so precious and desirable a fellow-creature. And all the while their acquaintances look on in stupor, and ask each other, with almost passionate emphasis, what so-and-so can see in that woman, or such-an-one in that man? I am sure, gentlemen, I cannot tell you. For my part, I cannot think what the women mean. It might be very well, if the Apollo Belvedere should suddenly glow all over into life, and step forward from the pedestal with that god-like air of his. But of the misbegotten changelings who call themselves men, and prate intolerably over dinner-tables, I never saw one who seemed worthy to inspire love—no, nor read of any, except Leonardo da Vinci, and perhaps Goethe in his youth. About

295

women I entertain a somewhat different opinion; but there, I have the misfortune to be a man.

There are many matters in which you may waylay Destiny, and bid him stand and deliver. Hard work, high thinking, adventurous excitement, and a great deal more that forms a part of this or the other person's spiritual bill of fare, are within the reach of almost anyone who can dare a little and be patient. But it is by no means in the way of everyone to fall in love. You know the difficulty Shakespeare was put into when Queen Elizabeth asked him to show Falstaff in love. I do not believe that Henry Fielding was ever in love. Scott, if it were not for a passage or two in *Rob Roy*, would give me very much the same effect. These are great names and (what is more to the purpose) strong, healthy, high-strung, and generous natures, of whom the reverse might have been expected. As for the innumerable army of anaemic and tailorish persons who occupy the face of this planet with so much propriety, it is palpably absurd to imagine them in any such situation as a love-affair. A wet rag goes safely by the fire; and if a man is blind, he cannot expect to be much impressed by romantic scenery. Apart from all this many lovable people miss each other in the world, or meet under some unfavourable star. There is the nice and critical moment of declaration to be got over. From timidity or lack of opportunity a good half of possible love cases never get so far, and at least another quarter do there cease and determine. A very adroit person, to be sure, manages to prepare the way and out with his declaration in the nick of time. And then there is a fine solid sort of man, who goes from snub to snub; and if he has to declare forty times, will continue imperturbably declaring, amid the astonished consideration of men and angels, until he has a favourable answer. I daresay, if one were a woman, one would like to marry a man who was capable of doing this, but not quite one who had done so. It is just a little bit abject, and somehow just a little bit gross; and marriages in which one of the parties has been thus battered into consent scarcely form agreeable subjects for meditation. Love should run out to meet love with open arms. Indeed, the ideal story is that of two people who go into love step for step, with a fluttered consciousness, like a pair of children venturing together into a dark room. From the first moment when they see each other, with a pang of curiosity, through stage after stage of growing pleasure and embarrassment, they can read the expression of their own trouble in each others' eyes. There is here no declaration properly so called; the feeling is so plainly shared, that as soon as the man knows what it is in his own heart, he is sure of what it is in the woman's.

This simple accident of falling in love is as beneficial as it is astonishing. It arrests the petrifying influence of years, disproves cold-blooded and cynical conclusions, and awakens dormant sensibilities. Hitherto the man had found it a good policy to disbelieve the existence of any enjoyment which was out of his reach; and thus he turned his back upon the strong sunny parts of nature, and accustomed himself to look exclusively on what was common and dull. He accepted a prose ideal, let himself go blind of many sympathies by disuse; and if he were young and witty, or beautiful, wilfully forwent these advantages. He joined himself to the following of what, in the old mythology of love, was prettily called nonchaloir; and in an odd mixture of feelings, a fling of self-respect, a preference for selfish liberty, and a great dash of that fear with which honest people regard serious interests, kept himself back from the straightforward course of life among certain selected activities. And now, all of a sudden, he is unhorsed, like St. Paul, from his infidel affectation. His heart which has been ticking accurate seconds for the last year, gives a bound and begins to beat high and irregularly in his breast. It seems as if he had never heard or felt or seen until that moment; and by the report of his memory, he must have lived his past life between sleep and waking, or with the preoccupied attention of a brown study. He is practically incommoded by the generosity of his feelings, smiles much when he is alone, and develops a habit of looking rather blankly upon the moon and stars. But it is not at all within the province of a prose essayist to give a picture of this hyperbolical frame of mind; and the thing has been done already, and that to admiration. in 'Adelaide', in Tennyson's 'Maud', and in some of Heine's songs, you get the absolute expression of this midsummer spirit. Romeo and Juliet were very much in love; although they tell me some German critics are of a different opinion, probably the same who would have us think Mercutio a dull fellow. Poor Antony was in love, and no mistake. That lay figure Marius, in *Les Misérables*, is also a genuine case in his own way, and worth observation. A good many of George Sand's people are thoroughly in love; and so are a good many of George Meredith's. Altogether, there is plenty to read on the subject. If the root of the matter be in him, and if he has the requisite chords to set in vibration, a young man may occasionally enter, with the key of art, into that kind of Beulah which is upon the borders of Heaven and within sight of the City of Love. There let him sit awhile to hatch delightful hopes and perilous illusions.

One thing that accompanies the passion in its first blush is certainly difficult to explain. It comes (I do not quite see how) that from having a very supreme sense of pleasure in all parts of life— in lying down to sleep, in waking, in motion, in breathing, in continuing to be—the lover begins to regard his happiness as beneficial for the rest of the world and highly meritorious in himself. Our race has never been able contentedly to suppose that the noise of its wars, conducted by a few young gentlemen in a corner of an inconsiderable star, does not re-echo among the courts of Heaven with quite a formidable effect. In much the same taste, when people find a great to-do in their own breasts, they imagine it must have some influence in their neighbourhood. The presence of the two lovers is so enchanting to each other that it seems as if it must be the best thing possible for everybody else. They are half inclined to fancy it is because of them and their love that the sky is blue and the sun shines. And certainly the weather is usually fine while people are courting. . . . In point of fact, although the happy man feels very kindly towards others of his own sex, there is apt to be something too much of the magnifico in his demeanour. If people grow presuming and self-important over such matters as a dukedom or the Holy See, they will scarcely support the dizziest elevation in life without some suspicion of a strut; and the dizziest elevation is to love and be loved in return. Consequently, accepted lovers are a trifle condescending in their address to other men. An overweening sense of the passion and importance of life hardly conduces to simplicity of manner. To women, they feel very nobly, very purely, and very generously, as if they were so many Joan-of-Arcs; but this does not come out in their behaviour; and they treat them to Grandisonian airs marked with a suspicion of fatuity. I am not quite certain that women do not like this sort of thing; but really, after having bemused myself over *Daniel Deronda*, I have given up trying to understand what they like.

If it did nothing else, this sublime and ridiculous superstition, that the pleasure of the pair is somehow blessed to others, and everybody is made happier in their happiness, would serve at least to keep love generous and great-hearted. Nor is it quite a baseless superstition after all. Other lovers are hugely interested. They strike the nicest balance between pity and approval, when they see people aping the greatness of their own sentiments. It is an understood thing in the play, that while the young gentlefolk are courting on the terrace, a rough flirtation is being carried on and a light, trivial sort of love is growing up between the footman and the singing chambermaid. As people are generally cast for the leading parts in their own imaginations, the reader can apply the parallel to real life without much chance of going wrong. In short, they are quite sure this other love-affair is not so deep-seated as their own, but they like dearly to see it going forward. And love, considered as a spectacle, must have attractions for many who are not of the confraternity. The sentimental old maid is a commonplace of the novelists; and he must be rather a poor sort of human being, to be sure, who can look on at this pretty madness without indulgence and sympathy. For nature commends itself to people with a most insinuating art; the busiest is now and again arrested by a great sunset; and you may be as pacific or as cold-blooded as you will, but you cannot help some emotion when you read of well-disputed battles, or meet a pair of lovers in the lane.

Certainly, whatever it may be with regard to the world at large, this idea of beneficent pleasure is true as between the sweethearts. To do good and communicate is the lover's grand intention. It is the happiness of the other that makes his own most intense gratification. It is not possible to disentangle the different emotions, the pride, humility, pity and passion, which are excited by a look of happy love or an unexpected caress. To make one's self beautiful, to dress the hair, to excel in talk, to do anything and all things that puff out the character and attributes and make them imposing in the eyes of others, is not only to magnify one's self, but to offer the most delicate homage at the same time. And it is in this latter intention that they are done by lovers; for the essence of love is kindness; and indeed it may be best defined as passionate kindness: kindness, so to speak, run mad and become importunate and violent. Vanity in a merely personal sense exists no longer. The lover takes a perilous pleasure in privately displaying his weak points and having them, one after another, accepted and condoned. He wishes to be assured that he is not loved for this or that good quality, but for himself or something as like himself as he can contrive to set forward. For, although it may have been a very difficult thing to paint the marriage of Cana, or write the fourth act of *Antony and Cleopatra*, there is a more difficult piece of art before everyone in this world who cares to set about explaining his own character to others. Words and acts are easily wrenched from their true significance; and they are all the language we have to come and go upon. A pitiful job we make of it, as a rule. For better or worse, people mistake our meaning and take our emotions at a wrong valuation. And generally we rest pretty content with our failures; we are content to be misapprehended by crackling flirts; but when once a man is moonstruck with this affection of love, he makes it a point of honour to clear such dubieties away. He cannot have the Best of her Sex misled upon a point of this importance; and his pride revolts at being loved in a mistake.

He discovers a great reluctance to return on former periods of his life. To all that has not been shared with her, rights and duties, bygone fortunes and dispositions, he can look back only by a difficult and repugnant effort of the will. That he should have wasted some years in ignorance of what alone was really important, that he may have entertained the thought of other women with any show of complacency, is a burthen almost too heavy for his self respect. But it is the thought of another past that rankles in his spirit like a poisoned wound. That he himself made a fashion of being alive in the bald, beggarly days before a certain meeting, is deplorable enough in all good conscience. But that She should have permitted herself the same liberty seems inconsistent with a Divine providence.

A great many people run down jealousy, on the score that it is an artificial feeling, as well as practically inconvenient. This is scarcely fair; for the feeling on which it merely attends, like an ill-humoured courtier, is itself artificial in exactly the same sense and to the same degree. I suppose what is meant by that objection is that jealousy has not always been a character of man; formed no part of that very modest kit of sentiments with which he is supposed to have begun the world: but waited to make its appearance in better days and among richer natures. And this is equally true of love, and friendship, and love of country, and delight in what they call the beauties of nature, and most other things worth having. Love, in particular, will not endure any historical scrutiny: to all who have fallen across it, it is one of the most incontestable facts in the world; but if you begin to ask what it was in other periods and countries, in Greece for instance, the strangest doubts begin to spring up, and everything seems so vague and changing that a dream is logical in comparison. Jealousy, at any rate, is one of the consequences of love; you may like it or not, at pleasure; but there it is.

It is not exactly jealousy, however, that we feel when we reflect on the past of those we love. A bundle of letters found after years of happy union creates no sense of insecurity in the present; and yet it will pain a man sharply. The two people entertain no vulgar doubt of each other: but this pre-existence of both occurs to the mind as something indelicate. To be altogether right, they should have had twin birth together, at the same moment with the feeling that unites them. Then indeed it would be simple and perfect and without reserve or afterthought. Then they would understand each other with a fulness impossible otherwise. There would be no barrier between them of associations that cannot be imparted. They would be led into none of those comparisons that send the blood back to the heart. And they would know that there had been no time lost, and they had been together as much as was possible. For besides terror for the separation that must follow some time or other in the future, men feel anger, and something like remorse, when they think of that other separation which endured until they met. Someone has written that love makes people believe in immortality, because there seems not to be room enough in life for so great a tenderness, and it is inconceivable that the most masterful of our emotions should have no more than the spare moments of a few years. Indeed, it seems strange; but if we call to mind analogies, we can hardly regard it as impossible.

'The blind bow-boy,' who smiles upon us from the end of terraces in old Dutch gardens, laughingly hails his bird-bolts among a fleeting generation. But for as fast as ever he shouts, the game dissolves and disappears into eternity from under his falling arrows; this one is gone ere he is struck: the other has but time to make one gesture and give one passionate cry; and they are all the things of a moment. When the generation is gone, when the play is over, when the thirty years' panorama has been withdrawn in tatters from the stage of the world, we may ask what has become of these great, weighty, and undying loves, and the sweethearts who despised mortal conditions in a fine credulity; and they can only show us a few songs in a bygone taste, a few actions worth remembering, and a few children who have retained some happy stamp from the disposition of their parents.

GEORGE MOORE

George Moore is one of the greatest—and most neglected—writers of English prose. He was born at Moore Hall, County Mayo. As a young man he went to Paris to become a painter.

He was a familiar figure in that city, as familiar in the 1870's as was James Joyce in the 1920's. Although he failed in his object of becoming a painter he knew Monet, Degas, Zola, Huysmans and Mallarmé intimately. He returned to London in 1880 to that flat in Ebury Street, near Victoria, from which he wrote so many letters to his friends. He disliked the telephone and refused to have it installed. In the event of an emergency a message could be got through to him by means of 'the apothecary Huckle-bridge' whose shop was opposite.

Moore returned to England from Paris with 'the avowed intention of liberating English fiction from its Victorian shackles'. He published *A Mummer's Wife* in 1885. His greatest books were *The Brook Kerith* and *Heloise and Abelard*. These two books have been described as touching 'a point of almost flawless artistry and nobility that have rarely been reached before in the history of English prose'.

He met Lady Cunard in 1894 probably at the Savoy Hotel. Maud was wearing a pink-and-grey shot-silk dress. Unfortunately no letters from her have survived but, from the evidence of Moore's letters to her, she would seem to have been half-hearted over a love affair which to Moore was life-blood and lasted until he died. He tried for years to dedicate one of his books to her, without success. This is not surprising if his suggested dedication of *Avowals* to her is any indication. In a letter of September 1919, he writes the following proposed inscription. 'For Maud, the incarnate Spring, whom I love as the goats love the spring.'

Maud Alice Burke was born in San Fransisco, as far as can be ascertained, on 31st August 1872. In 1893 she was passionately in love with Prince André Poniatowski of Poland, but he is said to have jilted her. She married Sir Bache Cunard in 1895 and he took her back to his house, Nevil Holt, near Market Harborough in Leicestershire. But hunting and shooting were not for Lady Cunard. Anyone who could play Chopin so beautifully, who admired the painters of the time and who even read a page or two of George Moore's books when he sent her copies, was made for better things than the dull rural pursuits of red-faced, hard-drinking squires. She became one of the greatest hostesses of the age. Her great passion was Opera. She passed elegantly through the Society of the day on the arm of an ambassador, or a statesman. Indeed, what affairs of state may not have been settled by the charm of her wit and intelligence over one of those sumptuous banquets which were the order of the day at that time!

When she died at the Dorchester Hotel on 10th July 1948, *The Times* wrote of her, 'Small and fair and invariably dressed in the latest fashion (she once told an interviewer that her dressmaker's bill might run into thousands and that, as she was generally in a hurry, she would order ten or twenty dresses at once, wear perhaps two, and give the rest away) Lady Cunard was perhaps the most lavish hostess of her day, and through her patronage of the best musical talent at her house might be met, and often heard, practically every musical celebrity, especially at her musical suppers, which were famous. . . . Her like will hardly be seen again in the years ahead and she did much to deserve her place in the social and artistic history of her time.'

Lady Diana Cooper, in the third volume of her Autobiography, *Trumpets from the Steep* (Rupert Hart-Davis, 1960), gives a picture of Emerald Cunard, whose real name was Maud, but whom everyone seemed to call Emerald, in 1942, when she had come back from the States and was at the Dorchester. 'Emerald had the hopping gait of a bird as she moved, a little restlessly, from perch to perch. You wanted to lure her to your hand, but she kept herself clear of human touch. Her hands were elegant little claws, her legs and feet of the slimmest and most shapely workmanship. There was nothing rushed about her modelling; everything was as finished as *biscuit de Sèvres*. Her skin and bosom were of the whitest, finest *pâte*. To my eyes she had scarcely changed in twenty-five years.'

What is remarkable in Diana Cooper's Autobiography are the letters of Conrad Russell, who was in love with her in the same way as George Moore was with Lady Cunard. His letters dealing with county matters—he farmed at Mells—his reading and his visits to Diana, can stand beside those of Lamb, Cowper and FitzGerald.

222   *George Moore to Lady Cunard*

Kirkstall Grange, Headingley, Leeds
6 October [1904]

Dearest Maud, dearest Primavera!

I do not know what primavera means, or if I have spelt it sufficiently for you to recognise the word. It means Spring, doesn't it? It means joy, the joy of green leaves with the flutter of wings among the leaves. And you, dearest, mean all these things to me, for you are not, I am convinced, a mere passing woman but an incarnation of an idea—we are all types more or less defined, we all represent an idea, but you do more than faintly represent an idea. You are the idea. In you Nature has succeeded in expressing herself and completely. We perforce make, if we would make them at all, poems out of words or musical notes or chalk lines or pigments. You take yourself and make a poem out of your body and out of your spirit. You are at once the poet and the poem, and you create yourself not with silks and pearls, though these things are beautiful upon you, but by your intense desire of beauty and life. I am thinking of you, that goes without saying, but today I am wondering what you would think of Strauss. The Festival has been going on for three days but today is the first musical impression I received. He captured me at once just as Whitman did and much in the same way, by telling me about life, telling me interesting things about life. Brahms bores me. Brahms I am convinced n'est pas grand'chose—he has thought and read and his writing is full of happy turns of expression, but what are happy turns of expression to me, when behind them there is no irresistible fountain of life? There is no fountain in Brahms, no spring of enchanted life, bubbling, singing, creating a green spring tide. In simple words Brahms is a pedant no better than Tennyson. The miserable Poet Laureate [Alfred Austin] is here and he asked me if I didn't prefer Brahms to Strauss. I said I would as soon read—the poor little wretch thought I was going to say 'you'. I said 'your predecessor'. Dear Maud, write to me about your mother and look into your affairs; if you do not apply yourself to understanding your affairs I am afraid that your money will melt away.

Always affectionately yours GEORGE MOORE

Sir Hedworth Williamson is here. I like him very much—he is really very intelligent.

223   *George Moore to Lady Cunard*
4 Upper Ely Place, Dublin
Thursday [26th January 1905]

Your letter arrived here last night and I answer it at once, though there will not be a mail before Saturday. I must write my letter for I can think of nothing but your dear mother. There was a bond of sympathy between us three. I don't know if you and she were as sensible to it as I was—I suppose you must have been. Your mother never tried to come between you and me; instinct seems to have told her that we were destined to be friends for life, and she knew that such predestined friendships must follow their own courses. She was so much occupied with her own husband that I never really knew her till he died—till last summer, thrice happy summertime for ever remembrable by me. It was late August that I began to love her—there is no other word, for all affection is love; and I began to see you in her; and her love for you and her appreciation of you endeared her to me. You say that she was devoted to me! That happy summertime—was god or mortal ever favoured as I was, living between you two women for one whole month in that beautiful house overlooking the wide terrace. I remember the balustrade and the mysterious green land beyond it flowing away, dipping; and the valley stretching for miles and miles—the hillside opposite with its long woods and the house which King John once lived in—Rockingham. My room is well remembered—the oak passage outside and the beautiful eastern rugs that your mother brought from America. Do you remember that sunny afternoon in June when we unpacked her innumerable boxes and found jam-pots and chintz curtains, fish-hooks and suede gloves, fire-irons and fiddles? Do you remember our laughter? That part of our life is over and done —how intensely one remembers—my room hung with Italian engravings, and the round table at which I used to sit writing, and your ringing voice calling me away, or your mother's, or dear Nancy's—those green swards! The ash tree within whose circular shade the shepherd and his flock used to gather—'a Leicestershire Abraham' I used to say, for life changes little in essentials. Dearest Maud, you are all I have, it is through you that I know that I am alive. There was a bond of sympathy between us three . . . Yes there was. Your mother thought of you as I think of you—hardly as a human being; you always seemed to us more like a fairy, a sprite—Abraham reappears in the Leicestershire shepherd and you represent some dream, heroism or beauty, one of those everlasting states of consciousness which do not die with the individual but pass on from generation to generation, a beauty that never perishes, a fire that never wanes. Your mother always thought of you as Primavera—the idea is as much hers as mine. Dearest Primavera, it is sad to think that your mother has gone—only you and I really mourn her; who else understands as we understand? All the love I had for giving I have given to you. My heart is overflowing—I must stop writing. I cannot think today, I can only feel. When shall I see you? Shall I come to Cork or will you come to Dublin and see your pictures

and yours ever GEORGE MOORE

Imperial Hotel
Castlebar
13 July 1905

How many years ago is it since I wrote some French verses for you? I remember saying that you would never find another Englishman to write French verses for you. And today I say you will never get a letter from another sent from the above address. No one will ever write to you from the Imperial Hotel Castlebar but I. I like to be exceptional even in little things, and I like to confer favours on Castlebar. I have just put aside Wagner's letters to Mathilde. They roll on seemingly for ever yet without wearying one. I wonder what one would think of them if the author were not Wagner. Was there ever so garrulous a man? Was there ever a man so interested in himself? Well, he had the right to be, for he was the most interesting thing alive and he clearly knew it; and egotism is the god that inspires the letter-writer and good letters are all about the letter-writer. And if I were a letter-writer I should tell you how it worries me to come here and dine with judges and drive to Moore Hall with my brother who dearly loves the Georgian house on the hilltop. I should tell you about *The Lake*, tell you that I fear I shall never be able to write the book at all, and I should copy pieces from the proofs, and the following day I should write telling you that I had received some rusks which when dipped into hot milk inspire the dull lagging brains of authors. But I am not sufficiently interested in any of these details of my daily life to write them. It would interest me much more for me to find expression for my feelings for you, were I able to find expression for them. I should like to express my gratitude to you for the extraordinary kindness and sympathy you give me. Other women have wished to be kind to me, but I did not want their kindness and tried to escape from it; but your kindness delights me—it does far more than delights me, it fills me with wonder and with a double wonder. I wonder what god selected me for happiness and why he selected me. For I am the most fortunate of men; surely the most fortunate man in the world is he who meets a woman who enchants him as a work of art enchants. I find in you Manet, Berthe Morisot, Tourgueneff, Balzac, Shelley,

308

and the works I cannot write but would, were I the George Moore that George Moore sees in front of him, beguiling him, luring him like a will-o'-the-wisp. If I have failed to write what I dreamed I might write, one thing I have not failed in—you. You are at once the vase and the wine in the vase. You are the music and the instrument which produces the music, and you are a prodigious virtuoso, and while thinking of you one thinks of all that one loves most intimately. I said to Howard, [Baron Howard de Walden, patron of the arts] 'She is like music, like Wagner's music', and he said 'No, not a bit like Wagner's music'. 'You are quite right', I answered, 'she is more like Mozart. The Symphony in G Major. She is as joyous as it.' Howard didn't know the G Major Symphony or he thought my remark foolish. Very likely I am foolish but I am less foolish than many another, for I am wise enough to delight in my folly and to take pride in it. You are my folly, and what an exquisite folly, and how happy I am in my folly and how I marvel at it! For very few men have seen their ideal as close to them and as clearly as I have seen mine. Very few have possessed all they were capable of desiring of beauty and grace; I have possessed more, for the reality has exceeded the desire. You seem to me as marvellous as a rose, as a tea rose in its prime, as Shelley's hymn to Pan, as a bust by a Greek or Florentine sculptor. A sky full of stars does not astonish me more than your face, your marmoreal eyes. 'Time cannot wither nor custom stale', and for twelve years the wonder has never grown less. A man said yesterday, 'None has enjoyed life as much as you, for you relive your life again and again in memory.' Et c'est vrai, j'ai le culte du souvenir, and for weeks and months, for years I shall remember how you came down to Seaford House in your electric brougham. That vehicle is for ever enshrined in my memory. You can never —and for this I pity you—you can never form an idea of the wonder it is to me to see you—to think you and dream you. I do not know if it be the eternal idea of joy which you represent on earth, or its outward form that delights me most—the gold of your hair, your hand like a spray of fern. You come into a room filling the air with unpremeditated music. The best comparison I can think of is the indefinite hum of a fountain and its various colour transformations—you are as unreal as a fountain and as spiritual. The water surges compelled by a force unknown and we are cooled, refreshed, soothed and charmed; the water falls back full of fleeting iridescent colour. Would that I could restrain my pen, for you will not be won by exaltations. But I cannot keep myself from thanking you for your kindness; I want you to know that I am grateful; it would be terrible if I did not appreciate—I mean if you did not feel that I understood. I must praise, for it is a pleasure to praise, and he who is happy must speak his happiness even though he loses it by speech. The loss of happiness through speech is one of the oldest stories in the world. Prudence tells me I would do well to tear up this letter but I cannot listen to the voice of Prudence.

As ever yours GEORGE MOORE

I have just read Mathilde's letters and I have read them with tears in my eyes. Sorrow is more beautiful than happiness, more wistful and much deeper, and in these letters one perceives the depth of the relation that may exist between men and women—in a word these letters tell us again that love of man for woman (better still the love of woman for man) is the most beautiful thing in the world.

225   *George Moore to Lady Cunard*

4 Upper Ely Place

6 April 1907
Dublin

One is not always fortunate, and the last time I saw you was an unlucky day. But you shouldn't allow an unlucky day to prejudice you, there are unlucky days in every life, and we have known each other so long that your memory can easily find a happier occasion to rest upon. You said that I was not a true friend of yours—you could not have meant what you said, you could not have been deceived: you know that I prize nothing on earth as much as you and that I shall die thinking of you. Do write me a line, for I am really unhappy.

Yours always GEORGE MOORE

[Extract]

4 Upper Ely Place,
Dublin

31 August [1907?]

. . . But how am I to live many months without seeing you? Candidly I don't know. I have seen so much of you lately that I am demoralised—in the sense that I am no longer independent. My eyes turn to Leicestershire as the sunflower turns to the sun. Could you come to Ireland in the autumn? Lady Burroughs I am sure would be delighted to see you—you know who I mean, Howard's aunt. I think Howard and I are sincere friends, and I owe him to you. Dear friend, when I think of the joy you have been to me, the benedictive hopes and aspirations you have inspired, I am overcome; I cannot understand how such a thing could have come across my life's way, such a spirit, such a fountain of delight. The hours I spend with you I look upon as a sort of perfumed garden, a dim twilight and a fountain singing to it. But months will have to pass without my seeing you. Shall I be able to endure this long exile? I met a man in the train I knew, one of the partners in the firm of Agnew, and he complained I had not been writing. I answered, I have been living. You and you *alone* make me feel that I am alive

As ever GEORGE MOORE

227   *George Moore to Lady Cunard*

4 Upper Ely Place,
Dublin

25 May [1908]

Dear vision, dear and divine, come down to me through many generations from the time when there were gods upon the earth, but losing nothing in this long transmigration of the original loveliness, I write to thank thee for thy last kindnesses to me a mortal but a worshipper of the essential. These lines will seem exaggerated to thee, for among ages which accept nothing as divine the goddess forgets her divinity without however losing any particle of it. But of such heavy substance is our human life made that it may rise above the earth only a little way; it must fall back soon from thou to you under penalty of seeming ridiculous, so turning from the immortal to the mortal I beg to say that tomorrow I hope to send you twenty-four Wedgwood green dessert plates, vine-leaf pattern; the dishes which are the most beautiful part of the service are unprocurable for the moment: I hope to obtain one which will serve as a pattern, and some of the London dealers will be able to get five more for you. Your health continues to cause me much uneasiness and it is my belief that a short season in town would suit you better than a long one; were you to go away at the end of June for a rest cure a good deal of firm health might come of it. Of course rest is a bore but ill health is the greatest bore of all. If I could only persuade you. About myself there is nothing to say except that I am here among my pictures writing *Sister Teresa*, but you know nearly as much about her as I do myself. My secretary is as satisfactory as ever, and we are working away beginning at 10.30 and ending every day at 5.30. She was interested to hear about Lord Howard, for she knows him well through me and she knows you, and our visit to Meredith impressed her very much, but like ourselves she doesn't care much for his novels. His poetry is the better part of him; when one is a poet one is always a poet and all that is good in his novels is the poetry they contain. . . . The Huntingtons are away now. Poor little woman! She too would like adventure, so you say, and to be watched or looked after is always a bore, especially when the watching is inspired by moral intentions. Dear vision, dear and divine, how shall I tell anew the one thing which seems to me worth telling, that all I am capable of conceiving of immortality I see in thee. Other men it is said have seen angels but I have seen thee and thou art enough. A light, a beauty, a grace—how often I have used these words. Divine vision, if not divine in all men divine at least to me, au revoir.

GEORGE MOORE

Seaford House
Belgrave Square

4 September [1909]

My dear Blue Bird,

Why did you say that I didn't seem sorry to lose you? Because I don't wear my heart always on my sleeve . . . is that necessary? And do you not know that no one ever will appreciate you and admire you as I do—never with the same truthful fervour, for you come out of the ends of my life—everything led up to the moment when I first caught the glint of those beautiful wings; and have I not followed the light of those wings ever since? And would not the truthful picture of me be, a man following with outstretched arms? And shall I not die seeing a blue bird—when sight of all else is gone your beautiful wings will float in the dimming twilight; beautiful in the beginning, more beautiful in the end. Unworthy suggestion that I was not grieved at losing you after a month of happiness—happiness such as only the blue bird's wings can give.

Always, O my blue bird, thy devoted and ecstatic follower

GEORGE MOORE

229   *George Moore to Lady Cunard*

121 Ebury Street
21 August [1921]

An hour's talk with you alone, dearest Maud, brings all my love of you back again; an inexpressible joy, a drenching sadness it is, and all that is most essential and real in me.

I enclose the *Fragments from Heloise and Abelard* and write 'as ever', feeling that the words cut to the centre when I address them to you.

GEORGE MOORE

1858   1944

DAME ETHEL SMYTH

Ethel Smyth was born in London on 23 April 1858. She studied music at Leipzig and her first opera, *Fantasio,* was produced at Weimar in 1898. She was an energetic and robust composer (she might equally have been an explorer or a brilliant games player) who took a prominent part in the suffragist movement. In 1911 she composed a 'theme' song for the movement, 'The March of the Women'. She was created D.B.E. in 1922.

In her Autobiography, *Impressions that Remained,* she gives these charming letters from a schoolboy admirer of hers when she herself was a young girl. Writing of him and them she says, 'S.D was the son of country neighbours of ours. His great obsession was to be "gentlemanly"—an ambition which somewhat tempers the ardours of his thirteen years; nevertheless our relations, though tender, seem to have lacked the repose characteristic of the type he aimed at. It will be noticed that the references to Mary [her sister] grow more and more insistent, and as No. 8 is the last letter of the series, I imagine that soon after it was written the usual transfer of affection took place.'

[no date]

My very dearest Ethel,—I beg and beseech you not to be angry with me for not writing before, but I do assure you on my word of *honour* that I have not a bit of time in this beastly place to write letters, not *even* to *you*. I took your sentence and read it over again several times, and when I found out what it meant I was *very glad*. Hurrah, hurrah, the holidays are soon coming and then *won't* we have a lark? Why I declare it will be as good as donkey riding to see you skating away as gracefully as a swallow skims the earth, doing the outside and inside edge which I hear you do *splendidly*. I mean to learn and skate and then *perhaps* I may have the long looked-for pleasure and honour of skating with *you*. I hope you have quite forgiven me for my ungentlemanly conduct, but I assure you I did not mean to be hauty and grand, in fact it never entered into my mind. I have another thing to ask, if Mary has quite forgiven me for getting her into such a scrape and *not getting her out of it.*
    With the old usual fond love I remain ever
            Your most devoted *loving* friend *for ever,*

S.

[no date]

My dearest Ethel,—I must say I was greatly offended, but however there is an old saying 'all's well that ends well' and as you have greatly *improved* my *temper* I have quite forgotten it. Please do not say anything more about the locket, it was hardly worth giving to *you* and you know I hate flattery, but then of course I don't mind it from *you*. How is that *dear darling* BEAST R.S.? I hope very ill. If you go to see the Mater will you give my poor old dog a kiss from me, and tell Mary to give Jack's dog Sailor one. I know Brin will not bite *you*, because, like his master, he is very *particular*. . . .

232 *S.D. to Ethel Smyth*

[no date]

. . . Have you been riding that *happy* donkey again, and have you been up in the Royal Ethel[1] again? Do you remember our seat at the top? Oh those happy rides even on donkeys!! Jack has gone back to Harrow. I forgot to tell you one of the R—— girls is in love with him but of course he does not return it as *his views are somewhere else!!!* . . .

I will wear the *ring always* for your own *dear* sake. . . .

233 *S.D. to Ethel Smyth*

[no date]

. . . I hope you don't think I was rude that evening in not paying you any attention; it was because you were painting and I thought you would not care to talk. Now I am going to ask you a serious question, but think it *well* over before you reply; and that is have you forgiven me enough to ride with me in the holidays, not on donkeys but on ponies? Because I am going to ask the Governor to borrow that pony again for me, as he is better than nothing and goes splendidly with spurs. *Mind you think before you answer.*

In case you should hear of it I daresay you will wonder why I do not wear the ring, but *that is far* too precious to wear at school: why, the fellows would have it off and break it in a very short time. Was it not odd the other day when some of the fellows were

---

[1] An oak-tree.

telling us ghost stories that one of them should tell the one *you* told me in that *dear darling* oak tree where I have spent some of the happiest hours of my life about?

With the fondest love *possible*, I remain ever my very dearest Ethel your *most loving* friend for *ever*.

S.

P.S.—The scratchings out are only mistakes.

234   *S.D. to Ethel Smyth*

[no date]

. . . Now that we are friends again I must tell you something I was *not quite* honest about, that is I *lost* the ring, but still I thought I would not tell you just then but wait and see if I would not find it: imagine my *delight* and *joy* when I found it lying on the washing-stand, where it must have been lying several days, and now it is looking as pretty as ever on my finger, with the white stone upwards. I am in such spirits about finding the ring that I have been jumping about, and have just fallen off my chair: of course that is not the only reason; the great reason is that *sweet* letter from you. . . .

I am sorry to hear Mary and Neaner have colds: colds are such horrible things are they not? . . . I heard Alice looked charming, but I should think she felt rather nervous when she was making her bow. I should like to see you at your first Drawing Room: *you* would not feel nervous, would you? nor would Mary I should think. . . . I hope you saw your name in Sheldrake's paper. I am pleased to hear he told the truth for once, because of course *you* played *beautifully* as you always do, because you couldn't help it. . . . Remember me kindly to Mary. I dare not send my love because old Jack *would be angry*. . . .

[no date]

Dearest Ethel,—A million thanks for your *charming* note; it
seems a year since I saw you last; not that I shall ever forget the
happiest days I ever spent in my life, which were at Frimhurst! oh
it was a jolly time was it not? I am going with the J's to see a
cricket match between Harrow and Aldershot. I expect we shall
get an awful licking (I mean Harrow) as they have got the weakest
eleven that was ever known; at least I should think so. But then
you see they make up for it by football, which they can lick any
school Colledge or university at in the world. . . . We are going to
the W's which is about nine miles off Frimley, and as he has a
pony perhaps we shall be able to have what I have *so long* wished
for, a pony ride together. . . . It is all humbug about my liking the
youngest Miss J. I only did it to chaff you, only I am afraid I have
offended you. Knowing your SWEET temper I know you will
forgive me because I am *awfully* sorry about it.

Your loving friend,

S.

[no date]

. . . I am riding such a beautiful cob; people say he does his 18
miles in the hour. I thought of you and how you would enjoy it. I
do wish I could come over and see your *darling* self, but you see
people won't lend their ponies to do 26 miles, for its 13 from here
at least. . . . Please, as old Jack is not there, give my love to Mary
if I may venture to send it. . . .

[no date]

My dearest Ethel,—I daresay you wondered why I did not keep my promise in coming to see you, but the Governor made us come up to London or you may be sure I should not have missed the pleasure of seeing *you*. . . . I went to a Pantomime last night and enjoyed it as much as I could without *you* being there. . . . I am longing for the pleasure of seeing you, once more only. I brought the little squirrel up here with me, he is just as tame as ever and hops about like a child. . . .

Please write to me if you can spare the time. I must not ask *Mary* to write or dear old Jack may not like it. . . .

1874   1936

GILBERT KEITH CHESTERTON

Chesterton and, with him, Belloc are now out of fashion. They
were protagonists of common sense and the Catholic faith. A year
between the two world wars was not complete without a new book
from one or both of them and they did things and wrote books we
all wanted to do and to write. Belloc owned a mill-house on the
Sussex Downs; Chesterton on account of his size was the butt of
the cartoonists, on account of his wit was always backed to defeat
the misery-mongers and faint hearts. They were rather like two
very good, very interesting uncles who might have slipped you a
guinea when you visited them before returning to school. They
were great lovers of children, old pubs, exercise and talking.

If you were an open-air man you read Belloc's *Path to Rome* or his
essays (nearly always one on sailing and walking) in such books as
On Nothing. Chesterton was, to the average reader, rather less
serious. We enjoyed his 'sensible' poems and his epigrammatic
style. Even the reader of very low intelligence could appreciate
such remarks as 'There is a great deal of difference between the
eager man who wants to read a book, and the tired man who wants
a book to read', and who, in those far-off days of the early thirties,
has not gone walking in Sussex and Kent, shouting to his companions the famous lines from Chesterton's poem 'The Rolling
English Road':

Before the Roman came to Rye or out to Severn strode,
   The rolling English drunkard made the rolling English road.

For all Chesterton's biographical works on Robert Browning and Dickens (by which he is best judged), it was his fiction that we most enjoyed. Books such as *The Napoleon of Notting Hill*, *The Man Who Was Thursday* and the stories of his delightful and original Father Brown.

Chesterton was born in London on 29th May 1874. At St. Paul's School he won the 'Milton' prize for English verse. Later he became a freelance journalist and, in 1901, he married Frances Blogg. The love letters he wrote her are very much 'period' pieces when it was possible to set up a joint home in a country cottage for eight shillings a week and imagine you were living in luxury.

238   *Gilbert Keith Chesterton to Frances Blogg*

[189–?]

. . . I am looking over the sea and endeavouring to reckon up the estate I have to offer you. As far as I can make out my equipment for starting on a journey to fairyland consists of the following items.

1st. A Straw Hat. The oldest part of this admirable relic shows traces of pure Norman work. The vandalism of Cromwell's soldiers has left us little of the original hat-band.

2nd. A Walking Stick, very knobby and heavy: admirably fitted to break the head of any denizen of Suffolk who denies that you are the noblest of ladies, but of no other manifest use.

3rd. A copy of Walt Whitman's poems, once nearly given to Salter, but quite forgotten. It has his name in it still with an affectionate inscription from his sincere friend Gilbert Chesterton. I wonder if he will ever have it.

4th. A number of letters from a young lady, containing everything good and generous and loyal and holy and wise that isn't in Walt Whitman's poems.

5th. An unwieldy sort of a pocket knife, the blades mostly having an edge of a more varied and picturesque outline than is provided by the prosaic cutler. The chief element however is a thing 'to takes stones out of a horse's hoof.' What a beautiful sensation of security it gives one to reflect that if one should ever have money enough to buy a horse and should happen to buy one and the horse should happen to have a stone in his hoof—that one is ready; one stands prepared, with a defiant smile!

6th. Passing from the last miracle of practical foresight, we come to a box of matches. Every now and then I strike one of these, because fire is beautiful and burns your fingers. Some people think this waste of matches: the same people who object to the building of Cathedrals.

7th. About three pounds in gold and silver, the remains of one of Mr. Unwin's bursts of affection: those explosions of spontaneous love for myself, which, such is the perfect order and harmony of his mind, occur at startlingly exact intervals of time.

8th. A book of Children's Rhymes, in manuscript, called the 'Weather Book' about ¾ finished, and destined for Mr. Nutt. I have been working at it fairly steadily, which I think jolly creditable under the circumstances. One can't put anything interesting in it. They'll understand those things when they grow up.

9th. A tennis racket—nay, start not. It is a part of the new regime, and the only new and neat-looking thing in the Museum. We'll soon mellow it—like the straw hat. My brother and I are teaching each other lawn tennis.

10th. A soul, hitherto idle and omnivorous but now happy enough to be ashamed of itself.

11th. A body, equally idle and quite equally omnivorous, absorbing tea, coffee, claret, sea-water and oxygen to its own perfect satisfaction. It is happiest swimming, I think, the sea being a convenient size.

12th. A Heart—mislaid somewhere. And that is about all the property of which an inventory can be made at present. After all, my tastes are stoically simple. A straw hat, a stick, a box of matches and some of his own poetry. What more does man require? . . .

When we set up a house, darling (honeysuckle porch, yew clipt hedge, bees, poetry and eight shillings a week), I think you will have to do the shopping. Particularly at Felixstowe. There was a great and glorious man who said, 'Give us the luxuries of life and we will dispense with the necessities.' That I think would be a splendid motto to write (in letters of brown gold) over the porch of our hypothetical home. There will be a sofa for you, for example, but no chairs, for I prefer the floor. There will be a select store of chocolate-creams (to make you do the Carp with) and the rest will be bread and water. We will each retain a suit of evening dress for great occasions, and at other times clothe ourselves in the skins of wild beasts (how pretty you would look) which would fit your taste in furs and be economical.

I have sometimes thought it would be very fine to take an ordinary house, a very poor, commonplace house in West Kensington, say, and make it symbolic. Not artistic—Heaven—O Heaven forbid. My blood boils when I think of the affronts put by knock-kneed pictorial epicures on the strong, honest, ugly, patient shapes of necessary things: the brave old bones of life. There are aesthetic pottering prigs who can look on a saucepan without one tear of joy or sadness: mongrel decadents that can see no dignity in the honourable scars of a kettle. So they concentrate all their house decoration on coloured windows that nobody looks out of, and vases of lilies that everybody wishes out of the way. No: my idea (which is much cheaper) is to make a house really *allegoric*: really explain its own essential meaning. Mystical or ancient sayings should be inscribed on every object, the more prosaic the object the better; and the more coarsely and rudely the inscription was traced the better. 'Hast thou sent the Rain upon the Earth?' should be inscribed on the Umbrella-Stand: perhaps on the Umbrella. 'Even the Hairs of your Head are all numbered' would give a tremendous significance to one's hairbrushes: the words about 'living water' would reveal the music and sanctity of the sink: while 'Our God is a consuming Fire' might be written over the kitchen-grate, to assist the mystic musings of the cook—Shall we ever try that experiment, dearest? Perhaps not, for no words would be golden enough for the tools you had to touch: you would be beauty enough for one house. . . .

240 *Gilbert Keith Chesterton to Frances Blogg*

[189–?]

You say you want to talk to me about death: my views about death are bright, brisk and entertaining. When Azrael takes a soul it may be to other and brighter worlds: like those whither you and I go together. The transformation called Death may be something as beautiful and dazzling as the transformation called Love. It may make the dead man 'happy', just as your mother knows that you are happy. But none the less it is a transformation, and sad sometimes for those left behind. A mother whose child is dying can hardly believe that in the inscrutable Unknown there is anyone who can look to it as well as she. And if a mother cannot trust her child easily to God Almighty, shall I be so mean as to be angry because she cannot trust it easily to me? I tell you I have stood before your mother and felt like a thief. I know you are not going to part: neither physically, mentally, morally nor spiritually. But she sees a new element in your life, wholly from outside—is it not natural, given her temperament, that you should find her perturbed? Oh, dearest, dearest Frances, let us always be very gentle to older people. Indeed, darling, it is not they who are the tyrants, but we. They may interrupt our building in the scaffolding stages: we turn their house upside down when it is their final home and rest. Your mother would certainly have worried if you had been engaged to the Archangel Michael (who, indeed, is bearing his disappointment very well): how much more when you are engaged to an aimless, tactless, reckless, unbrushed, strange-hatted, opinionated scarecrow who has suddenly walked into the vacant place. I could have prophesied her unrest: wait and she will calm down all right, dear. God comfort her: I dare not. . . .

1878   *1945*

CARADOC EVANS

Caradoc Evans was born on 31st December 1878 at Pantycroy, Llandyssel, in Wales, the son of an estate agent. In true Welsh fashion he became a draper's apprentice in Carmarthen at 14. After twelve years of 'the trade' he moved to Cardiff and then to London where, by studying the Bible, he perfected his English.

He was a satirist of his own people. Indeed, his first book of short stories, *My People* (1915), was so vitriolic that it was banned in Wales. Arthur Machen writing about the book, said, 'Never have I come into so wild and dark a country as that shown in *My People*. Black savagery, black magic, black superstition, all pretending to be Methodism; Witch Doctors and Medicine Men more dread and powerful than any such to be discovered in Africa; and these calling themselves Respected Religious Teachers! If you would shudder and be thrilled and drink of the very Cauldron of the Sabbath . . .'

When Caradoc died, in 1945, Gwyn Jones wrote of him in *The Welsh Review*: 'A man here and there becomes a legend in his lifetime, and in their register is Caradoc Evans. With his death a great stormy petrel has fallen out of the Welsh sky.'

In 1933 Caradoc married the Countess Barcynska, an Englishwoman who wrote novels under the name of Oliver Sandys. She also wrote Caradoc's biography from which the following letters are taken.

325

Richmond
[Undated]

My lovely one,

You hung up on the telephone last night and I do not know what made you or how I have offended you and I cannot rest for thinking and wondering what was wrong with you or me. If you turn your face from me now, or stop coming to see me I shall not be able to stick it. I waited all afternoon for you to come in and toast your little toes at my fire and I burnt a whole bucketful of the office coal and I closed the window to make it a hot-house for you, but you came not. I am afraid to ring you tonight lest you do not answer my call. Then I shall not dare to go home.

> The stuffing in your bed is my good wishes.
> The down in your pillow is my breath.
> The sleep on your eyelids is my soul.
> Therefore your pillow is too soft for sorrow.
>   Your

CARADOC

Richmond,
June 9, 1930

My darling,

I am sorry I was late to-day. I had no business to be late. You know I like to be on time. I met Nat Gubbins in a pub and we got talking. I had three sherries only. You ticked me off and I said unkind things to you. I provoked you and went on provoking and could not stop myself. You looked so beautiful. It pleased me to make you cry.

I went away from you. I have had three more sherries. I vowed I would never see you again, but I cannot keep my vow.

Albeit I come back to my love for you.

CARADOC

Queens Square House,
Aberystwyth,
September 5, 1935

My little one,

I loved you the first moment I saw you and since then it has grown and grown and grown and will outlast eternity. I loved my first kiss and sweet it was. The kisses that came after were just as sweet.

I loved your voice and your eyes and your hair and I shall love them forever. I love your company and I shall never want to part from it, however wild be the periods of storm.

Your

CARADOC

244   *Caradoc Evans to his wife*[1]

36a North Parade,
Aberystwyth
January 6, 1945

My darling

For all the travail and unhappiness I have brought into your life I entreat your forgiveness. You have never failed me.

When I die I would like you to arrange to rest beside me.

My clothes are for Josi and I know that you will care for him out of your great and loving heart.

Do as you wish with my books and papers. Destroy, sell or keep. There is nothing else except the wherewithal to bury me.

CARADOC EVANS

[1] This letter was found in a drawer amongst his papers.

KATHERINE MANSFIELD

Katherine Mansfield was born at Wellington, New Zealand, and her first short story was published when she was 9 years old. Although she spent her young days in New Zealand it was really no good, in those days, for an artist to live anywhere but Paris or London, so she came over to Queen's College, London, where she edited the college magazine.

She was a brilliant and perfect short story writer and her influence extended far beyond the D. H. Lawrence 'circle' in which she moved. No one will ever forget, in the twenties and thirties, reading her collections *Bliss* and *The Garden Party*. She was also a fine critic. She married John Middleton Murry in 1913, after her divorce from her first husband, George Bowden.

Katherine Mansfield died of tuberculosis at Fontainebleau in 1923. Her letters to her husband make a vast collection. It is said that she wrote to him every day from her various nursing homes and clinics. And speaking of her, Middleton Murry said that she suffered, in rather the same way as Keats, from, 'the fearful alternations between confidence and despair which are the characteristic of the phthisic patient'.

Cholesbury,
[Summer, 1913]

Dear Jack,

This is just 'good morning' to you.

It has been a warm bright day here—very quiet. Immediately you had gone the house fell fast asleep, and it refuses to wake up or so much as smile in a dream until next Friday. I feel that I have been here a long time—and that it's New Zealand. I'm very happy, darling. But when you come into my thoughts I refuse you, quickly, quickly. It would take me a long time away from you before I could bear to think of you. You see, when I am not with you, every little bit of you puts out a flaming sword.

[Summer, 1913]

Jack dearest,

I sent your glasses yesterday, packed—I hope—carefully enough. Thank you for the money: I'm going to start again keeping a strict account of every penny I spend and then we can see where the screw is loose or the shoe pinches—or whatever it is.

Last night as I got into bed the bed refused to have me and down I flew with my feet up in the air. I was terrified but I couldn't help laughing—and once started I kept on. It seemed no end of a joke to be all alone in what R.C.[1] would call 'the profound stillness of the June night' and to be served that age old trick.

'Mrs Walter' is here today and we're having clean pinnies from head to foot. Such relief that I've written my reviews again and started my *Epilogue*.[2]

I went in to see Baby Gomm this morning. He was sucking. Such a pretty sight as a rule. But Mrs. Gomm's sharp worn face above him somehow filled me with horror.

You poor darling! Having to write to me at such 'impossible hours'. Well, assert yourself and 'be hanged if you will'. I'd rather

---

[1] Richard Curle.
[2] Katherine was contributing sketches under this title to *The Blue Review*.

wait for the afternoon post or until you feel 'I want to talk to Tig'.
So treat me like that in future.

I'll phone you when I get to London tomorrow, but I know
Wednesday is your busy day and I don't want on any account to
disturb you.

Things have straightened out in my mind and I'm rather
ashamed that I told you . . . what I did yesterday. It sings in my
ears rather like the wail of the little girl left behind on the fence
. . . more anger than anything else.

I kiss your eyes and your soft furry ears and your darling
frightening mouth.

I am your

TIG

Cafe Royal at 10.30 if I don't hear from you tomorrow.

247   Katherine Mansfield to John Middleton Murry

1st Morning   13 Quai aux Fleurs, Paris
                                              [Friday, 19th March 1915]

My dearest darling,

I have just had déjeuner—a large bowl of hot milk and a
small rather inferior orange—but still not dressed or washed or at
all a nice girl, I want to write to you. The sun is very warm today
and lazy—the kind of sun that loves to make patterns out of
shadows and puts freckles on sleeping babies—a pleasant creature.

Bogey, I had a vile and loathsome journey. We trailed out of
London in a fog that thickened all the way. A hideous little
Frenchwoman in a mackintosh with a little girl in a dirty face and
a sailor suit filled and overflowed my carriage. The child combed
its hair with a lump of brown bread, spat apple in our faces—
made the Ultimate impossible noises—ugh! how vile! Only one
thing rather struck me. It pointed out of the window and peeped
its eternal 'Qu'est-ce?' 'C'est de la *terre*, ma petite,' said the
mother, indifferent as a cabbage. Folkestone looked like a picture
painted on a coffin lid and Boulogne like one painted on a sardine
tin. Between them rocked an oily sea. I stayed on deck and felt

nothing when the destroyer signalled our ship. We were 2 hours late arriving and then the train to Paris did not even trot once— sauntered—meandered. Happily an old Scotchman, one time captain of the 'California', that big ship that went down in the fog off Tory Island, sat opposite to me and we 'got chatting'. He was a Scotchman with a pretty, soft accent; when he laughed he put his hand over his eyes and his face never changed—only his belly shook. But he was 'extremely nice'—quite as good as 1s. Worth of Conrad. At Amiens he found a tea-wagon and bought ham and fresh rolls and oranges and wine and would not be paid, so I ate hearty. Paris looked exactly like anywhere else—it smelled faintly of lavatories. The trees appeared to have shed their buds. So I took a room (the same room) and piled up coats and shawls on my bed to 'sleep and forget'. It was all merely dull beyond words and stupid and meaningless

But today the sun is out: I must dress and follow him. Bless you my dearest dear. I love you *utterly—utterly*—beyond words— and I will not be sad. I will not take our staying in our own rooms for a little as anything serious. How are you? What are you doing?

Address my letters to the post until I give you another address.

This is a silly old letter—like eating ashes with a fish-fork— but it is not meant to be. I rather wanted to tell you the truth. I read last night in the *Figaro* that the 16th Section (Carco's) are to be sent to TURKEY Alas, the day!

Jaggle, Bogey, love—tell me about you, your book, your rooms—everything.

Your

TIG

248 *Katherine Mansfield to John Middleton Murry*
[Extract from letter from Paris]
[19th March 1915]

. . . *The same night*. Very strange is my love for you tonight. Don't have it psycho-analysed. I saw you suddenly lying in a hot

331

bath, blinking up at me—your charming beautiful body half under the water. I sat on the edge of the bath in my vest waiting to come in. Everything in the room was wet with steam and it was night-time and you were rather languid. 'Tig, chuck over that sponge.' No, I'll *not* think of you like that. I'll shut my teeth and not listen to my heart. It begins to cry as if it were a child in an empty room and to beat on the door and say 'Jack—Jack—Jack and Tig.' I'll be better when I've had a letter.

Ah, my God, how can I love him like this! Do I love you so much more than you love me or do you too . . . feel like this?

TIG

Saturday morning. Just off to see if there are any letters. I'm all right, dearest.

249   *Katherine Mansfield to John Middleton Murry*

Friday evening
[26th March 1915]

Dearest darling,

I am in such a state of worry and suspense that I can't write to you tonight or send you anything. When I came back from the fruitless search for letters the concierge began a long story about an Alsatian in the house who had received yesterday a four page letter for the name of Bowden.[1] 'Another came today,' said she; 'I gave it back to the postman'. I literally screamed. I have *written* this name for her and she'd utterly forgotten it, thinking of me only as Mansfield. Since then I've simply rushed from post-office to post-office. The Alsatian is out. I'm waiting for her and the postman now. My heart dies in my breast with terror at the thought of a letter of yours being lost. I simply don't exist. I suppose I exaggerate—but I'd plunge into the Seine—or lie on a railway line— rather than lose a letter. You know, Bogey, my heart is simply crying all the time and I am frightened, desolate, useless for anything.

[1] Katherine's married name.

332

Oh, my precious—my beloved little Jag, forgive Tig such a silly scrawl.

But life ought not to do such things to you and me. I could *kill* the concierge—yes, with pleasure. 'Une lettre d'Angleterre dans un couvert bleu.'

Courage! But at this moment I am simply running as fast as I can and crying my loudest into your arms.

I will write you properly tomorrow. This is just to say that I love you and that you are the breath of life to me.

TIG

250   *Katherine Mansfield to John Middleton Murry*

[28th March 1915]

Jack, I shan't hide what I feel today. I woke up with you in my breast and on my lips. Jack, I love you terribly today. The whole world is gone. There is only you. I walk about, dress, eat, write—but all the time I am *breathing* you. Time and again I have been on the point of telegraphing you that I am coming home as soon as Kay sends my money. It is still possible that I shall.

> Jack, Jack, I want to come back,
> And to hear the little ducks go
> Quack! Quack! Quack!

Life is too short for our love even though we stayed together every moment of all the years. I cannot think of you—our life—our darling life—you, my treasure—everything about you.

No, no, no. Take me quickly into your arms. Tig is a tired girl and she is crying. I want you, I want you. Without you life is nothing.

Your woman

TIG

Sunday before Xmas
[19th December 1915]

My dearest love,

I have just got the letter that you wrote me on Thursday night, with the money in it. Papers have come, too, which I have not opened yet, and other letters are waiting—but I want to speak to you très sérieusement. Your letter made you 'real' to me in the deepest sense of the word, I believe, almost for the first time. You say just those things which I have felt. I am *of* you as you write just as you are *of* me.

Now I will say Toujours because now at last I know you. We are in a world apart, and we always shall be in a world apart—in our own kingdom which *is* finer and rarer. Shut the gates of it for a minute and let us stand there. Let us kiss each other, we three. Yes, Bogey, I shall love you *for always*.

TIG

Sunday night
[27th January 1918]

My love and my darling,

It is ten minutes past eight. I must tell you how much I love you at ten minutes past eight on a Sunday evening, January 27th 1918.

I have been indoors all day (except for posting your letter) and I feel greatly rested. Juliette has come back from a new excursion into the country, with blue irises—do you remember how beautifully they grew in that little house with the trellis tower round by the rocks?—and all sorts and kinds of sweet-smelling jonquils. . . . The room is very warm. I have a handful of fire, and the few little flames dance on the log and can't make up their minds to attack it. . . . There goes a train. Now it is quiet again except for my watch. I look at the minute hand and think what a spectacle I shall make of myself when I am really coming home to you. How I shall sit in the railway carriage, and put the old watch in my lap and pretend to cover it with a book—but not read or see, but just whip it up with my longing gaze, and simply make it go faster.

My love for you tonight is so deep and tender that it seems to be outside myself as well. I am fast shut up like a little lake in the embrace of some big mountains, you would see me down below, deep and shining—and quite fathomless, my dear. You might drop your heart into me and you'd never hear it touch bottom. I love you—I love you—Goodnight.

Oh, Bogey, what it is to love like this!

V. SACKVILLE-WEST

Victoria Sackville-West was born at Knole Castle, Kent, a house reputed to have 365 rooms, one for each day of the year. She was the daughter of the 3rd Baron Sackville.

In 1913 she married Harold Nicolson.

Her poem 'The Land' was awarded the Hawthornden Prize in 1927 and, in 1946, 'The Garden' received the Heinemann Prize. She will be remembered best for the perfect garden she made at her home, Sissinghurst Castle, and for her highly sophisticated gardening articles in various leading periodicals. 'She spent every penny she could spare on the garden at the expense of the house,' says her son Nigel Nicolson in the introduction to his father's *Diaries and Letters*, vol. 1, 1966.

Harold Nicolson and his wife wrote to each other daily when they were apart. The following is one of the tenderest of all love letters collected in this book.

253   *V. Sackville-West to Harold Nicolson*

25th June, 1929
Long Barn

What is so torturing when I leave you at these London stations and drive off, is the knowledge that you are *still there*—

that, for half an hour or three-quarters of an hour, I could still return and find you; come up behind you, take you by the elbow, and say 'Hadji'.

I came straight home, feeling horribly desolate and sad, driving down that familiar and dreary road. I remembered Rasht and our parting there; our parting at Victoria when you left for Persia; till our life seemed made of up partings, and I wondered how long it would continue.

Then I came round the corner on to the view—our view—and I thought how you loved it, and how simple you were, really, apart from your activity; and how I loved you for being both simple and active in one and the same person.

Then I came home, and it was no consolation at all. You see, when I am unhappy for other reasons, the cottage is a real solace to me; but when it is on account of *you* that I am unhappy (because you have gone away), it is an additional pang—it is the same place, but a sort of mockery and emptiness hangs about it—I almost wish that just *once* you could lose me and then come straight back to the cottage and find it still full of me but empty of me, then you would know what I go through after you have gone away.

Anyhow, you will say, it is worse for you who go back to a horrible and alien city, whereas I stay in the place we both love so much; but really, Hadji, it is no consolation to come back to a place full of coffee-cups—there was a cardboard-box lid, full of your rose-petals, still on the terrace.

You are dearer to me that anybody ever has been or ever could be. If you died suddenly, I should kill myself as soon as I had made provision for the boys. I really mean this. I could not live if I lost you. I do not think one could conceive of a love more exclusive, more tender, or more pure than I have for you. I think it is immortal, a thing which happens seldom.

Darling, there are not many people who would write such a letter after sixteen years of marriage, yet who would be saying therein only one-fiftieth of what they were feeling as they wrote it. I sometimes try to tell you the truth, and then I find that I have no words at my command which could possibly convey it to you.

EDITH THOMPSON

On 6th December 1922 one of the most dramatic and controversial murder trials opened at the Old Bailey. Before Mr. Justice Shearman were Edith Thompson and Frederick Bywaters, accused of jointly murdering Edith's husband, Percy Thompson, at midnight on 3rd/4th October as they were returning home from the West End to their house in a street called Kensington Gardens, Ilford. As they were walking along Belgrave Road, Frederick Bywaters, Edith's lover and some eight years her junior, followed them. When he approached them Bywaters drew a knife from his coat and stabbed Percy Thompson to death. He ran away. Edith, too, ran to get help and when she returned Percy was dead.

The Thompsons' life was not happy. They earned their living separately. Percy was a London shipping clerk and Edith was employed by a wholesale milliners in Aldersgate Street. They left home each morning at 8.15 and did not return until 7 p.m. They had no children and Thompson was often violent in his attempts to force sex on his wife. There were bitter quarrels and Thompson became disagreeable and mean towards his wife.

Frederick Bywaters got to know the Thompsons when they moved to 41 Kensington Gardens and, indeed, in June 1921 he came to lodge with them. Bywaters was in the Merchant Marine and he was often away from England on board the S.S. *Morea*. It was while he was away on his various voyages that Edith Thompson (Peidi) wrote him the letters which, eventually, caused her to be hanged, with her lover, on 9th January 1923. Edith received

338

many letters from Frederick but, having read and answered one letter, she destroyed it. She was constantly referred to, at her trial, as a 'femme fatale', a woman who had driven Bywaters to commit murder for her sake. It is now thought that she was nothing of the kind but only a frustrated working girl with a very vivid imagination. Perhaps Bywaters, so much younger than she, took her letters seriously. These letters which are full of what she was doing each day, are those of a mother as well as a mistress, indeed, at times, almost of a slave. Unfortunately for Edith they were also full of references to her attempts to poison her husband. Yet we shall never know whether she actually carried out the poisoning attempts she describes so vividly. She would include, too, cuttings from newspapers dealing with murder cases of the day. The entire correspondence, their whole love, is summed up in one sentence from one of Edith's letters. 'He has the right by law to all that you have the right to by nature and love.'

The following letters are a selection from the book of the trial by Filson Young. Only three letters of Bywaters were found and brought in as evidence. And reading the trial, which seems to have been mismanaged, it is impossible to believe that Edith intended her lover so blatantly to kill her husband. It is clear that she had no idea the impression her suggestible letters were having on the young man who was only 21 when he died.

254   *Edith Thompson to Frederick Bywaters*

Dec. 6, 1921

Darlingest boy I know,

I saw in the paper yesterday you touched Aden on the 28th, I suppose tomorrow or Sunday you will arrive in Bombay & I believe Bill left today, perhaps you will just manage to see him tho'.

I am feeling very blue today darlint, you havn't talked to me for a fortnight, and I am feeling worried, oh I don't know how I'm feeling really, it seems like a very large pain that comes from that ceaseless longing for you, words are expressionless—darlint, the greatness, the bigness of the love I have, makes me fear that it is too good to last, it will never die, darlint don't think, but I fear —how can I explain—that it will never mature, that we, you & I will never reap our reward, in fact, I just feel today darlint, that our love will all be in vain.

He talked to me again last night a lot, darlint I don't remember much about it, except that he asked me if I was any happier. I just said I suppose as happy as I shall ever be, & then he frightened me by saying—oh I don't think I'll tell you.

I left off there, darlint—thought—thought for $\frac{1}{2}$ an hour & I will tell you now. He said he began to think that both of us would be happier if we had a baby, I said 'No, a thousand times No' & he began to question me, and talk to me & plead with me, oh darlint, its all so hard to bear, come home to me—come home quickly and help me, its so much worse this time. He hasn't worried me any more, except that once I told you about, darlint, do you understand what I mean? but things seem worse for all that. You know I always sleep to the wall, darlint, well I still do but he puts his arm round me and oh its horrid. I suppose I'm silly to take any notice, I never used to—before I knew you—I just used to accept the inevitable, but you know darlint, I either feel things very intensely or I am quite indifferent just cold—frozen.

But to write all this is very selfish of me, it will make you feel very miserable—you can't do anything to help me—at least not yet, so I'll stop.

What else can I talk about? only ordinary things darlint, but to talk about even those perhaps will help to deaden the pain. We went to the theatre in the week to see 'Woman to Woman' at the Globe. I had the tickets given me. Darlint, it was a lovely play, I think I liked it as much as 'Romance' altho the plot is not the same. I have written you a description of it—I should like you to discuss it with me, but better still I should like to see it again with you, but I cant, so I have talked to you about it, that's the next best thing, isn't it darlint?

Also I finished the book 'The Trail of 98' & liked it ever so much, I have also written to you, about it. Darlint you have quite a lot of mail from me at Aden, I think, I do hope you will feel pleased—not too miserable, I don't want you to darlint, just forget all the miserable things I've said to you.

Its been terribly cold here, & foggy—thick real old fashioned

340

fogs for 4 days. I've had & still got such a bad chilblain on the back of my heel—its been there a fortnight now & I cant get rid of it. I think I've tried 5 different things. The worst of it is any shoes I have—the tops of them cut it—the chilblain right in half.

Darlint, have you written to the 'B.I.Co.' yet, please do—I want you to, you know—if we are going to win, we must look forward understand darlint?

Yesterday I was taking a country buyer to Cooks, St. Pauls, & passing the 'Chapter House' he said to me 'Would you care for a glass of wine here, its quite a nice place.' Imagine darlint, me being told its quite a nice place. I said 'No thanks, really I'd rather not' & yet if it had been anywhere else I should have said 'Yes.' Do you know, darlint, when you were home last time we didnt go there once, I feel sorry when I think about it, I should like to have gone, but we will next time, say 'Yes' darlint I do so hope you'll be home longer than a fortnight this next time. Isn't it funny the feelings we have about going into the places with strangers that we have been in together. I feel very strongly about it, I *couldn't* no I simply couldn't go & sit in either of those corner seats at the Strand without you nor at the Holborn, nor 'Chapter House' nor the 'Coronetion' nor anywhere else, where you & I have been *and talked*, really talked. Do you remember us talking together in the 'Chapter House' one Friday night, about my life being happy, living with only 2 people beside myself. I don't remember what I answered then—Yes, I believe I do, but the answer would not be the same today, it would be with only 2 people, 2 halves, one whole, darlint, just you & me, say 'Yes it's right, & it will be so,' I want telling so many times darlint.

What do you think he is going to learn dancing—to take me out to some nice ones, won't it be fun—as the song says 'Aint we got fun,' while you are away. About myself, darlint, its still the same & I've not done anything yet—I don't think I shall until next month, unless you tell me otherwise, after you get this letter, or the one I wrote previously.

Darlint I got a letter, or rather 2 in 1 envelope on Saturday morning. You say that you can't write but you will try from Port Said. Is this correct? The envelope of these is stamped Port Said. No, you're quite right darlint, when you say you cant talk to me, you can't, these letters are only writing, they are not talking, not the real talking I was looking forward to.

Why is it? darlint, what is the matter? you do still feel the same, don't you? Oh say Yes, I feel so sad & miserable about it. I seem to be able to talk to you always & for ever, but you, I don't know, you don't seem the same as when you were away before, you did talk to me a lot that trip, but this time you don't seem to at all. Why is it darlint? You do still feel the same don't you? Am I horrid to expect so much, tell me if I am but darlint I feel that I could give all, everything & I can't read between the lines of your letters this time that you even want to accept that all.

One part that did amuse me was over the argument. That expression 'I do love 'em, etc.' made me think of old times, you remember the Shanklin times, when neither of us had any cares, or worries, personal ones I mean, altho' we hadn't learned to know ourselves or each other, which were the best times darlint? now or then, just tell me, I shant mind. That was a funny dream you had, wasn't it? I wonder what it means or if it means anything. Why do you tell me not to get excited darlint, do you think I would. I don't think I should darlint, over that, you & I have too much at stake, to take too many risks. But I don't think there is any risk, darlint, it doesn't seem so at any rate. But I feel that I could dare anything, and bear everything for you, darlint.

That's all now, darlint, I've got such a great lump come in my throat & I'll have to swallow it somehow. Peidi does want you now.

255 *Edith Thompson to Frederick Bywaters*

Feb. 15, 1922

I was so pleased to get your letter, darlint, it came on Friday midday. Miss Prior took it in & examined the seal—all the time she was bringing it down the stairs. I was looking at her Darlint, you say I cant know how you feel, when you failed cant I darlint? don't I know didn't I fail once? I do know darlint, its heartbreaking to think all the schemeing—all the efforts are in vain. But we'll be patient darlint the time will come we're going to make it just you & I our united efforts darlint, I shall be very very interested in all you will have to tell me. I can understand darlint how difficult it must be—all that underwork. I wonder if I could do any more I believe I could somehow women usually can in these things but I'm counting on you putting all my faith in those persuasive powers that I know you possess, because you've used them on me. Darlingest Boy you say 'Am I right' I don't know it's what I think happened—darlint—but I don't know, I've never had any experience in such matters and I can never discuss them with members of my sex as so many girls do therefore I suppose I'm rather ignorant, on such subjects but I'll tell you everything about it when I can look at you & you mustnt be cross with me darlint about getting up. I can say I did know it was dangerous or whether I didn't I just didn't think about it at all, I fought and fought with myself to make myself keep up & I think I succeeded, darlint. Put yourself in my place darlint & see how you would feel if you thought by stopping in bed and not making an effort a doctor would have been called in would have said well what have you & I think he would someone else not you would have taken both the blame & the pride for the thing they did not do.

I imagine how I would feel about it, I'm afraid darlint I would not have been able to keep silent. Please dont worry, darlint I'm alright really now—only a bit shaky—& I dont like the way you say 'It was ridiculous for you to get up' etc. because I'm not going to let you bully me so please take note monsieur & dont transgress again.

Darlint that Friday night you wouldn't have 'gone under to anything' would you and left me by myself. I understand how you felt, but cheer up darlint it wont always be like that & all we get in future darlint, we shall appreciate the more because we have had to climb so many stiles in 'Our glorious adventure' & have fallen the other side so many times, that when we dont stumble when we land on our feet oh wont it be gorgeous darlint the thought of it is the only thing that keeps us up sometimes eh, I understand darlint, the one pal you've got understands everything.

It is as if our thoughts and minds & actions were just one even tho' we are miles apart. Do you feel like that darlint I do when I'm doing anything by myself. I always think & say to myself that you are doing it & thinking it with me.

Darlint when you are home next time you must ask your

sister to play that song for you because it wont matter that she does know who gave it you then will it & I shall never be able to play it so darlint please do.

Fancy darlint you doing such a dreadful thing as to discuss those truly awful matters with me. I am ashamed of you. Am I? you know & darlint I am glad you altered (in your own mind) that word *good* to fortunate because you also have to utter the word 'Bad' to unfortunate.

I've been reading a perfectly glorious book darlint 'The Business of Life' by R. W. Chambers. It is very like in detail 'The Common Law' but in the *one* question it is exactly opposite.

I did enjoy it so much I believe I liked it better than 'The Common Law' no I'm not quite certain. Anyhow I want you to read it & tell me what you think of it if you liked it better etc it seemed to me more human in many ways, than the other one.

Shall I send it to your home for you to read over weekend March 18th or shall I keep it & give it to you. I'd like to send it to you now, I'm so anxious for you to read it.

Darlint is my letter to Bombay awaiting you on your arrival, or do you have to wait a week for it, I believe you do. This morning I think you arrive and you'll see Bill & I'll be thinking of & about you all this coming week darlint such a lot. I know you'll be careful you said you would.

I want to tell you about a dream I had last week I received a letter by hand by Avis & the envelope was addressed in Harry Renton's writing only inside was a letter from you.

It wasn't your writing darlint it was a large round hand just like a schoolboy's. I read & read for a long time not recognising from whom it came until I came to the word Peidi & then I called out 'Why its from my own boy.' I dont know if I did really, but I did in the dream.

Even now I cant determine in my own mind whether you sent the letter to him to send on to me, or whether he got hold of it somehow.

Tell me what you think darlint. There's nothing but ordinary every day things to tell you darlint oh except one thing just that I love you so much but you know that dont you darlint, I wish you were here that I could tell you but you will be one day each day is gradually dragging on.

PEIDI

June 2, 1922

Since I have posted the first letter to Sydney darlint a whole night & day has gone by & Ive been thinking & thinking such a lot & feeling so awful about it—I couldnt sleep for one little minute—thinking about you & what you would think of me & how you would feel when you received it.

I am sorry darlint—but I wrote how I felt it was awful—& sometimes when you feel so terrible you write & think very unjust and bitter things your feelings at the time carry you away they did me please, please, darlingest boy forgive me.

Pals should never feel hard & cross with one another—should they? & we are still pals in spite of that letter, aren't we? do write and tell me it has made no difference; I feel an awful beast about it: I wish I had not posted it at once but kept it for a day then I should have torn it up. Please forgive me & try to excuse your pal. She did feel so awfully down in the world when she found that or felt that the best pal a girl ever had had forgotten or neglected her.

She'll try hard not to transgress again

PEIDI

[20th September] 1922

Darlint darlint pal—I'm so happy Ive heard from you—such a lot it seems like the very first time I have really heard since you have been gone. I don't know what to say to you—I really dont —but you know how I feel dont you? Today is the 20th and I've got tons of work to do—it is statement day and its also nearly H—so I must post this now. I will talk to you properly and answer your letter—& keep it until you tell me where to send it— you will wont you? One thing I must say darlingest pal—Im a thought reader—I must be—you'll think so too when you get

345

your parcel at Plymouth. Must it be pals only darlint? if you say
'Yes' it shall be.

PEIDI
(still loves you.)

258   Edith Thompson to Frederick Bywaters

1922

Darlingest Boy,

Thank you—ever, ever so much for all those things I
received—are they all for me tho? there seems such a lot & what
am I to do about them? Wear them now? or wait, I know when
you sent them you wanted me & expected that I would wear
them, but now—well I suppose its not to be.

Ive nothing to talk about darlint, not a tiny little thing—
Life—the Life I & we lead is gradually drying me up—soon I'll
be like the 'Sahara'—just a desert, like the 'Shulamite' you must
read that book, its interesting—absorbing, arent books a consolation and a solace? We ourselves die & live in the books we read
while we are reading them & then when we have finished, the
books die and we live—or exist—just drag on thro years & years,
until when? who knows—I'm beginning to think no one does—no
not even you & I, we are not the shapers of our destinies.

I'll always love you darlint,

PEIDI

259   Edith Thompson to Frederick Bywaters

[no date]

Darlint, I did have a doubt about Australia—doesnt doubt
show great love sometimes? I think it does, its that sort of doubt I
had—perhaps 'doubt' is the wrong word—its fear more—fear of
losing you—a woman is different for a man—a man says 'I want it

346

—I'll take it'—a woman wants to say that—but an inborn feeling of modesty is it? makes her withhold her action perhaps you'll not understand this. Men are carried away on the moment by lots of different actions, love, hate, passion, & they always stand by what they have done.

Darlint, Australia frightens me, memories, with faces, return & humans cannot control their own Fate.

Supposing Fate has it written down that you & I are never to be happy, you'll fight against it, but you'll have to give in & perhaps you'll come back, perhaps you wont. Darlint I'm going to forget there is such a place from the day you sail this time, till the day you return.

On the evening you said to me 'Au revoir' in January—you told me you still had something—something in connection with Australia. All the time you were away I wondered why you mentioned it what made you remind me about it.

Darlint before you go this time send me everything connected with Australia & when you *come back to me from Australia* I'll give them all back to you, to do with what you like.

Whatever you think about this will you talk to me about it please darlint.

Nothing, nothing on this earth ever will make a teeny scrap of difference to our love.

Darlint, it is real & for all time too large—too great—too grand for anything to destroy it.

I'll keep those things, at least for you to see the first time, but darlint if its possible for us to go out this Thursday, I'm going to wear one set, & on the day you come home I'm going to wear the other set. Yes, you want me to? or not?

Why and how was I a 'little girl'—darlint I always feel that I want you to take care of me, to be nice to me, to fuss hold me always in your 2 arms, tight, ever so tight, & kiss me, keep on doing it darlint.

An organ outside now, playing 'Margie'.

Darlint I'll try not to be cynical, hard I'll try always to be just a 'little girl' a tiny little girl that you call

PEIDI

Darlingest boy I know always and ever, after all I shant be with you on our birthday—darlint I shall think of you such a lot & you will too eh?

I want to leave every little thing to you darlingest boy, I know you will decide and do what is best for two halves, only I should like to know all your thoughts and plans darlint, just to help me beat up & live, to exist thro this life, until it is time for us to be joined together. Could you write to me from Marseilles & tell me everything. Am I selfish? I believe I am because I am always thinking of myself & yet right deep down in my heart I want to do what is best for you.

Its fearfully hard to decide, thats why I want you to pour moi & whatever you say or do I shall accept without fear or doubt or question, & think all the time, even if it seems wrong to me, that you know it will, at some indefinite period be, best for us. This is right, isn't it?

It gets harder and harder every time doesnt it. I seem to have lived years & years in that little one from 27.6.21 to now.

Goodbye darlingest—I want you to have every success in everything darlint, you know that dont you? if only I could help you in that success, but I cant, so you must go on by yourself and know always that you are loved and trusted by

PEIDI

261 *Frederick Bywaters to Edith Thompson*

Bombay,
1st December, 1921

Dear Edie,

Do you remember last Xmas you wrote to me wishing me all the best. I never wrote you so this year I'm going to make sure of it, I want to wish you all that you can wish yourself. I know all those wishes of yours will run into a deuce of a lot of money. Such items as fur coats, cars and champagne, will be very prominent on the list—anyhow, good health and I hope you get it. Have a very real good time, the best that is possible. I shall be about 2 days this side of Suez. Never mind I will have a drink with you. Once more the very very best at Xmas and always.

Yours very Sincerely,

FREDDY

262   *Frederick Bywaters to Edith Thompson*

Gomme
[no date]

Darling Peidi Mia,

Tonight was impulse—natural—I couldnt resist—I had to hold you darling little sweetheart of mine—darlint I was afraid—I thought you were going to refuse to kiss me—darlint little girl—I love you so much and the only way I can control myself is by not seeing you and I'm not going to do that. Darlint Peidi Mia—I must have you—I love you darlint—logic and what others call reason do not enter into our lives, and where two halves are concerned. I had no intention darlint of doing that—it just happened thats all—I'm glad now chere—darlint when you suggested the occupied carriage, I didn't want to go in it—did you think that perhaps I did—so that there would have been no opportunity for me, to break the conditions that I had stipulated—darlint I felt quite confident that I would be able to keep my feelings down—I was wrong Peidi. I was reckoning on will power over ordinary forces—but I was fighting what? not ordinary forces—nothing was fighting the whole of me. Peidi you are my magnet—I cannot resist darlint—you draw me to you now and always, I shall never be able to see you and remain impassive. Darlint Peidi Mia Idol mine—I love you—always—always Ma Chere. Last night when I read your questions I didn't know how to answer them—I have now Peidi?

Darlint I dont think I can talk about other things tonight—I want to hold you so tightly. I'm going to tonight in my sleep. Bon Nuit Ma Petite, cherchez bien pour votre

FREDDY

[no date]

Peidi Darlint.

Sunday evening, Everybody is out and now I can talk to you. I wonder what you are doing now my own little girl. I hope that Bill has not been the cause of any further unpleasantness darlint. Darlint little girl do you remember saying 'the hope for all.' 'Or the finish of all.' Peidi the finish of all seems terrible even to contemplate. What darlint would it be in practice? Peidi Mia I love you more and more every day—it grows darlint and will keep on growing. Darlint in the park—our Park on Saturday, you were my 'little devil'—I was happy then Peidi—were you? I wasn't thinking of other things—only you darlint—you was my entire world —I love you so much my Peidi—I mustnt ever think of losing you, darlint if I was a poet I could write volumes—but I'm not—I suppose at the most Ive only spoken about 2 dozen words today I dont try not to speak—but I have no wish to—Im not spoken to much so have no replies to make.

Darlint about the watch—I never really answered your question—I only said I wasnt cross. I cant understand you thinking that the watch would draw me to you—where you yourself wouldnt—is that what you meant darlint or have I misunderstood you. The way you have written looks to me as though you think that I think more of the watch than I do of you darlint—Tell me Peidi Mia that I misunderstood your meaning.

Darlint Peidi Mia—I do remember you coming to me in the little room and I think I understand what it cost you—a lot more then darlint than It could ever now. When I think about that I think how nearly we came to be parted for ever,—if you had not forfeited your pride darlint I dont think there would ever have been yesterday or tomorrow.

My darlint darlint little girl I love you more than I will ever be able to show you. Darlint you are the centre—the world goes on round you, but you ever remain my world—the other part some things are essential—others are on the outskirts and sometimes so far removed from my mind that they seem non existent. Darling Peidi Mia—I answered the question about the word 'Idle' on Saturday—I never mentioned it.

Yes darlint—I remember you being asked if you had found

350

'The great lover'. It was when you sang 'A Tumble Down Nook.'

What have I found darlint? The darlingest little sweetheart girl in the whole world and 'The Only Pal.' Now darlint pal— Im anxious about Avis—I hope you have found out all there is to know of the other night—I want you to tell me. Supposing she did stay with some fellow and she tells you and asks you not to tell anybody—are you going to tell me Peidi?

Darlint I'm enclosing a slip for you for the books in case I am unable to get them myself—also will you get the 'Tempting of Paul Chester' Alice and Claude Askew. There is 13/- to pay on the others—but darlint I hope to be able to get them myself, also and principally I want to drink Beaune with you.

Good night now darlingest—dearest little sweetheart and big pal.

FREDDY

DYLAN THOMAS

Dylan Thomas was born on 22nd October 1914, at 5 Cwmdonkin Drive, Swansea, and he died in New York on 9th November 1953.

Between these two dates a considerable literature has grown up of a poet who was an angel when he was young and uncorrupted, and a devil when he was in drink which, in later years, was more often than not. The guilt of an entire generation between the wars and after has been thrown on the shoulders of this brilliant poet who was incapable of managing (indeed despised) what he would have called 'ordinary' life. Anyone can perceive his faults—they are no longer of any consequence. What matters is his poetry, much less read today than twenty years ago.

The love affair between Dylan Thomas and Pamela Hansford Johnson has been made 'famous' by Constantine FitzGibbon in his books on Dylan Thomas in which he says, speaking of Thomas's life, 'There have probably been more legends and myths about Dylan Thomas than about any other poet since Byron. As a friend of his I am anxious that the true story can be told before the myth has got quite out of control.'

I am tortured to-day by every doubt and misgiving that an here-ditarily twisted imagination, an hereditary thirst and a commercial quenching, a craving for a body not my own, a chequered education and too much egocentric poetry, and a wild, wet day in a tided town, are capable of conjuring up out of their helly deeps. Helly deeps. There is torture in words, torture in their linking & spell-ing, in the snail of their course on stolen paper, in their sound that the four winds double, and in my knowledge of their inadequacy. With a priggish weight on the end, the sentence falls. All sentences fall when the weight of the mind is distributed unevenly along the holy consonants & vowels. In the beginning was a word I can't spell, not a reversed Dog, or a physical light, but a word as long as Glastonbury and as short as pith. Nor does it lisp like the last word, break wind like Balzac through a calli-graphied window, but speaks out sharp & everlastingly with the intonations of death and doom on the magnificent syllables. I wonder whether I love your word, the word of your hair—by lov-ing hair I reject all Oscardom, for homosexuality is as bald as a coot—the word of your voice. The word of your flesh, & the word of your presence. However good, I can never love you as earth. The good earth of your blood is always there, under the skin I love, but it is two worlds. There must be only half a world tangible, audible, & visible to the illiterate. And is that the better half? Or is it the wholly ghostly past? And does the one-eyed ferryman, who can-not read a printed word, row over a river of words, where the syllables of the fish dart out & are caught on his rhyming hook, or feel himself a total ghost in a world that's as matter-of-fact as a stone?

? 26th May 1934
Sunday morning
Bed

Question One. I can't come up.

Two. I'm sleeping no better.

Question Three. No I've done everything that's wrong.

Four. I daren't see the doctor.

Question Five. Yes I love you.

I'm in a dreadful mess now. I can hardly hold the pencil or hold the paper. This has been coming for weeks. And the last four days have completed it. I'm absolutely at the point of breaking now. You remember how I was when I said goodbye to you for the first time. In the Kardomah when I loved you so much and was too shy to tell you. Well imagine me one hundred times worse than that with my nerves oh darling absolutely at the point of breaking into little bits. I can't think and I don't know what I'm doing. When I speak I don't know if I'm shouting or whispering and that's a terrible sign. It's *all* nerves and more. But I've never imagined anything as bad.

And it's all my own fault too. As well as I can I'll tell you the honest honest truth. I never want to lie to you. You'll be terribly angry with me I know and you'll never write to me again perhaps. But darling you want me to tell you the truth don't you. I left Laugharne on Wednesday morning and went down to a bungalow in Gower. I drank a lot in Laugharne & was feeling a bit grim even then. I stayed in Gower with a friend of mine in the waster days of the reporter's office. On Wednesday evening his fiancée came down. She was tall and thin and dark and a loose red mouth and later we all went out and got drunk. She tried to make love to me all the way home. I told her to shut up because she was drunk. When we got back she still tried to make love to me, wildly like an idiot in front of Cliff. She went to bed and my friend and I drank some more and then very modernly he decided to go and sleep with her. But as soon as he got in bed with her she screamed and ran into mine. I slept with her that night & for the next three nights. We were terribly drunk day and night. Now I can see all sorts of things. I think I've got them.

Oh darling, it hurts me to tell you this but I've got to tell

354

you because I always want to tell you the truth about me. And I never want to share. It's you & me or nobody, you and me and nobody. But I have been a bloody fool & I'm going to bed for a week. I'm just on the borders of D.T.s darling and I've wasted some of my tremendous love for you on a lank, redmouthed girl with a reputation like a hell. I don't love her a bit. I love you Pamela always & always. But she's a pain on the nerves. For Christ knows why she loves me. Yesterday morning she gave her ring back to Cliff. I've got to put a hundred miles between her and me. I must leave Wales for ever & never see her. I see bits of you in her all the time & tack on to those bits. I've got to be drunk to tack on to them. I love you Pamela and must have you. As soon as all this is over I'm coming straight up. If you'll let me. No, but better or worse I'll come up next week if you'll have me. Don't be too cross or too angry. What the hell am I to do? And what the hell are you going to say to me? Darling I love you & think of you all the time. Write by return and don't break my heart by telling me I mustn't come up to London to you becos I'm such a bloody fool.

XXXX Darling. Darling oh

ALUN LEWIS

Alun Lewis was born at Aberdare on 1st July 1915 and he grew up in the atmosphere of bitterness which surrounded the impoverished Welsh miners of those days. 'I used,' he wrote in one of his short stories, 'to watch the wheel of the pit spin round year after year, after school on Saturdays and Sundays; and then from 1926 on I watched it not turning at all, and I can't ever get that wheel out of my mind.'

Lewis loved Wales with a deep passion and he loathed the narrow Puritanism which sought to suppress such things as the real folk poetry, the creativity of the Welsh people. In 1932 he went to Aberystwyth University to read history, to dabble in left-wing politics and to write his first poems. In 1935 he won a Research Studentship to Manchester University. In 1939 he became engaged to Gweno Ellis, a teacher of German in the local grammar school at Mountain Ash and, by 1940, he was conscripted into the army. He spent much time training at Woodbridge and Aldeburgh. Later he was posted to India and, in February 1944, his unit moved from Burma to confront the Japanese in the Arakan. On 5th March, in mysterious circumstances, after he had joined his battalion on the Mayu Range, Lewis died.

Alun Lewis was one of the most promising poets of the Second World War. His books include *Raider's Dawn* and *Ha! Ha! Among the Trumpets*. The most recent book on the poet is by Ian Hamilton from which the above details have been taken.

POSTSCRIPT: FOR GWENO

If I should go away,
Beloved, do not say
'He has forgotten me'.
For you abide,
A singing rib within my dreaming side;
You always stay.
And in the mad tormented valley
Where blood and hunger rally
And Death the wild beast is uncaught, untamed,
Our soul withstands the terror
And has its quiet honour
Among the glittering stars your voices named.

GOODBYE

So we must say Goodbye, my darling,
And go, as lovers go, for ever;
Tonight remains, to pack and fix on labels
And make an end of lying down together.

I put a final shilling in the gas,
And watch you slip your dress below your knees
And lie so still I hear your rustling comb
Modulate the autumn in the trees.

And all the countless things I shall remember
Lay mummy-cloths of silence round my head;
I fill the carafe with a drink of water;
You say 'We paid a guinea for this bed,'

And then, 'We'll leave some gas, a little warmth
For the next resident, and these dry flowers,'
And turn your face away, afraid to speak
The big word, that Eternity is ours.

Your kisses close my eyes and yet you stare
As though God struck a child with nameless fears;
Perhaps the water glitters and discloses
Time's chalice and its limpid useless tears.

Everything we renounce except ourselves;
Selfishness is the last of all to go;
Our sighs are exhalations of the earth,
Our footprints leave a track across the snow.

We made the universe to be our home,
Our nostrils took the wind to be our breath,
Our hearts are massive towers of delight,
We stride across the seven seas of death.

Yet when all's done you'll keep the emerald
I placed upon your finger in the street;
And I will keep the patches that you sewed
On my old battledress tonight, my sweet.